Tito Gobbi

on His World of
Italian Opera

Also by Tito Gobbi:

MY LIFE

Tito Gobbi

on His World of
Italian Opera

HAMISH HAMILTON LONDON

TO MY WIFE

First published in Great Britain 1984
by Hamish Hamilton Ltd
Garden House, 57–59 Long Acre, London WC2E 9JZ

Copyright © 1984 by Tito Gobbi and Ida Cook

British Library Cataloguing in Publication Data

Gobbi, Tito
    Tito Gobbi on his world of Italian opera
    1. Gobbi, Tito   2. Singers – Italy –
    Biography
    I. Title
    782.1'092'4   ML420.G/

    ISBN 0-241-11257-5

Photoset in Great Britain by
Rowland Phototypesetting Ltd, Bury St Edmunds, Suffolk
and printed by St Edmundsbury Press
Bury St Edmunds, Suffolk

Contents

List of Illustrations 7

Acknowledgements 9

Preface: Windows on Italian Opera 11

1 The Gift of a Voice 15
2 The Small Part 19
3 Make-up 23
4 Don Giovanni 29
5 The Two Figaros 38
6 William Tell 57
7 Ernani 67
8 Rigoletto 76
9 La Traviata 95
10 Simone Boccanegra 109
11 Don Carlo 125
12 Otello 142
13 Falstaff 157
14 I Pagliacci 168
15 La Bohème 177
16 Tosca 194
17 Il Tabarro 214
18 Gianni Schicchi 222
19 Some Composers of My Time 236

Index 257

Contents

Preface and Acknowledgement

Acknowledgement

Prologue: Windows on Indian Opera

Chapter one ...

1 The Setting ...

2 Make-up ...

3 Love Potions ...

...

List of Illustrations

Between pages 64 and 65

Tito Gobbi as:

Falstaff. (Zoe Dominic, London.)
Ford in *Falstaff*. (Richard Levin, B.B.C. Television.)
Gobbi's sketch of his own face: creating Iago for *Otello*.
Gianni Schicchi. (Teatro Dell'Opera, Roma.)
King Nebuchadnezzar in *Nabucco*. (Maria-Jeannette, Los Angeles.)
Baron Scarpia in *Tosca*. (Fayer, Wein.)
Rigoletto. (Richard Levin, B.B.C. Television.)
Simone Boccanegra. (Zoe Dominic, London.)
Simone Boccanegra. (A. Villani and Figli, Bologna.)
Prologue in *I Pagliacci*.
Tonio in *I Pagliacci*. (Oscar Savio, Roma.)
Figaro in *The Barber of Seville*.
Count Almaviva in *The Marriage of Figaro*. (Houston Rogers, London.)
Don Giovanni. (Richard Levin, B.B.C. Television.)
William Tell.
Peter in *Hansel and Gretel* (Barzacchi.)
Amonasro in *Aida*. (Fayer, Wein.)
Wozzeck. (Teatro alla Scala.)
Jack Rance in *La Fanciulla del West*.
The story-singer in *Il Tesoro*. (Oscar Savio, Roma.)
Michele in *Il Tabarro*. (Houston Rogers, London.)

Between pages 128 and 129

With Tito Schipa in *The Barber of Seville*. (Oscar Savio, Roma.)
With Renata Tebaldi, Anna Maria Canali and Giulietta Simionato in *Falstaff*. (Nancy Sorenson, Chicago.)

With Mirella Freni in *The Marriage of Figaro*. (Donald Southern, London.)

With Geraint Evans in *Don Giovanni*. (E. Gustie.)

With Maria Callas in *Tosca*. (Zoe Dominic, London.)

With Mario del Monaco in *Otello*. (Donald Southern, London.)

Rehearsing *Simone Boccanegra*. (Stephen C. Archetti, Keystone, London.)

With Boris Christoff in *Don Carlo*. (Zoe Dominic, London.)

Recording with Placido Domingo and Ileana Cotrubas. *Gianni Schicchi* for C.B.S. (Clive Barda, London.)

With Marie Collier in *Il Tabarro*. (Richard Levin, B.B.C. Television.)

With Renata Scotto in *Rigoletto*. (Richard Levin, B.B.C. Television.)

With Elizabeth Robson in *Gianni Schicchi*. (Richard Levin, B.B.C. Television.)

Between pages 192 and 193

Otello: Placido Domingo. (Clive Barda, London.)

La Traviata: Joan Sutherland. (Paul Popper Ltd.)

La Traviata: Amelita Galli-Curci.

La Traviata: Maria Callas. (Zoe Dominic, London.)

La Bohème: José Carreras and Katia Ricciarelli. (Stuart Robinson.)

La Bohème: Neil Shicoff and Ileana Cotrubas. (Catherine Ashmore, London.)

La Bohème: Luciano Pavarotti and Kiri Te Kanawa. (Donald Southern, London.)

The Marriage of Figaro: Thomas Allen. (Clive Barda, London.)

Mario Persico.

Riccardo Zandonai.

Bernardino Molinari.

Ildebrando Pizzetti.

Tullio Serafin. (Levi, Firenze.)

Ermanno Wolf-Ferrari.

Dedication on *Canzoniere*.

Umberto Giordano, Lorenzo Perosi and Pietro Mascagni.

Acknowledgements

I make no apologies for this book being personal. I am writing in the light of my own experience of what was *my* world of Italian opera. For example, to me both *William Tell* and *Don Carlo* are Italian operas, and so they were usually treated in my day. Naturally during their long history and in various countries they have sometimes been given with their original French libretti. Anyway, for me they are Italian, and I have a pleasing suspicion that in any discussion I should probably find both Rossini and Verdi on my side.

My thanks to my friends Ida Cook and Gian-Carlo Bartolini Salimbeni.

I am grateful to Macdonald, the publishers of MY LIFE, for permission to quote five passages taken from my autobiography, and to the photographers whose work is reproduced in this book.

The drawings which introduce each chapter are by
Gian–Carlo Bartolini Salimbeni.

Preface: Windows on Italian Opera

Many years ago I had occasion to visit San Gimignano, that famous Tuscan hill town where thirteen of the mediaeval towers (there were over seventy during the time of the rival factions of the Middle Ages) still rear their proud heads, like some fourteenth-century anticipation of Manhattan. I was in a sight-seeing mood and, finding a guide, asked to be conducted to the top of one of the highest towers.

He agreed, with the enthusiasm of one who took a pride in the beautiful place in which he lived, and together we began to mount the inside staircase, which went up and up in almost total darkness.

Then, when we were rather near the top, my guide paused, threw back the wooden shutters at one window and simply said, 'Look at that!' and I found myself gazing out on a scene of such indescribable sunlit beauty that I think I must have gasped aloud.

Before me lay a tremendous stretch of the Tuscan countryside in all its magic. The fields were a patchwork of varied colours, broken up by the wooded hills and valleys, while the farms and villages looked like beautiful toys. It was a landscape not unknown to me but, viewed like this, the exquisite panorama of colour and form was something quite different.

I had never seen it like that before!

Then the guide said, 'On some days you can even see the sea.' And in that moment I *saw* the sea. For my stimulated imagination reached beyond the confines of mere physical sight, in a flash of revelation. Physical, mental and perhaps even spiritual awareness combined to give me a sort of vision, which I have remembered for the rest of my life.

When I came to write this book I thought a lot about that experience, and that is why I have called this preface 'Windows on Italian Opera'. I make no claim to be a deeply learned musicologist, though music has, of course, been my life. But I have been fortunate enough to live that life among some of the greatest maestri and teachers of the century. I have also known some of the composers and librettists and can, without presumption, claim that I have some idea of what they really wanted.

During my forty-seven years in opera I have been privileged, like all devoted interpreters, to give some light to the genius of those much greater than myself – the originators of the works we serve. This is not conceit. It is a matter of recognising the proud responsibility laid upon every interpreter who seeks to follow the true path. If this seems a high claim, please reflect that the finest musical masterpiece *unperformed* remains no more than a manuscript, abandoned among others gathering dust on some obscure shelf. We, the performers, are the lucky ones permitted to give that essential light to the work and, in so doing, are ourselves illumined.

My simple aim is to tell about opera and its world – its problems and its hopes, its beauties and its ugliness, its traditions and the new ideas which flourish within its compass. It is a marvellous, magical world, a world of dreams and hopes, a world which many would like to enter and know, and which too many still do not appreciate.

Everyone, including myself, has his own ideas, his own personal approach – mental, moral and physical, his own way of thinking and feeling. Thus there are countless different realisations of a character, which still must remain faithful to the original music and text. I write, therefore, from my own point of view, which has naturally changed and developed during my years of life in opera. I do not seek to arouse animosities, still less to provoke violent argument. I merely hope to open a few windows – for performers and audience alike – and say, like my guide in San Gimignano –

'LOOK!'

I

The Gift of a Voice

What *is* a voice?

In itself it is just air passing through the vocal cords. But beautified by mind and heart it becomes the art of expressing all human feelings – a gift from God which, like all God's gifts, carries with it a great responsibility.

It is no credit to you personally that you have a lovely face, wonderful muscles, a fine brain or a beautiful voice. The question is – what are you going to do with that gift? Waste it? Exploit it for your own aggrandisement? Ignore it and let it wither? Or humbly, diligently and with love and intelligence endeavour to perfect it for the joy of others as well as yourself?

Well, let us suppose you have a voice of some distinction, and that your hopes have been confirmed by someone with knowledge and authority. This is important, for it is not enough that you and your family think you are as good as many people already before the public. You may be, but the chances are against it.

Before involving yourself and your family in expense, anxiety and disappointment, face the fact that the voice alone is not enough. Also – though you may not welcome this piece of practical cynicism – it is wise to have the possibility of an honourable retreat should things not turn out as you have hoped.

Now make a severe analysis of all your gifts. What a singer needs is excellent health, well controlled nerves, natural musical instinct, good intonation, a first-class sense of rhythm, good stage presence and, above all, humility. Only with humility does one learn from one's many, many mistakes.

Beware of unknown teachers with gimmicky methods of approach. If lying on your back with a toothpick between your front teeth were really the secret of bel canto someone else would have discovered it before now. Use your observation, your intelligence, your perseverance, and remember that every decision of importance will ultimately be yours alone.

Breathe properly, as a sportsman does; concentrate every minute of your life on this world of opera you are seeking to enter. But don't become a bore or a fanatic about it. And don't give yourself airs. You are just someone very lucky who is trying to justify that luck.

When you have a toehold on the first rung of the operatic ladder never underestimate the importance of that tiny role which has come your way. Acquaint yourself with the *whole* work, even if only a line and a half is yours. Let your mind range over that little character. He or she had a life before coming on to the stage and (unless killed onstage – an occupational hazard of operatic characters) a life afterwards.

It is not your business to display more than the importance allotted to that character by composer and librettist, but it *is* your business to know that character so well that you would recognise him or her in the street. In this way you begin to build up a convincing portrayal *in your own mind*. This is splendid practice for later successes. Characters are not just funny or touching, noble or devious in their own way. The Sacristan in *Tosca* is not funny in the same way as Melitone in *Forza del Destino*. Why? Well, work that one out for yourself. It is a good opening exercise.

If a certain phrase seems specially difficult you must find out the reason. More often than not your anxiety about it made you pay too little attention to the proper placing of the *previous* note. Take Rodolfo's aria in Act 1 of *La Bohème*, where that dreaded high C seems much higher than it is and presents a great temptation to force and push. In forcing you almost inevitably open the mouth too much, dropping the jaw and therefore closing the throat, cutting off the sound.

Instead, for a well rounded 'La-a-spe-e-ranza' relax, and start climbing the vocal staircase, lifting the sound into the high position from 'ma il furto non m'accora', be lighter in . . . 'poichè v'ha preso stanza', avoiding too much weight on the previous notes – you are already up there in position for the high C.

Another pitfall for an inexperienced singer is the temptation to start a *pianissimo* too weakly, in 'Una furtiva lagrima', for instance. Immediately he is in danger, for he cannot reduce the volume and has not sufficient support to increase it. Consequently, he starts to wobble. The solution is to start with a real note, rich, well projected and strong; then as soon as possible reduce the *quantity* of sound, while supporting with more breath and controlling the *quality* and the intensity.

This chapter is not intended to be a singing lesson *per se*. We are just opening a few small windows as we ascend. So here are a few hints rather than dogmatic rulings. They are the result of forty-seven years of experience and much thought.

Always go through a role silently and mentally beforehand and answer all the questions *then*. It is true that an opera singer walks a tightrope and with one false step can tumble over into the ridiculous, but try not to be too tense about this during the actual performance. Good, calm preparation beforehand helps you to relax and give of your best. You can think ahead and many problems can be avoided – in almost everything. Try not to listen anxiously to yourself or you will not project your voice properly and will tend to go flat. Rather like a man on a bicycle who nervously watches only the road immediately in front of him and, therefore, fails to see the danger ahead.

Physically speaking, you must from the waist downwards be like a rock. But keep the neck flexible and relaxed.

Breathe through the nose.

Keep the sound always in focus till the last consonant.

Light a fire when you sing! A performer's nervous system is ten times more alert than normal, and if you call on it with intelligence it will respond with brilliance.

A smile on the face (when appropriate of course) brings radiance to the tone of the voice. Sing with joy, and remember that beauty comes from the inside. Even a physically ugly person can be artistically beautiful.

Always give close attention to rhythm and tempo, carrying over phrases. And remember that silence too is music and must be well balanced.

Melody must never be hampered by stage movement. (Producers who send their singers galloping up and down stairs please note.) The audience went to see your facial expression; keep your muscles relaxed so that there is no distortion of sound. And *walk tall* as though your hair touches the ceiling.

Where words or phrases are repeated always vary the shading and tone. Too much sameness in this respect cannot fail to be boring. The audience is a monster who must be served and kept awake; if it shows the slightest sign of boredom – *do* something, quickly.

Do not get too emotionally involved, for this will exhaust you and smother the voice, and then the vocal fire is lost. You can do your crying at rehearsal, so that you know how far you can go while remaining totally in command.

Play for the audience *always*. They will remember you.

As in all careers – all ways of life – it is vital to be able to assess the importance and the unimportance of what one is doing. There is no such thing as a totally unimportant role, but in a virtual beginner a little seemly modesty is acceptable. The gift as such may be an important one – indeed, I hope it is – but, as I said in the beginning of this chapter, it is what you do with it that matters.

There is immense power in a voice well used, and by that I do not mean personal pomp and pride. Towards the end of the War, I went quite often to military hospitals to sing to the wounded, who were of varying nationalities. On one occasion among them was a young fellow, very ill, who asked me in a whisper to sing 'Ave Maria' for him.

So young, so frightened, so far from home, poor lad. Sitting down by his bedside, holding his hand, I began to sing 'Ave Maria'. And while I was singing he died – smiling.

2

The Small Part

All children are born good. Ask their mothers! But then, in the
course of time, circumstances and unresisted temptation introduce
some evil into most of them. Even so, one drop of distilled
goodness, one gem of the initial splendour, appears from time to
time, rousing a deep human emotion.

It is for us, the performers, to discover these emotions in even the
smallest of characters, and reveal them to the audience, giving to
each any possibility of human feelings: nobility or wickedness,
good or evil, cruelty, arrogance, intelligence or foolishness, modesty or pride. Not all to be discovered in one character, of course!
Only what the personality requires. Then it must be presented
without distortion, giving some touch of humanity to even the
most negative actions.

In this Verdi is perhaps the greatest teacher of all. When he has
Macbeth singing: 'Pietà, rispetto amore,' he transforms a criminal
into a poor ageing man, lonely and weeping. His overwhelming

sense of compassion for poor suffering humanity opens even the cold heart of Philip II to the Marquis of Posa when, on a moving impulse, he entrusts his wife and son to him. Oh, there are countless instances of this human touch in Verdi.

To an interpreter it should be a genuine joy to take advantage of contrasting actions and reactions, the rapid changes as one state of mind almost melts into another. It is as though an uncontrollable force, an irresistible urge to be sincere, overwhelms the negative forces which are in us all, though often concealed or controlled.

As a young man I dived headlong into this foaming sea of contrasting emotions, and I have for many years swum happily among the rocks, the depths, the shallows, discovering for myself the winding paths, the secrets, the treasure.

In 1936 I started as a *comprimario*, and at the same time had the opportunity to study many roles in which I had to be ready at a moment's notice to 'cover' for indisposed singers. I was only too eager to undertake the long weeks of rehearsals which allowed me to penetrate a role and acquire confidence in it. A sudden opportunity to play was extremely exciting, and in those days at the Teatro Reale in Rome the risk was minimal. This was due to the invaluable assistance of a legion of excellent *répétiteurs* in the wings and the generous co-operation of colleagues on the stage.

A so-called 'small' role was much more perilous. These nearly always consist of a few phrases scattered at intervals through the acts, and are full of pitfalls. I am not the only one who viewed them with terror.

If a *comprimario* slips up in his one or two phrases he seldom has a chance of making good again. And it is over him that the conductor will discharge the vials of his wrath, which he will hesitate to pour upon one of the so-called stars. Yet these small roles are nearly always entrusted to beginners or ageing singers. Those *comprimarios*, those heroes of the stage, have my fullest sympthy. They are the protagonists of a fugitive instant. And if things go wrong they will need all the protection of Santa Barbara (the patron saint of the artillery)!

Then there are, of course, the *Comprimarios* with a capital C, the king-sized ones who can split a demi-semi-quaver in two, true masters of rhythm and diction. They are precise in stage action, always well dressed and faultlessly made up. They are the ones on whom you lean in moments of uncertainty: de Paolis, Nessi, Nardi, Zagonara, Santafé, Andreolli, Giorgetti, Velis, Lanigan, Ercolani, Mariano Caruso and many, many others who were not only colleagues to me but dear friends. A similar legion of ladies added to performances the beauty of their voices and the truth of their characterisation.

Many have now left the stage and few are the ones who come along to replace them. And I ask myself – why? why? The career of a *comprimario* is a beautiful one, of the utmost importance, dignity and responsibility. It is also, incidentally, a very rewarding one financially. For every performance of a leading singer the *comprimario* will very probably have three or four. And his ability to discharge the lesser vocal demands of his type of role will probably enable him to go on singing long after many a 'star' has ceased to twinkle.

It is not always in the leading roles that you build up a reputation and a career. In fact, if I were producing *Otello* today I should count Cassio and Emilia among my principal worries. Or what about Arturo in *Lucia*, Arlecchino in *Pagliacci*, Flora in *Traviata*, and so on?

I always advise my young singers to be well prepared in roles of this calibre, for they are likely to offer the first chance to get into an opera house. Similarly, there are instances of distinguished singers who, after a brilliant career in leading opera houses, feel unwilling to leave the stage; and so they give to it the benefit of their experience and intelligence in bringing new distinction and life to minor roles.

I still remember my real joy when I was producing *Tosca* at the Lyric in Chicago and learned that, out of old friendship and affection, that splendid artist, my good friend Italo Tajo, had come to be my Sacristan.

It does not always work that way, however! There is a story of the great Caruso who, generously replacing Arlecchino in *Pagliacci* for an ailing colleague who had lost his voice, sang the Serenade from behind the scenes. Next day an indignant critic wrote with angry contempt about 'this donkey who dared to imitate the great Caruso – and badly at that!'

Most audiences today are fairly knowledgeable about the actual story of the standard operas. But we, the interpreters, must go farther than that. We must know the limits allowed within which we can express the varied emotions, without indulging in the over-acting or buffoonery which will make the audience laugh or cry in the wrong place.

It is, of course, part of the legitimate enjoyment of an audience to weep, tremble – and laugh, in feelings shared with the interpreter. But it must be appropriate and in proportion. The performer who deliberately attracts attention by cheap buffoonery may possibly earn a laugh – but never esteem. If this comment brings a guilty blush to your cheek – pause and reflect, admit your guilt and *never* do it again.

Shaming instances of this type of exaggeration spring to mind. The Don Basilio in a performance of *The Barber of Seville* whose 'La Calunnia' was greeted by Don Bartolo with 'But this is the atomic bomb!' The Sergeant in the same opera who, ostensibly coming to restore order in the house of Don Bartolo, entered as though dead drunk, allowed his hat to fall off, replaced it the wrong way round, fell down because he got his sword entangled between his legs – and finally addressed himself to the wrong person. Quite a performance, but totally pointless and irrelevant.

Imagination is always free to add expression, but *only* with full respect for the opera which generates it. And, I might add, full respect for the colleagues who are sharing the stage with you. The most elementary politeness and camaraderie absolutely forbid anything achieved at the expense of another. Worth must be established for itself and never by diminishing someone else.

One of my most valued memories of Mario del Monaco is the time when he impulsively exclaimed, 'My best performances of Otello were the ones I sang with Tito.' Though both of us were animated by the determination to play our respective roles to the very best of our ability we always supported each other with the greatest respect for both our colleagues and the work.

While still on the subject of the small or assisting role I must allow a few words for those who do not sing at all, but whose presence is vital to the scene and the action. Their responsibility must not be underestimated. It can be almost terrifying. Inexplicably, the audience seem to expect nothing short of perfection from them! A star may be forgiven a bad note or an awkward stumble. But no sooner does something happen to the poor devil who has nothing but his silence and his dignity to sustain him than the whole house falls on him.

I well remember a performance of *Don Carlo* when, just before the Auto-da-Fé, an officer of large and splendid proportions had to cross the stage towards the cathedral. Magnificent in armour and plumes, alone and without escort, he proceeded with measured step to the centre of the stage, where he stopped suddenly, began shaking like a spaniel emerging from the water and uttered a tremendous sneeze. At which half the house shouted a delighted 'Bless you!'

3
Make-up

In my view it is highly important that an opera singer should be able to make up his own face; or at least be able to suggest to the make-up man what he knows from experience to be to his advantage. No one knows a face better than its owner: the possibilities for telling expression, the intensity and the rate with which he passes from one emotion to another.

It is not through narcissism that a good actor spends hours in front of the mirror. It is to study and learn what he requires in order to express sorrow or joy with those small, almost imperceptible changes. Only by this severe self-criticism, accompanied by intense inner feeling, does he avoid mediocre and unconvincing grimaces.

The thought goes behind the face, transforming it and immediately altering the expression in a way which anticipates the words. Poker faces are of no interest on the stage, unless specifically required for the portrayal of a particular character.

Look at yourself, then, in one, two or three mirrors, and get to know your features from every angle, never forgetting that the audience observes you from all sides. Then you will be able to change and correct your expression with the help of make-up and attitude.

While changing into a new human being it is not enough to paint your face; you must change your thoughts and character, becoming *inside* what you want to appear *outside*. Start by imagining your new character and build him up in your mind. Model him in clay if you can. Close your eyes and try to see him alive as you sit in front of the mirror. Then open your eyes and look at that poor face of yours, colourless and without character. Make a firm mental note of all you have to change, correct or add. Have fun realising your new self. You will never have better company.

If you have a good supply of photographs of yourself chalk or paint on them the alterations you propose to make. If, on the other hand, economy is your admirable watchword, use a piece of glass, *one* photograph and paints which will wash off. It was in this way, incidentally, that I worked out my Scarpia profile.

The mad impulse to draw wrinkles with lines of black and white must be firmly controlled. Better still, throw away and never buy again those non-colours. Wrinkles and other marks which characterise a human face must be done with lighter or darker shades of the same colour as your foundation. Lines must follow the hills and valleys of the muscles, where inevitably one day art will no longer be needed to age the face, only to rejuvenate it.

In the long series of characters I have performed very rarely have I accepted the help of a make-up man – and then only to be aimiably co-operative. But my refusal to trust my face blindly to the hands and talent of someone else does not mean that I wish to denigrate this type of collaboration, so important for the good result of the performance. Indeed, today, as producer, I work in willing collaboration. First comes the careful study of the character and then I entrust the carrying out of our joint decision to the expertise of the make-up man.

Think of make-up as a bridge which takes you to the other side of fantasy; into a magic world where everything is possible, where for a few hours imagination, ambition, excitement become a reality. In my silent dressing-room, concentrating during the four or five hours before a performance, I used to bring before me that second self. I would build him slowly inside me so that he would take actual form, until I felt and, above all, *believed* what I wanted to be.

Every night there would be something different. A mark more or less strong on the brow, the nose, the lips, according to my state of mind. I believe it is absolutely necessary to change the character very slightly night by night to fit and support the stage action and the colleagues with whom one shares the burden and the honours of the evening. I mean this literally, while always, of course, preserving the essence of the character. It is a balance between flexibility and fidelity to the basic character.

For instance, some attitudes or actions of Scarpia were different if I was singing with Maria Caniglia, Maria Callas, Renata Tebaldi, Zinka Milanov, Eleanor Steber . . . oh, the list is endless, for, indeed, I sang with almost every Tosca from 1943 to 1977. And how different were those divas in appearance, voice and interpretation.

For the ladies of the operatic stage the make-up presents fewer problems, although they too have to know their faces very well; how to enhance beautiful features, how to reduce small faults. A long face should be properly framed by hair, for wigs and head-dresses make the face look rounder and wider. For a round, wide face the opposite treatment is of course required.

Very seldom should ladies enlarge the mouth with heavy lipstick, and this should never be too dark. Pay special attention to the eyes, which should be beautiful, alive and expressive to a degree. Do not detract from their brightness by lifting the brows too much. In any case, brows should be lifted very little near the temple to avoid a Mephistophelian look.

Never draw in the eyebrows with a single line. Draw the hairs of the eyebrows one by one where you want them marked. Then create effects of light and shade in the eye-socket and lids with colour. Avoid the temptation to darken too much. It is extraordinary how the eyes attract and centralise the attention of the audience. (Indeed, I have often thought that the veil worn by Arabian women disclosing only the eyes is an example of supreme coquetry, to distract attention from the often generous hips.)

But don't stop at the eyes. Take care of the cheekbones, the cheeks, the forehead and, above all, the nose with smoothly shaded dark colour.

The mirror is our frank friend, revealing what we must improve. So if the finished make-up does not make you feel satisfied with yourself be prepared to do it all over again without hesitation. It is not possible to play well feeling uncomfortable and dissatisfied with your appearance.

Don't expect to succeed at first. I still remember the astonished expression of the producer Carlo Piccinato as he stared at the red and blue marks I had lavished on my face in order to make myself look old.

'Have you been fighting with a cat?' he shouted – and sent me back to do it all again.

In my young days, at the Royal Opera House in Rome, we were inflamed by the spirit of eager competition. Italo Tajo used his colours like a portrait painter. Giulio Neri was sparing with marks and colours, having the advantage of a strong, naturally expressive face. Gino Bechi had a new invention for every character. Mario del Monaco was for ever engaged in passionate research. Mariano Stabile – ah, there was a master of make-up as of everything else to do with the operatic stage. I see him now as a stupendous Falstaff or an ice-cold Scarpia. Giacomo Vaghi was wonderful with imposing beards – and many, many others. We were a legion, all animated by the exciting spirit of emulation.

Tormented by our exacting demands, a band of wigmakers performed miracles: Ronchetti, Paglialunga, Maggi, Filistrucchi – they were all obliged to follow our whims and claims.

Later on, finances permitting, we wanted our own individual costumes, which look infinitely better than those which are 'custom made'.

Today this hardly ever happens. For good or ill, opera houses supply everything to the singer, and the make-up man puts on to his skin a face that does not belong to him. So to talk of make-up today may seem superfluous and pointless, but this is not so. I am still convinced that if you learn to do it yourself you can penetrate and interpret your character better.

I find no justification whatever for a singer growing a moustache or beard, imposing a hairy face on roles and periods in which cleanshaven faces were the norm. Also, it is discourteous to his female partners who have to put up with the disagreeable rubbing and perspiring of rough 'fur'. A real beard is identifiable whatever the role, which means that the singer is recognised but the interpretation of the role is lost. Admittedly there is a risk of losing a false moustache or – even worse – swallowing it. But this predicament can be avoided with due care!

I always used to draw my moustache on the upper half of my top lip, on the spot right under the nose, adding false hairs only at the corners of the mouth. I would arrange these in the required fashion and secure them with spirit gum. I then traced on the upper half of the top lip light separate marks with spirit gum, to look like light hair, then when this had dried I marked the 'hairs' with thin strokes of dark brown crayon. I must say that even in photographs this gave good results.

Securing the wig requires great care. The tulle on the forehead and sides must be scrupulously clean and must be prepared in good time, using acetone or some other solvent to remove all traces of spirit gum from the previous performance. The wig itself, smoothly combed with a little hair spray, must fit perfectly.

Then it will be enough to fix it with the spirit gum in no more than three or four spots. After that a few hairpins on the top of your head secured in your own hair – should you be so fortunate as to have some left – complete the delicate task. I dislike a wig pasted all the way round as it makes you perspire, and inevitably shows wrinkles which should not be there. If your wig has a tail, fix it high on the nape, then it won't bother you by getting inside your collar.

It is easy to add to a face, but exceedingly difficult to take away from it. Consequently 'anonymous' faces, without strong significant features, thick brows and showy noses, are the easiest to make up. For a role requiring strong characteristics you can go at it with a bold hand, adding pastiches and emphasising the effects of light and shade. But never make clean heavy marks which do not correspond to the natural facial movements, for they may well give the impression of dirt. When your dark mark has been made on the face gently smooth your finger over it, following the contour of the muscles.

Again, let me warn against the use of black. There are other dark shades which give a better result. Indeed, nothing looks more bogus than hair or beard tinted black in an attempt to make someone look younger.

The foundation colour should be compared with that of the other singers so that you all appear to belong to the same race – providing of course that this is the case. And naturally all must be according to the demands of the stage lighting.

It is very important to know the warm colours from the cold ones and to make good use of them. Thus you can depict the thin face of suffering or the large, jovial face of a Falstaff. You can give the effect of prominent cheekbones or an aggressive chin for, say, Scarpia. You can even distort and make assymetrical the eyes and lips and bulbous forehead of Tonio in *Pagliacci*, though this is a more complicated matter.

For Tonio I used to distend my nostrils with little bits of rubber, and I had a special denture made so that the side front teeth appeared longer and more prominent. The assymetry of the face was emphasised by the lifting of an eyebrow and an enlargement for one ear lobe attached with a light mark to the cheek. A shadow on the throat completed the effect.

Today's sophisticated stage lighting can perform miracles but it can also ruthlessly expose careless make-up. A white neck, unmade-up, or the cheeks badly shadowed – these are the unmistakable signs of someone who checked only the front view in the mirror, forgetting that vital if familiar warning; every side of you is exposed to the attentive glances of the spectator, not to mention the keen eye of the critic!

It is not always necessary to make up the hands, but they must be alive and in action, never with the four fingers rigidly together like fingers pasted on a puppet.

Remember also that the neck (which you have now conscientiously made up) must be flexible, loose, free to move and turn naturally. This adds grace and expression to the whole body, just as mobility of the eyes gives life to the face.

If there seem to be rather a lot of 'do's' and 'don'ts' in this chapter, please allow me that indulgence from the height of my nearly seventy years. I assure you that if you follow faithfully most of the rules laid down here no one will ever say of you, 'The voice is good, but he (or she) is just a block of wood on the stage.'

4

Don Giovanni

The final resting place of Wolfgang Amadeus Mozart is unknown. He was buried in the common grave of a cemetery in Vienna, with nothing to identify him. Thus the unique genius whose music has enriched humanity for two centuries has no tombstone on which today a devoted admirer can lay a single flower.

In one sense this is of course a matter for sadness and shame. And yet – is it not also the perfect answer to the mystery that was Mozart? He came into this world like a divine messenger, poured out the riches of his musical inspiration upon an often rather indifferent public and then, at an incredibly early age, returned to spirit, leaving no shred of his material self behind. But there *was* nothing material by which he need be remembered. His music is his eternal monument. And no monument erected by man could rival that.

In the years since his death scholars, commentators and directors have all offered 'interpretations' of *Don Giovanni*. Some have obviously been inspired by love and respect, others have been eccentric and perverse to the verge of insult. It is not for me to offer excuses on behalf of anyone else, but for myself I would beg some indulgence for entering at all upon this debatable field. Without making extravagant claims to exclusive knowledge, I hope to keep myself strictly to what, with devotion, I have learned through being an interpreter, and merely offer certain ideas which were born in me while studying the music and the Italian libretto.

In 1941 Maestro Serafin first asked me if I had ever studied the role of Giovanni. I said I had not, but expressed myself ready to start on the morrow, rather implying that I would be at his service in a matter of months.

'Perhaps in fifteen years' time,' was the reply. 'We shall see. But start now.'

It was quite kindly said, but conveyed to me immediately something of what it really meant to confront one of the most subtle, difficult and demanding roles in all opera.

Molière, Corneille, Shadwell, de Zamora, Goldoni and many other playwrights took inspiration from the first *El Burlador de Sivilla*, written by Tirso de Molina (1571–1641). But we need not confuse ourselves by studying them all! The Italian libretto of *Don Giovanni* was born of the collaboration between Mozart and da Ponte, and in this collaboration (spiced by Casanova) the highest form of the Don Giovanni story was undoubtedly reached. Scenes full of drama are in spectacular contrast with others full of comedy or romance, all guided by a deep knowledge of human nature, a psychology which binds truth and fantasy together with supreme grace.

Don Giovanni was not of course a Venetian – but da Ponte was, and there is much of Venice in this Spanish libretto. Venice is a world and a civilisation all its own, strong in the tradition of its way of living, which shows itself in the thoughts and actions of all its sons – and above all in its use of language. Nuances, veiled designs, subtleties, graceful double meanings are all there. And they are all in da Ponte's libretto too.

This is why I wince when the magical recitatives which are one of the glories of *Don Giovanni* are often flung headlong, like a hail-storm of notes, concealing the subtle meaning and revealing little knowledge of the Italian tongue. Not a major crime, perhaps – but certainly an offence against a beautiful and musical language. And, incidentally, an offence against commonsense too! To deliver words as though one already knows them all by heart is childish and ineffectual. Recitatives are not just links between arias and set numbers. They must be spoken (or sung) with a clear, calm pronunciation as if thought had that moment been translated into utterance.

Too often these recitatives are spoken in a childish way with the wrong cadence, without regard for the Italian, the value of punctuation or the rhythm suggested by the thought and action. It is not only what the performer says which is important but the meaning behind the words, reflecting his subconscious.

The essential minimum to be asked of any interpreter is that he should understand the meaning – and the full value – of every word he is singing. He cannot bury his head in the sand of ignorance. There are dangers ahead which even the most dedicated ostrich ignores at his peril.

Don Giovanni, Nozze de Figaro, Così fan Tutte all belong to the Italian repertoire, but the indifference of Italian singers – aided and abetted by conductors, managers and impresarios – has allowed these operas to fall under the influence of foreign singers who frequently mangle the language or, worse still, translate it into other tongues. Why, may I ask, did the Austrian Mozart write these works to Italian librettos if they were to be performed in German or even English? Translations, which move the words out of place, away from the melody related to them, always seem to me like a family group photograph in which the heads have been cut off and replaced on the wrong necks and shoulders. The plea that this makes the whole thing more understandable to the general public is paltry and verges on impertinence. Better surely to have some explanation in the programme and a truer and more faithful performance from the interpreters.

If I seem to grow a little hot in my championship of the original masterpieces, let me plead that I have at least served them to the best of my ability and devotion for more than forty-five years. I must, I think, be allowed a little affectionate partisanship.

Please follow me with some indulgence, then, as we explore the wonders and the characters of this masterpiece. We shall start at the bottom of the social ladder – for one of the great subtleties of this work is the insight, both musical and dramatic, with which the various classes are differentiated. First let us meet:

Zerlina, one of the most adorable feminine creations that even Mozart ever touched with musical immortality.

She is both troubled and charmed by her meeting with the Don. A handsome cavalier, a *gentleman*, who says things that no one has ever said to her before. He seems so anxious to please her, and she is gratified beyond expression. What simple country girl would not be? But she is disturbed all the same and thrown into great confusion between what she would like to do and what she knows she should not do.

The thought of her devoted but unglamorous Masetto worries her a little, but the light touch of the gentleman's perfumed and bejewelled hand arouses other sensations, not to be resisted. At least – not entirely. Zerlina is the complete portrait, both musically and dramatically, of the eternal woman, in whom naïve grace and an awareness of her own power combine. This dangerous combination is even enough to set her whirling in the dance with the handsome cavalier under the very eyes of her jealous fiancé. If he is angry it is because he is only a peasant. No class – no distinction!

Basically innocent, she nevertheless shows a natural coquetry – which almost lands her in disaster. But it also stands her in good stead when she wants to make it up with Masetto. 'Vedrai carino' (if you will promise not to distrust me) is the most exquisite expression of the innocent coquette smoothing down the ruffled feathers of her man with the promise of voluptuous tenderness.

At the end of the story life goes on again quite normally for Zerlina and Masetto. They have had a slight brush with both heaven and hell, but it has not really affected their serene way of living.

Masetto is the simple and credulous peasant, ignorant, inclined to violence when jealous but subdued by Zerlina's first caress. Without any subtlety, he yet knows instinctively that there are going to be difficulties in having a ravishingly pretty bride. He is the product of centuries of servile obedience to the nobility, with their riches, their rights and their privileges. And although furious when he sees his beloved falling an easy prey to the charm of the great libertine, he is unable to make any effective protest. The Don, with his feathered hat and sword, seems to Masetto almost literally like a rapacious falcon falling on his sweet dove.

Rebellious and vengeful, he gathers together a few friends – no more subtle than he himself – and plans an ambuscade for his enemy. Naturally it is a total failure, ending with the devilishly amused cavalier giving him a good drubbing just to remind him of the social distinctions.

Poor honest, stupid Masetto! But Zerlina will sooth those bruises of both body and self esteem. The seducer will disappear from the scene and they will live happily ever after. It is all there in the music.

★

At the other extreme of the social scale we have

Don Ottavio, the fiancé of Donna Anna. He is not a man in the first flush of ardent youth. On the contrary, he is a calm lover, dedicated to the relief of his beloved's grief and pain. He reassures the bereaved Anna with 'You have a husband and a father in me', words which describe his character in one sentence. After the Commendatore's death Don Ottavio is Donna Anna's sole protector, a role which he willingly accepts with almost paternal tenderness. Wise and self-controlled, he is ready to face sacrifices and dangers in order to carry out any responsibilities required of him.

His natural authority is reflected throughout in his composure and the accent of his expression. A man who commands respect and trust, he should not be too involved in the virtuosity of his singing. By nature noble, high-minded and generous, he is the living antithesis of Don Giovanni and, above all, he is extremely clear-sighted and aware of everything going on around him.

Donna Anna is in striking contrast to this man of self-restraint and composure; indeed, in striking contrast to all the other figures in the drama. Tragic, inspired by her filial love and her fierce desire for revenge, she is an almost neo-classic figure. Her father's murder has robbed her of all peace of mind, and thoughts of vengeance are stronger even than the offence to her own honour. Both heart and love are frozen, all softer emotions in abeyance. Only in the palace of Don Giovanni does she yield to an impetuous impulse when she snatches off her mask so that she shall be recognised by the guilty villain.

Always aware of her high social standing, she is haughty and distant. Even towards Ottavio she shows remarkably little affection and is in no haste to marry him. So much so that when the tragedy has ended and just fate has overtaken Don Giovanni, it is she who suggests that they postpone their wedding for a year. A proposition to which the self-controlled Ottavio characteristically agrees!

Donna Anna is the only one with the strength to resist Giovanni, who for the first time is faced with threatened disaster as she pursues him – as yet unidentified – with the air of a great tragedienne. She is like the goddess of justice herself. The natural antagonism between them is complete – she constant and resolute and he unstable and changeable.

At the turn of the century there was a typically romantic theory that Donna Anna was unconsciously attracted to her aggressor. While this idea may be pleasing to the psychoanalyst it has no real justification in either text or music. If even a vague sense of eroticism were required in the music of the Commendatore's daughter, Mozart would certainly have known how to give the necessary hint.

Donna Elvira is a gentlewoman, though without the aristocratic self-control of the haughty Anna. Beautiful and intense, she is passionately in love with Giovanni – the only one of the three women who is. In her desperation at being abandoned she pursues him and, encountering Donna Anna and Don Ottavio, joins forces with them. Not because of the cruel way Giovanni has treated her, and not primarily from any motive of revenge, but simply because she loves him to distraction.

Elvira is ready to pardon all his offences and forget all sorrow and tears for just one little sign of tenderness. And, instinctively, she is the one who knows that the Don is doomed. In the last scene, when she makes a final attempt to speak with him in his own palace, it is to implore him to repent while there is still time.

After the final tragedy all earthly joys for her are over. She is the only one who will be constant to his memory, as she returns to the convent life from which Giovanni had seduced her.

Leporello, who announces enviously in his very first utterance, 'Voglio fare il gentiluomo' (I'd like to be a gentleman), is a constitutional grumbler. He longs to break free but is really in thrall to the malevolent charm of his master. He mimics him and mocks him when he is alone, but no sooner is he in the Don's presence than he is ready to obey him in every particular.

Alternately arrogant and complacent according to circumstances, he tries to be a rough copy of Don Giovanni but does not make a very good job of it. He may criticise his master savagely to himself, but he would never leave him of his own accord. After all, they share some pleasant memories of times together. Like the Don, Leporello has become dissolute and enjoys their precarious life of unexpected adventures, even showing a sort of pride and cynical gusto when he keeps tally of his master's conquests in his famous Catalogue aria.

At times Don Giovanni's open mockery of the Almighty frightens Leporello and troubles his conscience, and he is appalled by the murder of the Commendatore. But more often than not he admires his master's brazen assurance, his success with women, his courage and his ability to cope with any situation. His mediocrity, both in good and evil, makes him the perfect foil for the large-scale attraction and wickedness of his master.

When all is over, like so many 'faithful' servants, he goes to the tavern to seek a better master. No regrets, no tears.

★

Surrounded by these characters and himself the centre of the drama is

Don Giovanni – an enigmatic, fascinating, repellent figure about whom endless questions have been asked and few authoritative answers given. There are many ways of interpreting and portraying him, while still remaining faithful to libretto and music. Within those limits, the one essential in my view is that the performer should be convinced to the depths of his being that *this* is how Giovanni really was.

For my part, I see Giovanni as a man who has outlived his magnificent virility and, when Mozart's opera opens, already suspects his own decline. Certainly, according to Leporello's catalogue, he has pushed his powers of conquest pretty hard! But no further name is going to be added to that famous list.

From the opening scene – his failure with Donna Anna – he never achieves success with any woman, not even with Elvira's humble maid. Admittedly, circumstances are against him each time, but previously, on more than two thousand occasions, it was he who conquered circumstances. Throughout the work he remains a towering figure and, from his brilliant audacity and his haughty charm, we are constantly aware of the powers he once wielded. But from the moment when the Commendatore points the accusing finger at him he starts the descent which eventually plunges him into the abyss.

Giovanni does not actually know the end in the beginning, but I think he has an inner awareness that his star has set. Supporting this belief is a growing conviction that the once virile conquering lover is a part he can no longer be sure of playing.

There is, it seems to me, both musically and dramatically, a certain feverish defiance, a desperation, of a man no longer sure of what had once been his irresistible powers. His repeated failures with all the women in the drama can only reinforce this agonising realisation.

Violent and ruthless in his adventure with Donna Anna, impatient and brutal with the discarded Elvira, careless and overplaying his part in his dalliance with the naïve Zerlina, he is angrily aware that he has somehow lost his touch. None of these reactions, it seems to me, is that of a man secure in his power to attract and conquer.

The fact that he did not actually intend to kill the Commendatore is important. The situation was forced upon him and was not of his choosing. Yet until that moment it was he who always dictated events. Now events are going to overtake him. Outwardly he may still be the dominating, arrogant, even defiant charmer, but something has begun to happen to the inner core of the man.

The gaiety and charm which we may legitimately presume to have been part of the young Giovanni's irresistible appeal changes subtly. The dominating figure is still there, it is true, but the glance is cold and haughty, the full, sensual mouth has a bitter curve, the whole air is menacing rather than beguiling. His hands are eloquent, but it is a nervous eloquence; his walk is still often dashing but there is a feline quality to his movements. The shadow of impotence is overtaking the once proud prince of virility.

If this is indeed the idea in da Ponte's characterisation – and I think it is – then Mozart adheres perfectly to it in his musical collaboration.

The supernatural happenings of the last scene are, again, capable of more than one interpretation. Both Giovanni and, to a lesser extent Leporello, are pursued by what we should nowadays call guilt complexes after the murder of the Commendatore. They do not speak about it to each other, but it weighs upon them both, and one might even ask if it is their guilty consciences which make them see the statue nod its head in acceptance of the cynical invitation to supper.

But this brings us to the one other role of great importance. That is – *Il Commendatore*, whose influence is felt throughout the evening, even though he dies only minutes after the curtain rises. He is in fact the *deus ex machina* of the entire drama. His death inspires Donna Anna to seek vengeance, but it is he himself who is the final avenger of the unrepentant libertine.

Insulted by Don Giovanni even in his grave, he accepts the defiant, mocking invitation to supper. And when the fearful apparition keeps the engagement he tells Giovanni that the time has come for him to appear before God and answer for his sins. In a last gesture of mercy he extends his hand to the sinner, entreating him to repent in this last hour of his life. But Giovanni rejects the hand and is precipitated into the inferno.

The very material appearance of the half-paralysed stone statue in person would, of course, be perfectly acceptable to many people – and it must not be forgotten that the alternative title for the work was 'The Stone Guest'. But equally I see no reason why we should not assume that the whole scene of the fatal supper party, culminating in the apparition, takes place in Giovanni's and Leporello's fevered imaginations.

Theatrically, I prefer something more nebulous than a block of stone, something suggestive rather than positive. A great deal can be done with steam, clever lighting, wind cloud effects and moonlight. And that which hovers between fact and fantasy is far more terrifying than a blunt presentation.

The actual ghost of the Commendatore – or the mental disturbance of a conscience loaded with guilt? It is a nice choice, and one which must be made personally. In leaving it undecided we are, after all, merely adding one more open question to those which have gathered over the centuries around the ever fascinating, ever provocative mystery of *Don Giovanni*.

5

The Two Figaros

The Barber of Seville The music gushes forth like a tidal wave, submerging everything, the almost physical impact enough to make one catch one's breath. Then as the wave retreats it leaves in its wake a cascade of notes glittering in the sunshine. Or rather, since they crackle and hiss, like drops of water sprinkled on boiling oil. Rossini, the inventor of savoury dishes, will not, I trust find the comparison disrespectful – though I believe fried foods were not his favourites. Today the vocal technique required is not respected; the correct rhythm, the elegance of gesture and singing, the clarity of diction and the liveliness of accent. The champagne has been replaced by – Seven-Up.

Recently I saw again the film of this opera which was made in Rome in 1947, with me in the title role. I enjoyed it afresh; if possible even more than when it was made. It belongs to another world, far away and lost – though not, I hope, for ever. Bewitched by the lightness and richness of the music, the matchless variety of rhythm, I revelled in my early study of this *Barber*, which was totally congenial to me. Even now I look back with nostalgic longing to those years of my artistic youth, when I was slim and agile, both physically and vocally, and still blissfully unaware of the great sense of responsibility and the ceaseless effort required for an operatic career. I did not particularly study the character of Figaro, nor did I think about it with special attention. He just came to me spontaneously and I had a lot of fun. But I did work prodigiously at the music and the singing.

From 1941 to 1943 I worked at Figaro almost daily with Maestro Ricci. Then the Rome Opera offered me the *Barber*'s opening night and the invitation was almost irresistible. But I am glad to remember that I had the strength of mind to ask for a delay, knowing that I needed longer to be truly ready and sure of myself. In those days the development of an artist was part of managerial planning. They were kind enough to allow me that postponement, and I sang my first *Barber* in February 1944.

It was a great step forward for me, and I had a good success, with praise for the purity of sound and the vocal agility. Maestro Fernando Previtali was the conductor, a man of almost fanatically exact tempi; in fact, we had to beg him not to beat time for the recitatives and even the pauses!

To Luigi Ricci must go much of the credit for my well based Figaro. Gigetto, as he was to his friends, was a legend for the last fifty years, and all of us owed to him a great part of our success. He died in 1981, but at over eighty he would still sit at the piano eight hours a day, just as he did twenty years before. We talked often and exchanged pupils. The very last time he telephoned to me he said, 'My dear Tito, this girl has a very good voice, but the face of a marble statue. I send her to you . . . see what you can do to make her look mobile and expressive.'

I miss Luigi, and am happy to make this acknowledgement of my debt to him. Hundreds of times we studied Figaro's music, and thousands of times repeated slowly the particularly difficult passages . . . then faster and faster until the desired tempo was reached.

'Oh, che volpe sopraffina' (Oh, the sly fox) and 'All'idea di quel metallo' (At the thought of that metal), then 'Ah, bravo, Figaro, bravo bravissimo' at a crazy speed. We would do a bit at a time and then put the whole together to form Rossini's marvellous work.

The 'fisic du role', a youthful spirit and an elegant appearance, are of course great assets to combine with a perfect vocal performance, giving the right balance between sight and sound. It all adds up to a pretty tall order! I made my voice lighter in order to achieve the exciting virtuosity which makes of every bar a bravura performance, and throughout my career I have used Figaro's cavatina as an exercise to put my voice right after singing heavy roles. I recommend this to all baritones.

That 1947 film of *The Barber of Seville* was the first full-length operatic film ever made. We were just out of the immense calvary of the War, all thin (literally from hunger), dashing and agile, and consumed by a great longing to resume our careers in full. We wanted to break out from the bonds which had confined us, and in fact that was exactly what we did – on the wings of Rossini's immortal masterpiece. In a matter of months the names Tito Gobbi, Ferrucio Tagliavini, Italo Tajo, Vito de Taranto, Nelly Corradi – and Mario Costa as a director – were known in every continent.

That first *Barber* film – which was of course in black and white – was still going the rounds when we made the second one, in colour. This was a clever combination of Beaumarchais' comedy with the music of Rossini, the cast being Nicola Monti, Giulio Neri and myself, with Irene Genna acting Rosina dubbed by the exquisite voice of Lina Pagliughi. Cesco Baseggio, the popular Venetian actor, played Bartolo.

Since 1816, the year when it first appeared, *The Barber* has proved itself indestructible, although it has had to stand up to some pretty coarse treatment in its time. There was a period when questionable liberties were allowed to performers, who even boasted of their excesses. Prima donnas held up the action while they indulged in canarylike displays. Basses, anxious to beat their colleagues at the game, clowned around as though in a circus, while baritones contented themselves with singing little more than half the notes Rossini had provided for them.

There were even conductors determined, literally, to 'get in on the act' who had the harpsichord lifted on to the podium so that they could strum endless arpeggios to accompany recitatives. But, in spite of it all, *The Barber of Seville* remains to this day an unblemished masterpiece, a masterpiece which repays every bit of loving care and discipline lavished upon it.

It is a work which singers should banish from their repertoire at the first sign of fatigue, doubt or lack of confidence. An *opera buffa* calls for more serious work than any high drama, for in it there is no way of hiding one's vocal shortcomings. Also, resisting all temptation to capture special notice, each performer must keep strictly within the framework of his or her character.

Figaro, in spite of his excellent opinion of himself and his boundless confidence as the 'factotum' of the city, is a barber. He must not forget it. Even if he does dare to make rather free with

Rosina, Don Bartolo or the Count Almaviva, it must be done with grace, moderation and at least apparent respect. Social stations must be properly underlined, for from them springs the comic or daring action. Even though we were not there in 1816 we must be aware of the customs and relationships of the period. That indefinable quality called style is based on knowledge of these things, and the music underlines this.

The wealth of recitative tells the story of great brilliance and keen wit. It does not require to be made funnier by clowning, gags, tricks and contrivances. Indeed we sometimes need to remove from the work all the encrustations which have accumulated over the years, choosing the interpretation most suited to our own histrionic vein.

I recall how in one provincial town – with an audience used to a rather rough performance – led by a conductor we all thought a bit dry and difficult, we gave a very fine *Barber* without a single added word or note but absolutely faithful to the score. We not only enjoyed it ourselves but had a great success, the audience quite obviously appreciating a refined performance to the full.

Towards the end of the War Figaro began to play an extraordinary part in our lives. We had been informed, of course, that we had been 'liberated', but naturally a 'liberator' is seen in the first place as a conqueror. *Vae victis* (woe to the conquered) was in the air and in our hearts, and the moral dejection was much heavier than any feeling of having achieved a 'freedom' which many of us neither knew nor understood. It can easily be appreciated therefore that the explosive liveliness of Figaro's cavatina transported everyone to a sense of mad elation.

At that very difficult time we singers followed the liberating armies as they advanced towards the north of Italy. We sang in ice-cold theatres in towns devastated by bombing, lived in hotels half shattered and without windows. It was a bitter winter, the roads covered with the snow, and we travelled by whatever means were available from one city to another. But we had suffered so much, endured so many privations, that we had been hardened like rocks. Our rude health stood up to every discomfort.

'Transport by any means available' usually meant driving in open trucks, through snow-covered mountain passes and valleys that were muddy in sun or rain. We would be dropped in front of some crumbling 'opera house' like statues of ice and mud. No hot water to clean ourselves, only the compulsion to be ready in a few hours to present *The Barber, Rigoletto, Tosca* . . . whatever. From Ancona to Terni, I remember, we crossed the Appennines in a heavy snow-storm in a motorcade of some twenty trucks barely covered by a tarpaulin. I had almost to scrape the mud and snow from my wife's face to discover her lovely smile.

I need not enlarge further on the daily drama and discomfort. But they explain the enthusiasm and impetuosity with which we threw ourselves into our work, glad to exchange grim reality for the representation of forgotten or forbidden joys, glad to pretend for a few hours that that hateful British sergeant who treated us to such humiliation did not exist. (He was like the ones you see in films and can't believe really happen. But they do! At least, one did – and we had him.)

The early response to our performances was cordial, even enthusiastic, but it was in some way – detached. The reception was not, and could not be, friendly. There was a barrier to be overcome between the audience and ourselves. We did not know each other.

In my case the barrier was crossed in one jump, with Figaro's cavatina. I sang it everywhere. Indeed it was, 'Figaro qua, Figaro la' (Figaro here, Figaro there) in very truth. I sang it for soldiers, officers and politicians. I sang it in hospital wards, among white beds, nurses and bandaged young bodies – victims like myself (though much more so) of the collective madness which so easily spreads through humanity. In every instance, and to an unbelievable degree, I brought a light of joy, friendship and gaiety, a breath from a better world which flew in on the wings of music. I was known as 'Figaro' at that time, and Charles Poletti, the US Governor of Rome at this period, was never tired of hearing me sing it. Indeed, he would jump from his seat, clap one hand against the other and shout, 'Titooo . . . Figaro!' I had friends by the thousand, and I used to think how I should love to be able to spread this 'Figaro qua, Figaro la' throughout the world, to make everyone laugh and never cry again.

I know myself what it means to be a listener as well as a performer at a first encounter with Rossini's *Barber of Seville*, for when I was only about twenty and knew little of the operatic world into which I was to plunge a few years later I went to hear a performance of it at the Rome Opera House. The brilliant cavatina sung by Carlo Galeffi, the suave serenade of Dino Borgioli, the miraculous aria of Toti dal Monte and the great 'La calunnia' of Ezio Pinza. I was overwhelmed by joy, filled with spiritual delight for the clean, elegant performance of that fabulous cast. It was an unrestrained sort of joy never experienced before. I had discovered *The Barber of Seville*.

It is a great moment in one's life and I could go on for several more paragraphs – but Rosina is waiting in the wings to make her appearance. She does say in the course of the opera, 'Figaro è un galantuomo, un giovin di buon cuore,' (Figaro is a good man with a good heart) but I fear she may change her mind if I neglect her longer.

Rosina, then, has just arrived in Seville with that boring guardian of hers, Don Bartolo. Meanwhile, Count Almaviva (alias Lindoro), ardent as a young Pamplona bull, has followed her from Madrid and spends his time serenading her and arousing in her all sorts of forbidden desires. Rebellion and cunning start their work in the pretty head of that almost imprisoned girl.

She is beautiful and lively and, although she is secluded within the four walls of her guardian's house, woe betide anyone who rouses her spirit and her will to fight. As she says in her first great aria, she is very sweet until roused. But then she becomes dangerous as a viper, and will set endless traps for her enemies. When she does decide to fight it is she who will win the battle.

So the comic plot takes wing. Love letters fly from the balcony under the very nose of Don Bartolo; Figaro acts as *postillon d'amour*, bringing messages to and fro. Poor Don Bartolo certainly has his suspicions – why is there a missing piece of paper? Why has Rosina a smear of ink on her finger? But his ward has demure answers to all his enquiries. In spite of all his suspicions, bolts and bars, he is threatened with the loss of his heart, his head and, above all, Rosina's handsome dowry.

In the end his consolation prize is to be the mature and homely Berta, his housekeeper, who grumbles her way through life, dissatisfied with her lot but ever hopeful. She is thoroughly sick of being ordered about, always under someone's feet when anything out of the ordinary happens. And indeed, in this work something happens every two or three bars. Her beautiful short aria before the storm, 'Il vecchiotto cerca moglie' (The old man seeks a wife) sets out very piquantly her curiosity about love – and her rebellious resignation.

Incidentally, the most unforgettable interpretation of that aria I ever witnessed was not by a woman. It was by the famous Russian producer Alexander Sanine when he was showing a young singer what to do. With eyes half closed because he was very short-sighted, and a grimace on the left side of his face as though he were winking, bent with age and moving heavily, he took out his handkerchief to dust around. And, to the amazement of us all, Rossini's Berta came to life before our eyes. Something never to be forgotten.

Lindoro, helped by the resourceful Figaro and his super-comic invention of several disguises – not to mention the judicious use of money, a ring and a pistol – earns even Don Basilio's interested co-operation. Throughout he finds himself sailing on tempestuous seas, and only in the short moments when he can reveal his own identity does he snatch a few moments of peace. Too many lies create such a bewildering tangle that precautions become useless. In conclusion, however, all is cleared for the happy ending.

The character of Don Basilio is gigantic – over life-sized. Wily cheat, peaceable crook, he threads his way through the most difficult and unforeseen situations unharmed, merely changing direction with the wind. The great aria 'La calunnia' is a master-piece, and explains his whole philosophy of life. It is pure gold for the true singing actor.

Indeed, the *melodramma buffo* by Cesare Sterbini gives to all the interpreters generous possibilities for characterisation, amusing as well as truly human. Then Rossini, the 'Swan of Pesaro', gave the opera elegance and humour with the divine, inexhaustible grace of his music. No wonder this masterly creation is so tense, so viva-cious in every musical aspect, inspiring all the performers with enthusiasm.

During some four hundred performances in which I took part I cannot recall one which did not animate all with a feeling of enthusiastic commitment, the mundane world forgotten in a wonderful, happy atmosphere. They were performances full of life, inspiring us all to do our best, and more than our best, in friendly competition with one another. The audience also identified with the characters, having their favourites, absorbed and overcome.

It is impossible to let the attention wander for one single second; there is so much to do and sing, and there is no let-up in the music. The recitatives must be given clearly and with expression. Once you are convinced of this axiom, you realise – as I have said but would like to repeat – that to add questionable gesture with the idea of amusing the audience is quite superfluous. What Rossini has put into the music is more than enough.

If, for instance, while Basilio is singing 'La calunnia' you watch just one face in the audience, you will learn exactly how Bartolo should react; without comment and over-excitement, which would be out of place. That is not to say that he should remain like a statue in order not to disturb his colleague's singing, just that he should present the normal attitude of someone listening to an extraordin-ary tale. Action and reaction in a brilliant comedy is the finest thing an actor-singer can achieve. To try to make a brilliant comedy even funnier is like adding salt to an already well-seasoned dish. You end by disliking it.

All the characters in *The Barber* are smiling ones, and their dilemmas must make the audience smile – right from the opening moments when we have the charming group of hired musicians assembled to serenade Rosina. Their exuberance at the sight of their pay grows to a tremendous crescendo of gratitude – the last thing Count Almaviva requires, and which he vainly tries to subdue.

Finally, they disappear, still embarrassingly vocal, just in time to leave the stage free for the striking entrance of Figaro. There follows the famous cavatina, the meeting with the Count, the second (more successful) serenade to Rosina and her reply.

The Count is impatient to see Rosina, and Figaro's genius begins to work, his agile brain producing innumerable ideas for penetrating Rosina's prison. The prospect of reward quickens his powers of invention. The rising phrase 'All'idea di quel metallo' (At the thought of this metal) mirrors his rising hopes as he imagines gold and silver landing in his pockets: 'Già viene l'oro, già vien l'argento' (Here comes the gold, here comes the silver). Innumerable sparkling notes are tossed into the air as though from some magic fountain.

Then the excitement takes practical shape as Don Bartolo makes a brief appearance, muttering that he is going to marry Rosina this very day. The two conspirators, delighted with the idea of frustrating his plans, watch him cross the stage and then take high-spirited leave of each other.

In the next scene we meet Rosina, who has already boldly written a letter to her 'Lindoro' and dreams of the serenade in which he declared his love. She is determined to have him, and relies on Figaro to help them. There is time, however, to exchange only a few words before Figaro has to hide, for in comes Don Bartolo, peering around suspiciously and cursing the barber.

Unexpectedly Don Basilio arrives; but not for the usual singing lesson with Rosina but as a sort of unofficial spy and information gatherer for Don Bartolo. He brings the unwelcome news that Count Almaviva is in town. Dispirited, the two men realise they must do something – and quickly. But what?

It is Don Basilio who finds the speedy answer. La calunnia! That little poisonous whisper of calumny which, properly handled, can grow into a cannon-shot loud enough to blast any man's reputation and ruin him. Voice, diction, the infinite range of colouring giving expression to every word, the crescendo in both voice and orchestra, the powerful cannon-shot, the description of the 'meschino calunniato' (the poor wretch thus calumniated) – all make of this aria a unique scene. It is a scene which reveals the masterly astuteness of Don Basilio, the music master – and tests to the full the taste and intelligence of the singer.

It is no surprise to us when Don Basilio concludes 'Vengan danari
. . . Al resto son qua io' (Let the money be forthcoming and leave
the rest to me.) They part in a state of mutual self-congratulation,
and Figaro emerges from hiding, having overheard all.

Almost immediately he is rejoined by Rosina. During the following very lively duet he makes a little free with her, but Rosina does
not seem to mind. She is thinking only of Lindoro and the letter she
must send him. There is quite a competition between them – the
genial Figaro and 'the cunning little fox', not only in the interpretation but even more in a rare and precious vocal challenge. There are
literally hundreds of notes to be sung prestissimo in the coloratura
style, intertwined in harmonious texture but every one as clear as
crystal.

Giulietta Simionato and I thoroughly enjoyed this gallant competition several times in Chicago in 1954. She is not only a
magnificent singer and actress but a woman of fine wit, and it
was wonderful! We were told it was a joy to see the two of us
together. (Excuse my modesty! I intend the compliment for the
lady.)

The letter which Figaro implores and encourages Rosina to write
has, of course, already been written. And he thought he could teach
the girl! He is charmed and amused beyond expression, reassures
her that all will be well, and goes off in very high spirits.

In comes the insufferable Don Bartolo, bullying Rosina with his
continual suspicions and questions. Finally, though she has an answer for everything, she can stand it no longer. Contemptuously
rejecting his threats of bolts and bars, she runs away upstairs.

There is a knock at the street door. Grumbling, Berta goes to
answer it, and finds, to her loud dismay, that there is a drunken
soldier outside armed with a billeting order. He forces his way in
amidst great noise and confusion, and we realise that he is the Count
in the first of Figaro's suggested disguises.

Attracted by the clamour, Rosina steals halfway down the stairs,
but is shooed off by her guardian who then searches for the papers
exempting him from billeting. He finds them at last, but the soldier
tosses the papers away, threatens Don Bartolo with his sword and
generally creates a tremendous confusion and uproar.

Everyone rushes around: Don Bartolo, Don Basilio, Berta, the
drunken soldier, the crowd who come in from the street attracted
by the noise, and finally the military police now summoned by
was wonderful! We were told it was a joy to see the two of us
Only a miracle can resolve the situation, and this our genius
provides. Suddenly Don Bartolo is struck dumb and motionless
like a statue. All concentrate on him, commenting one after

another. Then, with a terrific sneeze, he recovers his senses and the act ends in a splendid ensemble.

★

Before the beginning of the next act Don Bartolo has gone to the commander of the regiment and discovered that no one knows anything about the drunken soldier who came demanding a billet. He immediately suspects that Count Almaviva is in some way involved and, full of fresh doubts, he returns home angrier than ever.

Here he receives a fresh visitor – Don Alonzo, a young music teacher who describes himself mildly and respectfully as a pupil of Don Basilio who, being seriously ill himself, has sent him instead to give Rosina her customary singing lesson. Naturally the modest young priest is none other than Count Almaviva in yet another ingenious disguise thought up by the ever resourceful Figaro.

He bows right and left, wishing everyone 'Pace e gioia' at interminable length, until the exasperated Don Bartolo fetches in Rosina and the singing lesson begins under the tutelage of the false Alonzo. Marvellous though her aria may be to the singer, it is very tedious to Don Bartolo, who nods off to sleep, thus giving Almaviva and Rosina the chance to exchange a few loving and explanatory words.

Suddenly Don Bartolo wakes up, protests against this modern music and himself starts singing the 'arietta' which the famous singer Caffarelli used to sing in his youth. In the nick of time Figaro arrives, makes fun of the old man and insists that he must now shave him. No question of putting it off until tomorrow for he will be much too busy then with the nobility.

Figaro hopes to give the young couple a chance to converse while he literally has the tiresome guardian under his hand. Also he must get a few things organised for the wedding! Going to get fresh linen from a cupboard in the hall, he disturbs a quantity of china, and the tremendous crash brings Don Bartolo running. During their few minutes of welcome peace, Rosina and Almaviva agree on the escape plot for the next night.

Don Bartolo, pulling Figaro by the ear, comes grumbling back into the room. But, just as he would sit down for the completion of the shaving, Don Basilio, like an apparition of gloom and mystery, makes an appearance, causing consternation to all. He is stupefied to discover another priest and follows him around like a hunting dog while Rosina tries to hide 'Don Alonzo' with her wide-spread skirts. Meanwhile Don Bartolo makes anxious enquiries after the health of the bemused Basilio, and Figaro busies himself in repairing the situation with a thousand inventions.

Preceded by recitative, there follows a quintet in which music, words, questions and answers are interwoven like the links of a precious chain, all done with an ingenuity which leaves the audience breathless. A bag of money (the Count's medicine for the so-called sick Basilio) does wonders, and the rascally old priest agrees that the best thing is for him to go home to bed and take care of himself.

With a light touch (*tempo allegro*) the orchestra restores some degree of calm, and the shaving is at last resumed. To shave anyone in such a situation is not exactly simple, and the humour is bound to become a little heavier. But the stylish performer is the one who can contain and control his actions within the general tone of the comedy and its logical development.

I remember once taking part in Stockholm in a performance under the famous Russian conductor, Maestro Dobrowen, who was also producing. He saw it almost as a ballet, which at the time I thought exaggerated and in which I felt like a marionette. We had quite a discussion and eventually I did somewhat understand his point. The ballet idea can indeed create a balance between the players, with stylish and light action and a certain overall elegance. But, as I have said, in the shaving scene one inevitably becomes less elegant, particularly at the moment when, while watching the young lovers, Figaro energetically applies the lather to Don Bartolo's eyes.

Finally the old man escapes from Figaro's clutches, surprises the lovers in intimate discussion and breaks out in tremendous fury. He chases everyone around, slapping out at them with his towel, during the delightful finale 'La testa mi gira' (My head is spinning).

In great confusion they all rush out by the first available door, and the indescribable pandemonium is succeeded by the entrance of poor Berta, who has every reason to complain there is always commotion in this house, in her lovely aria, 'Il vecchiotto cerca moglie' (The old man seeks a wife).

Then comes the storm, magically evoked by Rossini with an amazing economy of expressive means. It is so engagingly realistic that one almost runs for shelter. The flutes give the effect of lightning, the cellos thunder with their tremolos, and the pizzicato of the violins provides the slackening raindrops as the small storm dies away. It is not a hurricane, not even a storm of any proportions, just a passing shower at the end of a hot summer day.

At the last drops of rain, Figaro and the Count appear, wrapped in cloaks, Figaro carrying a lantern. It is midnight, the hour when

Lindoro has told Rosina to expect him. But, alas, Rosina is angry and suspicious, for Bartolo has convinced her that both Figaro and Lindoro intended to abduct her and throw her into the arms of the Count Almaviva. She makes quite a scene with her refusal to be taken in; but the misunderstanding is short lived when Lindoro admits to being none other than Count Almaviva in person, come to marry her here and now.

There is general joy and astonishment on the part of the lovers, while Figaro basks in the success of his masterly stage management. He watches the happy pair, marvelling at his own genius. But fresh problems are already preparing to pile upon one another. The plotters discover that the ladder required for the escape has been removed from the balcony by the wily Don Bartolo. Then Don Basilio arrives with the notary who is to celebrate Rosina's marraige to her guardian.

But no matter! the ingenious Figaro immediately seizes on the notary to perform a marriage between Count Almaviva and his, Figaro's, 'niece'. Don Basilio would like to interfere but, offered the choice between a pistol and a valuable ring, decides to trim his sails to the prevailing wind. He accepts the ring and ends up as a witness to Rosina's marriage to Lindoro, otherwise Count Almaviva.

Poor outwitted Don Bartolo arrives in anxious haste, accompanied by soldiers and an officer – but too late. Even here, however, Figaro has the ready answer. He leads forth Berta as an alternative bride for Bartolo, who accepts her with a fairly good grace, particularly when he finds that the Count has renounced Rosina's substantial dowry.

The *Barber* story is so rich in invention, surprises and unexpected developments in rapid sequence that to add anything further is to overload one of the most superbly balanced comedies in the whole range of opera. As I have said, I always sang this work with boundless enthusiasm, surrounded by colleagues of like interest and enjoyment. But I have to add that when it was all over we were exhausted, only too glad to put up our feet in our dressing-rooms – though still in riotous good spirits.

In my score (Ricordi 1938) there is an aria for Bartolo 'Manca un foglio' (a sheet is missing) composed by Pietro Romani, which for years it was fashionable to substitute for Rossini's authentic 'A un dottor della mia sorte' (To a doctor of my kind). I also recall Rosinas singing just what they liked in the singing lesson, regardless of period or suitability.

Now, happily, the original arias have been restored – and quite right too! This is *Rossini*'s comic masterpiece. Let no one interfere in the mistaken belief that the master can be improved upon.

★

The Marriage of Figaro. In writing next of the other Figaro masterpiece I am, of course, stepping back in time so far as musical
composition is concerned. But I have chosen to do this since the
events of Mozart's *Marriage of Figaro* follow on those in Rossini's
Barber of Seville. Also – though I would not claim that this is at all a
matter of comparable importance – I myself had occasion to
approach the two great works in that order.

Both, of course, drew their inspiration from the Beaumarchais
play *Le Barbier de Seville* which appeared in 1775. Several lesser
composers based operas upon this work, but the only one of any
eminence was Giovanni Paisiello's *Il Barbiere de Siviglia*, which
appeared in 1782 and held quite a popular place in the Italian
repertoire until Rossini's work of the same name came along in
1816. Before then, as I have said, Mozart had given *The Marriage of
Figaro* to the world in 1786.

The superb libretto is by Lorenzo da Ponte – abbot, adventurer,
impresario and publisher, who was justly proud of his influence on
Mozart. 'I can never recall without pleasure and exultation,' he said,
'that largely because of my perseverance and firmness, Europe and
the world enjoy all the exquisite vocal compositions of this admirable genius.'

When the time came I was curious to pass from my young Figaro
to the other more mature, mordant and certainly less happy man,
attracted by the idea of following his development through the
years. But, to tell the truth, I found his later character heavier,
rougher, greedier about his future welfare and not so naturally
elegant. His mind, heart and spirit seemed to have lost their
freshness – and I decided to abandon him. I did not want to see
Rossini's Figaro getting older and I turned with quickened interest
to Count Almaviva, the fine gentleman who seeks to be the
absolute master in his own castle.

A very complex character. A seducer – not always successful
perhaps, but authoritative and jealous. He falls easy prey to traps
prepared for him but throughout he maintains an awareness of his
distinction of class and an unmistakable style in his reactions and
demeanour.

In representing this handsome, haughty gentleman, I admit that I
was sometimes inwardly amused – a little maliciously so – to watch
my colleagues make the role of Figaro more decadent than mine. In
my view, if you want true eighteenth-century style you must look

for it in the Count and Countess. It follows that Figaro is – and remains throughout – a subordinate. *They* are the real protagonists of the story.

My decision to abandon Figaro in favour of the Count received a strong 'push' owing to a genuine misprint. I had been engaged to sing Figaro and Italo Tajo to sing the Count. Then together we read on posters displayed all over the district that our roles had been switched! Hurriedly and happily Italo and I exchanged our projected roles then and there. We had to work like mad, of course, but felt much better in each other's shoes. The other person who was relieved beyond measure was the impresario, who had been in agony over the mistake until he found we were perfectly happy with our own re-casting.

Thus I became the Count. And the Count I remained throughout my career.

The construction of *Nozze* does not follow the usual form of the period, nor is it closely connected with Beaumarchais' comedy. It is in fact a world unto itself. But it captures us instantly and involves us willingly in the brilliant plot.

The opera opens on the day before the wedding of Figaro and Susanna. She is trying on a new hat, while he is taking the measurements of the room they are to share. (A good mark, by the way, to the Figaro who does this properly on his knees – unlike one illustrious singer who refused to assume such a menial position!) Their duet is purely conversational, and must be coloured vocally with the proper shades, the tones and expressions of both displaying the absent-minded accents of those who talk of one thing and think of another.

Then suddenly a problem rears its head and a small quarrel ensues. 'Se a caso Madama la notte ti chiama din . . . din . . . don . . . don . . .' (If by chance the Countess calls, etc.) In other words, the room allotted to them may be convenient should the Countess summon but – suppose it is Figaro who should be sent on a message and Susanna left alone? How far will the Count take advantage of that?

They have quite an acrimonious little exchange over this, and it is immediately observable that Susanna is the resourceful one and Figaro the one who is easily jealous. Indeed, when she has tripped off on her mistress's business, Figaro gives vent to his real feelings about his master in the brilliant, sarcastic cavatina, 'Se vuol ballare, Signor Contino' (If you would dance, my lord, I'll play the tune). Beginning with an irresistible waltzlike tune, it develops into a sort of challenge to the Count and his amorous exploits, showing more and more the anger of the justifiably jealous future husband.

The room assigned to the couple now becomes almost a meeting place for everyone, the goings and comings, the meetings and partings, being legion.

First enters Don Bartolo, muttering over his grievances against Figaro, whom he has never forgiven for having outwitted him. He expresses his longing for some sort of revenge in his aria 'La vendetta'.

Then appears the waspish old Marcellina, who has romantic designs on the attractive young Figaro. She has high words (though very dignified ones) with Susanna, both of them deadly sweet to the other but murderous in their bearing.

Next to appear is Cherubino, the page, dying of love for every woman in the place. Consumed with passion for Susanna, Barbarina (the gardener's daughter), even the Countess herself, he is prepared to sing about his feelings to anyone willing to listen. Or even if they don't want to. His amusingly immature personality is expressed in one of the loveliest and most popular melodies in the opera, 'Non so più cosa son, cosa faccio' (I don't know who I am or what I'm doing).

Susanna is teasing Cherubino and allowing a little flirting when the Count arrives, hoping to find the attractive maid alone. Only just in time she conceals Cherubino in a big armchair and throws a cover over him, thereby unwittingly preparing a situation worthy of a French farce. While fending off the Count's advances, she tries to draw him away from the fatal chair. Don Basilio sneaks in and the Count hides himself behind the same chair. At one point Susanna is even reduced to feigning a fainting fit when he seems about to sit down on the concealed page.

Eventual discovery is inevitable of course, and the astounded and angry Count decrees that Cherubino shall join his regiment and go to the wars. The Count has only just escaped looking ridiculous, and he is hard put to it to remain gracious when Figaro leads in a bevy of local beauties who stand there intoning their thanks to the Count for his graciousness as a master.

Apparently the Count has been vaguely thinking of relinquishing his *droit de seigneur* (his feudal right to sample any young bride before her husband). Figaro, no doubt with his Susanna in mind, forces his reluctant hand. For having been publicly acclaimed as the noblest of masters, the Count can hardly proceed to tarnish his halo without delay. He leaves the room in haughty disgust – dignified still, but with no friendly feelings for Figaro. Their relationship is indeed very different from that in Rossini's *Barber*.

The act ends with a burlesque martial tune, like a fanfare, in which Figaro sings a mocking farewell to Cherubino, now condemned to join the army – 'Non più andrai farfallone amoroso' (Here's an end to your philandering).

This is perhaps the moment to pause and warn that the many lovely arias which appear throughout this work – irresistible though they may be – are *not* for the beginner. That deceptive simplicity, those easy melodies, require a voice which is technically ready and virtually flawless, with the right projection, range and breath control. The risk of singing without proper support, losing the vibrations and the vocal commitment – these are an abyss all too ready to swallow up the inexperienced singer. Believe me, it is very, very difficult to sing Mozart well.

In Act 2 the Countess is alone. She is no longer the lively, brilliant Rosina of *The Barber of Seville*. Sad and forlorn, with no one to overhear her, she sings, 'Porgi amor qualche ristoro' (Love give me relief), anticipating the plaintive and even more nostalgic, 'Dove sono i bei momenti?' of the third act (Where are the lovely moments?)

With other people, she keeps up appearances, and does not forget her position as the Countess Almaviva. Only with her maid, Susanna – and that half unwillingly – does she reveal something of her inner feelings, for it is from Susanna that she knows of her husband's amorous attentions elsewhere.

To divert her mistress, Susanna introduces Cherubino into the room and then, taking her guitar, delicately accompanies him as he sings the bewitching 'Voi che sapete' (You who know). Infatuated by the graciousness of the Countess, the blushing page hardly minds Susanna's mockery. There is some enjoyable flirting, and Susanna makes a lot of fuss dressing the page up as a woman – 'Venite inginocchiatevi' (Come here and kneel before me). But, just as their amusement is at its peak, the jealous Count arrives outside the door and, finding it locked, imperiously demands admittance.

In extreme confusion at the prospect of being found alone with Cherubino in woman's attire, the Countess tries to play for time. Cherubino hides in the dressing-room, Susanna retires behind a screen, and the Countess finally opens the door of her room to admit her suspicious husband.

There is a lively and angry discussion in which he demands to have the dressing-room door opened. She vows that the key is lost but, taking her by the hand, he almost drags her away with him, declaring that he will find something with which to break open the door.

The moment they have gone Susanna emerges from behind the screen and releases Cherubino, who, now in his own attire, jumps down out of the window, breaking some glass as he goes. Susanna then shuts herself in the dressing-room a second or two before the Count and Countess return.

In spite of her pleas of innocence (though she knows she has been indiscreet) the Countess cannot restrain her husband from banging on the dressing-room door prior to breaking it down. To the stupefaction of both Count and Countess, the door is opened and out steps Susanna, as demure and innocent as a kitten who has eaten the cream. The Countess, breathing again, although she still does not know how she has been saved, adopts an air of injured hauteur towards her now abjectly apologetic husband. Then in comes Figaro, as fresh as a daisy, all ready to fix the wedding day.

Before anything can be settled, however, Antonio, the grumpy old gardener, comes in to complain that some young man has just jumped out of the window and broken some of his flower pots. Suspicion is immediately rekindled in the Count's mind but, in what is arguably the greatest operatic ensemble ever written, everyone competes to explain away Antonio's story.

Each character expresses his or her own thoughts and reactions with individual distinctness and yet the most magical fusion. And on this superb achievement the act ends.

The Count is now up to the neck in this imbroglio and cannot find a way out. His amorous assaults have become more tentative and he begins to look ridiculous. Every time he risks a new conquest he is anxious lest he be caught in the act by his wife, whom he still loves passionately in spite of his little escapades.

He has a brief meeting with Susanna, who appears momentarily rather more compliant; but then he is disabused of this pleasant thought by overhearing a conversation between her and Figaro which shows they are in concert against him. The aria he sings at this point, 'Vedrò mentr'io sospiro?' (Must I forgo my pleasure?) is marked *allegro maestoso*, but must not be allowed to lose dignity in the singing. Unfortunately, this is often the case. It becomes a rush, with gabbled words which detract from the impressiveness that should underline the Count's thoughts and attitudes.

Later comes the altercation between Marcellina and Bartolo during which it is disclosed that Figaro is no less than their own son. There is again a great deal of surprise, misunderstanding and confusion, framed and clarified in a beautiful sextet in which everyone comments on the extraordinary and comic discovery.

Meanwhile the sorrowing Countess, alone once more, sings her beautiful 'Dove sono' recalling in a moment of sweet melancholy the happy past. But with the re-entry of Susanna comes a happier mood. Together the resourceful maid and the Countess concoct a note of assignation to the Count – 'Che soave zeffiretto' (How soft the breeze) – for the meeting is to take place where the pine trees of the little wood sway in the soft breeze. Susanna writes the note to the Countess's dictation and, as the two singers pass the words to and fro between them, the music provides an effect of undulation, dreaming and poetic like the swaying of the pine trees. It is one of the many beautiful numbers in this beautiful opera.

The Countess and her maid agree that, if the Count falls for their little plot and accepts the invitation, then Susanna, disguised as her mistress, will keep the assignation.

Meanwhile, to complete the Count's discomfiture, Barbarina the gardener's daughter – who is really no better than she should be – inadvertently lets fall that the Count has been kissing her and making lavish promises to her. In short, there is a minor domestic revolution afoot to assail the Count's dignity from every side.

Yet as master of them all, and in ceremonies company with his Countess, he is called on to receive the two bridal couples: Marcellina now belatedly to be made an honest woman by Bartolo, and the happy Figaro and Susanna. During the brief parade, enlivened by a delicious Spanish rhythm, Susanna contrives to give the Count the famous note. It has been fastened with a pin, the return of which is to constitute his acceptance of the invitation. However, he pricks his finger with the pin and drops it.

Figaro, seeing his master with a note, is amused, assuming that some light girl has given it to him. But he is a little previous with his laughter, for he too is soon to be mocked.

At the end of the little ceremony the Count, on taking leave of them all, promises a big banquet for the evening, with dances and fireworks. Though plotting vengeance on those who have manoeuvred him into doing what they want rather than what he desires, he still preserves his dignity, appearing noble and paternal with a haughty, half jaundiced smile on his lips. Even so he is naïve enough to choose Barbarina to return the pledge of the pin. She immediately loses it in her turn, and sings the plaintive little cavatina 'L'ho perduta' (I have lost it, poor me!). Figaro, coming on her and trying to console her, receives the stunning information that the note to the Count was originally sent by his own new bride.

Bitterly disillusioned, he sings furiously of the duplicity of all women in his aria 'Aprite un pò quegli occhi' (Until your eyes are opened) and rushes from the stage. Once more he is proved mistaken, however, for he is succeeded by Susanna, who sings her beguiling aria 'Deh vieni non tardar' (Then come, my heart's delight) which is a pure love call.

In the paths of the little wood, among fountains and scented bushes – and all of it in the dark ! – the confusion of the interwoven plot is slowly reduced to simplicity. Mistaken identities, slaps and kisses in abundance, explanations and excuses – all combine to bring about the final unmasking of the Count and his amorous intrigues. Disconcerted but not humiliated, he gallantly falls to his knees and, in a touching and most beautiful phrase, public repents and asks for his Rosina's pardon.

A most lively and humorous finale 'Questo giorno di tormento' (What a vexatious day) ends in a mood of general rejoicing.

*

Lorenzo da Ponte's complicated and amusing comedy can hardly be understood if read in haste. Which is why, in the deplorable rush of some performances, with no proper time given for the recitatives or thought for clarity of diction, the whole thing degenerates into a muddle which does scant justice to the story. Yet the characters are all finely drawn, with an extraordinary harmony between the words and the divine music; the whole producing a richness of eloquence and depth of human feeling rare in even the most superb master-piece.

The role of Count Almaviva, in turn baffled and authoritative, was one I always loved playing. Of the many productions in which I took part I remember with particular affection the one at Covent Garden under Sir George Solti, with a wonderful cast.

The Figaro was Sir Geraint Evans, with whom I had a lot of fun. As in *Don Giovanni*, we two made a most happy match of it, with a mutual understanding and a shared joy in performance which was wellnigh perfect.

Susanna was Mirella Freni, delightfully coquettish with me as the Count while deceiving me shamelessly, the bad girl! Ilva Ligabue was the Countess, beautiful both vocally and personally, and Cherubino was that little devil Teresa Berganza, pulling faces at me as she hid in the chair, flirting so unashamedly with the Countess that Ilva could hardly stay serious.

Among a host of other roles I remember how Michael Langdon, as Bartolo, shone, and cannot help reminding him of it sometimes now when we meet for Master Classes at the Opera Studio. Happy relationships never to be forgotten! Happy memories which last a lifetime.

6

William Tell

Thirteen years after *The Barber of Seville*, and at the age of thirty-six, Rossini gave expression to his genius in another, entirely different masterpiece – *William Tell*. And although he was to live almost forty years longer, this was his last opera.

The original four-act libretto was written in French, by Etienne de Jouy and Hippolyte Louis-Florent Bis for the Paris Opéra. Later it was translated into Italian by Calisto Bassi and had its first Italian presentation in Lucca, the city which less than thirty years afterwards was to see the birth of another great opera composer – Giacomo Puccini.

Most people are well acquainted with the irresistible overture, beloved of leading orchestras and humble brass bands alike, but know little else of *William Tell*, which is a pity. For this great, this unique opera is, in fact, a seminal work. Like a snowclad mountain peak it towers into the sky, while fresh waters of inspiration descend from it in countless rivulets, bringing new life and ideas to numberless composers.

There is an inexhaustible creativity of musical expression in it and a totally new orchestral depth and sonority. Combined with these features the melodies, themes and ensembles make of this work, in my opinion, an unsurpassed musical monument, imparting to opera a grandeur not previously known. A new accent is achieved and with it the impulse to create what we call 'atmosphere'. Although the music is always of itself the main feature, in many scenes – and in Act 2 particularly – the drama actually *becomes* music. The superb balance between, and blending of, sound and word is little short of miraculous.

Also to be noted is a romantic tone new to Rossini, showing a deepened sensitivity. It can be said that with *William Tell* he brings to a close the music of the eighteenth century while throwing wide the doors to the romantic melodrama. In doing this he displays ideas and intentions of quite unexpected renewal.

For years I have tried to persuade companies like the Royal Opera of Covent Garden and the Lyric Opera in Chicago to mount *William Tell*. But with the disappearance of Sir David Webster and then Carol Fox I must admit that my hopes rest at zero. Generally it is the chorus masters who panic at the prospect, for this is a great and demanding choral work, and their negative reaction inevitably influences conductors, artistic directors and sponsors. There are also, of course, great difficulties for the principals. But these I think one might surmount in an age when excellent singers are not afraid to step out of their usual repertoire.

Certainly anyone willing to take the plunge would find their just reward in *Tell*, for it is an almost inexhaustible mine of vocal treasure for the heartfelt interpreter. In fact, I do not hesitate to cry shame on those who, while pretending to musical culture and knowledge, virtually ignore this gigantic masterpiece. To plead that it is a little difficult of approach is beside the point. *Any* worthwhile work requires on the part of the performers – and the audience, incidentally – a little education, preparation and good feeling. No one should expect just to hold out a passive hand and have a diamond dropped into it. That is not what life (and art) is about.

William Tell was the Swiss national hero of the early fourteenth century. In Switzerland there are monuments and squares dedicated to this man who liberated the country from the Austrian tyrant, uniting the cantons into the confederation which became the Switzerland we know today. Legend and historical truth are most happily united in a great story of patriotism, the yearning for human justice and the fight for freedom from the oppressor.

At the time when the opera opens the Swiss lie passive but bitterly resentful under the despotic rule of the Austrian invader. Then gradually they gather round the strong figure of William Tell, providing a heartlifting example of how the many can be moved to courage and strength by the inspiration of a good and steadfast man. Tell is a devoted husband and father, a loyal, generous friend and a support and comfort to all. He is not a man who likes fighting for fighting's sake. On the contrary, he is constitutionally a man of peace and still hopes that a calm and passive resistance may placate the arrogant enemy.

The local tyrant, Gessler, troubles the life of the village. His sinister shadow, and that of his brutal second-in-command, Rodolfo, lie continually across what would otherwise be the tranquil, simple life of harmless country people.

When the curtain rises the villagers are about to celebrate the marriages of three young couples. Tell leans on his spade, reflecting on the fate of his country lying beneath the conqueror's heel. Close by his wife, Edwige, is spinning, while his young son, Jemmy, practises shooting with his crossbow and arrows. Around are villagers and fishermen, singing of the coming village festivity. It is a deceptively peaceful scene.

There enters Melchtal, one of the most respected older men of the village, leaning on the arm of his son, Arnoldo. Edwige asks him as a favour to bless the wedding festivities and, on his agreeing to do so, Tell invites him to enter their home and rest from the heat of the day. He accepts the invitation, the family and Melchtal enter the house, the crowd disperses still singing, and Arnoldo is left alone.

This gives him the opportunity to describe in a beautiful aria his own cruel predicament. He, the son of a simple Swiss farmer, has fallen hopelessly in love with Mathilde, a Habsburg princess who he rescued from the path of an avalanche. Not only is she socially far above him but, even worse, though good and gentle, she is a representative of the hated invader and everything that his patriotic feelings bid him oppose. He loves his country – but he loves Mathilde too, and the warring emotions to which he is a prey are driving him to distraction.

Distant sounds of a hunting party are heard. He knows that she must be of the party, and curses the fact that the hated Gessler must be there too. He turns abruptly to go, and comes face to face with Tell, who, guessing that something is causing him guilty misery, seeks an opportunity to question the younger man.

There is a tense conversation between them in which Tell calls on

Arnoldo to show his patriotism and join the forces who are
gathering to oppose the enemy. Torn between patriotism and love,
the wretched Arnoldo prevaricates but cannot remain unmoved by
Tell's stirring words. He is saved from committing himself,
however, by the approach of the wedding couples and the re-entry
of his father, Edwige and Jemmy.

The simple service of blessing takes place, but the repeated sound
of hunting horns moves Tell to a fresh outburst of patriotic fervour
during which Arnoldo slips away. Deeply disturbed, Tell follows
him.

Village dances and games continue, during which Jemmy wins
an archery competition and is boyishly exultant. Suddenly there is a
tragic interruption. The shepherd Leutoldo staggers in, pale and
distraught. One of Gessler's party had attempted to abduct his
daughter and, in rescuing her, Leutoldo has killed the man.
Gessler's party are now in hot pursuit and his only chance of escape
is to cross the water. He implores a frightened fisherman to take
him, but the man protests that the current is too strong to risk the
passage at this time.

In vain Leutoldo repeats his pleas; then Tell, returning to the
scene, steps forward and undertakes to row him across the dangerous stretch of water. He hustles the shaking Leutoldo into the boat
and, accompanied by his wife's prayers, pulls away from the shore.
As he is seen disappearing towards the other bank all kneel in
supplication to Heaven to save the two men.

Rodolfo is heard approaching, breathing fire and slaughter.
Terrified, the villagers pray to God for protection, while giving
thanks as they see Tell and Leutoldo land safely on the other side of
the water and disappear among the trees.

Rodolfo enters and demands to know who took the fleeing man
to safety. No one replies. Only Melchtal exclaims contemptuously,
'Sciagurato! questo suolo non è suol di delator!' (Villain! This
country harbours no informers.)

Realising that he is the one who is stiffening the resistance of the
others, Rodolfo turns on him and orders his arrest. Then, having
further decreed that the villagers' houses be burnt to the ground, he
withdraws with his soldiers, taking the imprisoned Melchthal with
him.

Act 2 opens in a wooded valley on the shores of Lake Lucerne (the
Lake of the Four Cantons). Mountains tower in the distance.
Huntsmen and ladies and gentlemen of the chase pass across the
scene. Then, as the stage clears, Mathilde, the Austrian princess,
enters. She has slipped away from her companions in the hope of
meeting Arnoldo.

Meditating on her growing love for him, she sings her beautiful aria 'Selva opaca' (Sombre woods). Arnoldo comes as she had hoped and, although his approach is humble and shows a deep awareness of the social distance between them, she tells him that she in her turn loves him.

Despairingly he points out how hopeless it is, that they would ever be allowed to wed; but she replies that if he, brave man that he. is, would join the Austrian army and fight with the courage he displayed when he rescued her, he would undoubtedly win fresh laurels which would transform his position and enable them to marry. Forgetting for a moment his duty to his country, Arnoldo agrees and they exult together in the hope that this may be the answer to their dilemma. Then they part as footsteps are heard approaching.

Almost immediately Tell and Gualtiero, a fellow patriot, enter, and Tell challenges Arnoldo to admit that he has been meeting Mathilde who can only be regarded as one of the enemy. Proudly Arnoldo confesses his love, to the horror and revulsion of Tell and Gualtiero, who bring grim tidings with them. In the magnificent trio which follows they disclose to Arnoldo that, while he has been exchanging vows of love with one of the enemy, his own brave father has been murdered by Rodolfo because he refused to disclose the identity of the man who saved Leutoldo. Appalled by the news and overwhelmed by remorse for his planned desertion of country and kin, Arnoldo undertakes to join the others in any plan which will enable him to avenge his father's murder.

At this point distant sounds are heard of men approaching, and the words, 'Amici della patria, amici della patria' (Friends of our country) can be distinguished. It heralds one of the most moving scenes in all opera. Musically, dramatically and humanly it is, quite simply, a masterpiece. We of this troubled twentieth century, who have seen – and, in some cases experienced – the fight for freedom and country waged by the brave few against the seemingly over-whelming forces of tyranny, cannot possibly contain a throb of sympathy as we see and hear the gathering forces meeting by night, animated by the example of one brave man. The depth and power of Rossini's music at this point reflect the emotions which have always made people fight for freedom against the oppressor.

Echoing the calls of Tell and Gualtiero, the groups of each canton respond from the valley, arriving armed with scythes, forks and hoes.

First the men of Unterwalden cautiously emerge from the woods and are greeted by Tell with the words, 'O d'Unterwald voi generosi figli!' (O noble sons of Unterwald!)

Then a lone trumpet is heard and Tell exclaims, 'Degli amici di Schwitz ado la tromba risonar d'intorno' (The trumpet call of our friends from the canton of Schwytz) and the men of Schwytz appear from another direction.

Fresh greetings are exchanged and Walter says, 'D'Uri mancan soltanto i magnanimi amici' (Only our brave friends from Uri are missing), but at this moment several small boats are seen quietly approaching the shore.

'Who goes there?' Tell asks, and the triumphant reply comes as the men step ashore, 'Amici della patria, amici della patria' (Friends of the Fatherland).

In turn the men of the three cantons say, 'Guglielmo, sol per te tre popoli s'unir' (William, your inspiration has made three people one). They gather round Tell, who appeals to them in words of such eloquence and strength that he communicates his own enthusiasm to each one of them, and they swear war and death to the enemy.

How can I describe this great scene? I have lived through it and each time felt so great and so strong that it seemed that the stage could hardly contain me. I have even seen people in the audience instinctively straighten up in their seats as though wanting to take part in the great event. The music is so beautiful, the chorus so powerful . . . It is beyond me to describe the scene adequately. I only beg you to listen to it if you ever get the chance. Provided it is presented as it should be, and not mangled by some trendy producer, it is something you will never forget. It will become part of *you*.

This solemn oath closes Act 2. Everyone is now in agreement and only waiting for the right moment to rebel.

Act 3 opens with a short scene between Arnoldo and Mathilde, in which he tells her of his father's murder. All hope of their being united is over. There is no question now of his seeking glory in the Austrian army. He lives only to avenge his father. She begs him to beware of Gessler, that brutal, dangerous man, but he refuses to listen and they part on the words, 'Per sempre addio!' (Farewell for ever!)

The next scene – the most dramatic in the whole work – takes place in the main square of Altdorf, with Gessler's castle seen in the background. He himself, in an ugly mood, sits on a dais at the side of the square, while soldiers sing a chorus in his praise. The women of the village refuse to dance until forced to by the soldiers, and they murmur among themselves that one day the Princess Mathilde, who is always kind to them, will modify some of the harsh measures imposed upon them by the tyrant.

In spite of the undercurrent of resistance there is a certain atmosphere of festivity which provides the opportunity for a ballet of considerable beauty. The mention of this immediately transports me back in thought to performances in the open air in the Baths of Carcalla, when the great ballerina Attila Radice was the solo dancer. I could not resist watching her every time from the wings as I waited for my entrance. Although the stage was exceptionally steep I don't think I ever saw anyone execute more miraculous pirouettes, which she always brought to a stop at the exact moment and the exact place required.

Presently Gessler, seeking an outlet for his ill temper, orders his hat to be hung on a tree and humiliates the throng by demanding that everyone should salute the hat as though it were important in itself. Proudly, William Tell refuses to do so, and Gessler has him arrested. Then, knowing well that he is a famous bowman, he devises a cruel test. He promises Tell his life if he will undertake to shoot an apple from the head of Jemmy, his beloved only child.

Tell's heart trembles in his breast at the fearful thought that he may himself kill his child, and the cellos in tender unison mirror his anguish. Then in accents of ineffable love and reassurance he addresses the child, bidding him stand absolutely still and pray to God to guide the threatening arrow. 'Think of your mother,' he says, 'who is waiting at home. Fix your eyes on heaven so that no fearful movement shall deflect the arrow.'

This aria which starts with the invocation 'Resta immobile' (Remain quite still) is one of the most beautiful of all baritone solos, expressing a father's feelings in tones of great nobility. I always found it moving beyond expression. There are but a few lines of music, but they say it all. The whole story lies in this short divine melody. The heart of the opera beats here in unison with the heart-beats of the listeners.

In front of a quivering and silent crowd the famous bowman splits the apple. Then, as he turns away, he drops a second arrow which he has kept concealed. Gessler immediately asks the reason for the second arrow, and Tell proudly informs him that, had he failed in the test, the second arrow would have been for him – the Austrian governor.

Furious, Gessler retracts his promise of freedom for the successful bowman and orders the arrest of both Tell and Jemmy. But Mathilde steps forward and intervenes. Invested with the authority of her rank, she takes Jemmy under her protection and proceeds to lead him away in spite of his desire to share his father's fate. In the momentary confusion Tell manages to whisper to the boy that he must light a beacon fire to warn the men from the neighbouring cantons that the moment for revolt has arrived.

Then, by Gessler's command, Tell is put in chains and led away towards the lake, with the promise of a horrible death in the castle of Küssnacht. The scene breaks up in furious lamentation, the whole crowd crying in unison, 'Anatema a Gessler!' (May Gessler be accursed!)

Act 4 opens with a short scene in the house which Arnoldo once shared with his father Melchtal. Remorse and a desire for revenge still consume him, and as he sings of his grief and hatred he hears voices approaching outside. The news of Tell's arrest has prompted a spontaneous insurrection. The courage of the men is high, but they lack a supply of effective arms.

At last Arnoldo can give practical expression to his fierce desire for revenge. In an almost joyful rage he leads the men to a cache of arms which he knew that his father and Tell had accumulated against the day of battle. They go out to save Tell, singing triumphantly.

The second, and last, scene takes place on the shores of Lake Lucerne. A tempest is raging, but high on the rock where Tell's house stands the women of the village gather around Edgwige, praying for her husband's safety. They are joined by Mathilde, in whose mercy and goodness the women all trust. She is still protecting Jemmy but, after greeting his mother, he suddenly remembers his father's instructions to light a beacon fire to warn the rebellious men of the cantons.

Deaf to protests and questions he runs away, mounts the hill to his home and sets the house on fire. Then, snatching up his father's precious crossbow and arrows, he rejoins the group. The signal for the insurrection has been given.

At this point Leutoldo reappears on the scene crying aloud that the barge conveying Tell to the prison fortress is being driven towards the rocks. He is no more in chains but is at the helm of the boat. Gessler and his soldiers, terrified by the fury of the storm, have released Tell so that he can handle the boat, as only someone of his skill and strength can save them all.

The fury of the tempest increases and Tell is seen driving the barge towards the shore with Gessler and his soldiers inevitably relying on his skill. At the moment when the boat touches land, however, he jumps ashore and, with his great strength, pushes the barge back into the raging waters.

Gessler is heard cursing aloud, but Jemmy runs to his father and presses his crossbow and arrows into his hands. Tell climbs the rock and cries out in a great voice, 'La Svizzera respiri. A te, Gessler!'

The importance of make-up in the creation of character. This photograph (*above*) was taken to show details of the nose, wig and eyebrows I devised for Falstaff. *Below left:* Ford in *Falstaff:* I have frequently played both roles. *Below right:* My sketch of myself — building the face of Iago in *Otello.*

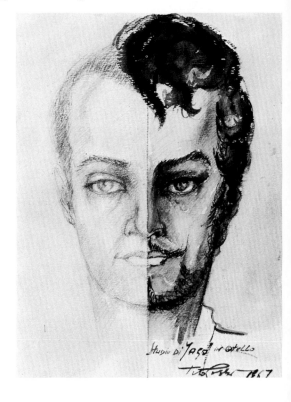

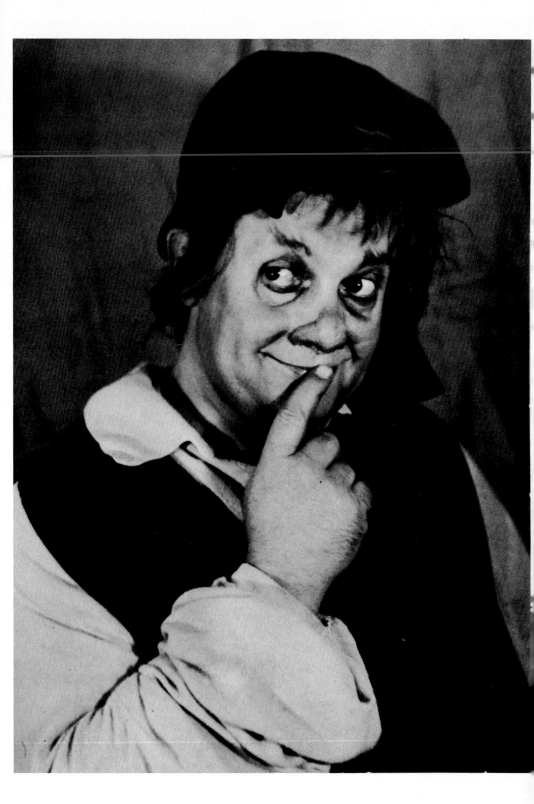

Study in noses. *Gianni Schicchi* (*left*),
King Nebuchadnezzar in *Nabucco*,
Baron Scarpia in *Tosca*,
Rigoletto (*right*). I always made
my own noses, out of cotton wool,
rubber and spirit gum, moulding
them sometimes on a finger
but more often "on site".
They should neither slip nor be
so fixed that they hamper the
expressiveness of the actor's face.

The mature Simone Boccanegra
(*above*), and the Simone of the
Prologue (*below*).

I Pagliacci: cleverly made-up for the
Prologue (*above*) and as Tonio
(*below*).

Don Giovanni (*above*) and Count
Almaviva in *The Marriage of Figaro*
(*below*).

William Tell (*above*) and Figaro in
The Barber of Seville (*below*).

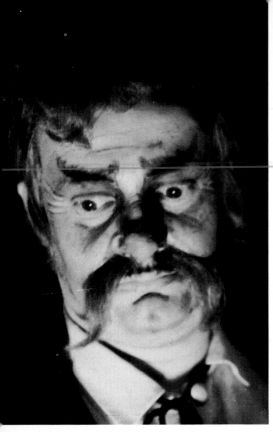

Amonasro in *Aida*.

Peter in *Hansel and Gretel*. I was in
my twenties.

Wozzeck.

Jack Rance in *La Fanciulla del West*.

The story-singer, the character I created in *Il Tesoro* by Jacopo Napoli.

Michele in *Il Tabarro*.

(Switzerland breathes again. This is for you, Gessler!) And, loosing his arrow with matchless skill, he shoots Gessler, who falls dying into the lake.

Led by Gualtiero, a crowd of the confederates enter, seeking Gessler and his forces, but the triumphant villagers explain that Tell has already despatched the villain to a well-deserved fate. All hail Tell as their liberator, though he warns them that they must not count themselves saved until the castle of Altdorf has been taken. Whereupon, right on cue, Arnoldo enters with the glorious news that Altdorf has fallen. His only regret is that his father did not live to see the day.

At this point the storm clouds begin to disperse and the sky becomes a clear blue. Everyone joins in a paean of praise to heaven's beauty and mercy. It is both a thanksgiving to God and an ode to the loveliness of nature. 'Tutto cangia, il ciel s'abbella' (All is changed and the sky is beautiful once more).

As will have been gathered, *William Tell* is not the easiest work to stage. There are quite a crop of difficulties along the way – but they are not insoluble. It is not, however, the achievement of tempests, crowd scenes or mountain prospects which intrigue most people. The one thing they want to know is: *How do you manage to split that apple?*

Well, I shall let you in on the secret. There are four stages.

1. We have a real rather large apple.
2. The fatal arrow never leaves the crossbow. It goes back inside at the moment Tell shoots, but so quickly that the sharpest eye is deceived.
3. Over Jemmy's head an inconspicuous little shelf has been fixed to the tree trunk and it is upon this that the apple really rests.
4. Jemmy, at the precise moment when his father shoots, presses a small concealed spring in the tree trunk and, like a sword-blow, a second arrow splits the apple, remaining with its point embedded in the trunk.

Simple, ingenious – and immensely effective.

Tell was always one of my favourite roles, the emotions ranging from the truly heroic to the tenderness of a loving and fearful father. To tell the truth, I thought that I was pretty good in it in my heyday, and in this connection there is a rather interesting story.

A few years ago, when my autobiography went into print, our friend Bryan Crimp then of EMI had the idea of issuing a record album at the same time. In the course of his researches he found in the archives several records (including two from *Tell*) made in the

1950s but rejected by me and Tilde at the time. He had them put on tape and sent them to us in Rome, asking us to listen to them and decide if we would now 'pass' them.

I remember we both shrugged rather disparagingly and said, 'We must have rejected them for *some* good reason.' But we sat down and listened to them; and slowly our expressions changed.

In the end we passed the lot, and Tilde said, 'What must our standards have been like then that we *rejected* these?'

I shook my head wordlessly. And at that moment I thought of our great Maestro Serafin, saying, 'Those were vintage years that we shared.'

7

Ernani

It was in the early months of 1982 that, yielding to the affectionate insistence of Maestro Boncompagni and Gennaro Orta, I gave up an eagerly anticipated holiday and embarked on the production of Verdi's *Ernani* for the Teatro San Carlo in Naples. The enterprise was a difficult one for me. I did not know the opera, had never seen it on the stage and had only sung the great aria 'Oh, de' verd' anni miei' (Oh for my youthful years once more) when I was myself in my youth, when impudence outweighs experience.

There is, of course, a school of thought today which holds that the less a producer knows about a work the more 'interesting' will his production be. It is not a theory which has ever commended itself to me but, be that as it may, I prepared to put my head in the lion's mouth and, after some harrowing experiences, I think I can say that the final result came out well.

The first difficulty which presented itself was that in this work the real protagonist is the chorus. No doubt that was all very well in

Verdi's day, when people talked less about their rights and had a certain regard for artistic discipline and the success of any enterprise in which they were involved. Today, in most countries of what is called the civilised world, it is a running fight, with endless discussions punctuated by vain pleas for silence and attention. Meetings are held during rehearsal time (with a consequent loss of time for the wretched producer) and the lack of disciplined work is almost unbelievable.

In the event, however, the San Carlo chorus proved to be an extremely good one, and at the actual performance they moved in and out as required. Naturally, for some scenes I should have greatly preferred to have half the chorus, or even a small group. But no – they had to be all together all the time, with the result that the stage was constantly overcrowded.

Fortunately I had the careful and very experienced collaboration of the Venetian designer Misha Scandella, and this was of immense help and comfort to me. The sets were beautiful and the costumes magnificent, which enabled me to work out splendid stage compositions based on the works of Spanish painters.

In *Ernani* the essence of Verdi is already there: youthful, spontaneous and vehement, with inexhaustible musical invention. Countless themes peep in and out almost at random, appearing once and not returning. (Later they will be found in other operas, more luminous, more developed.) The whole work is imbued with the spirit of the Risorgimento to which Verdi was so deeply committed. The great choruses which are such a feature of the work swept Italy at the time, as the people identified their own fight for freedom against the tyrant with events in the opera.

Indeed, as I came to know this beautiful opera well, I deeply regretted not having sung in it when I was the right age to do so.

The plot is complicated, with little action for the principals, all of whom are unpredictable to say the least. The story is based on Victor Hugo's drama *Hernani*, but little of his delicate irony remains in the libretto by Francesco Maria Piave.

Ernani himself is a dramatic tenor, fiery in temperament, romantically in love with Elvira.

Don Carlo, baritone, is Carlo I, King of Spain. He is proud, eager for power and is also in love with the unfortunate Elvira. In the course of the opera, at the age of nineteen, he becomes the Emperor Charles V of the Holy Roman Empire. Born in Ghent in Flanders in 1500 and dying in the monastery of Yuste at Estremadura, Spain in 1558, he was the son of Philip the Beautiful, Archduke of Austria and Joanna the Mad, Queen of Castille. Historically speaking, he was one of the great Emperors of that immense empire which was not all conquered by arms but mostly inherited or claimed as dowry. Many of these arrangements were made by his paternal grandfather, Maximilian of Austria. He is, incidentally, that same Emperor Charles V whom we meet briefly in another opera of Verdi, *Don Carlo*. By that time he has abdicated (in 1556) in favour of his son Philip II of Spain, and appears as a mysterious figure in the cloisters of St Just to save his nephew, the Crown Prince, from the clutches of the Inquisition.

In the course of *Ernani* he is variously alluded to as Don Carlo, Carlo I of Spain and the Emperor Charles V. But take heart! It is all the same person.

Don Ruy Gomez di Silva (bass), hard and obstinate to a degree which borders on the ridiculous, is Elvira's uncle. He too declares himself in love with her, telling the King so in resounding tones. No one seems to question this rather tricky relationship, and so we have poor Elvira with all three principal male characters in hot pursuit.

Elvira, who is of course soprano (what else, poor girl, with such a fate in store?) flutters like a gentle dove in a gilded cage with three handsome Alsatian dogs pushing and howling outside.

Hospitality, honour, hatred, pride and vengeance are invoked on every occasion, and Elvira has a hard time of it between the warring suitors. She implores them from time to time to stop fighting, but with little result. Death is asked for and exalted by all the lovers at the tops of their voices, and there is much grabbing of daggers and threatening of suicide.

Act 1 – The Camp
When the scene opens, the exiled Ernani is camping in the moonlight in sight of Silva's castle. Aware that Silva intends to marry his beloved, he has become so desperate that he determines to abduct her. He calls on his followers to assist him, and they all set off in the direction of the castle.

In the second scene we find Elvira lamenting her cruel situation. She sings her famous aria 'Ernani, Ernani, involami' (Ernani, save me) almost as though she senses his approach. Silva is absent from the castle, but precious gifts arrive from him to tempt Elvira into marrying him. Sad and dejected, however, she determinedly returns them.

At this point the young King enters and proceeds to make violent love to her in his beautiful aria, 'Da quel di'che t'ho veduta' (Since the day I saw you). She rejects him passionately and, seizing his dagger from him, is threatening suicide when Ernani enters and prevents her. The King recognises Ernani as the exiled Juan of Aragon and, somewhat inexplicably, bids him flee and save his life, since to linger in the castle of his enemy Silva is to court disaster.

Silva, however, is not the man to miss a scene like this, and makes an unexpected appearance, rushing in to surprise the two seducers in the room of his fiancée. He rants about her lost virtue, insults everybody and challenges both intruders to open combat. No one manages to do much explaining or commenting – but it is a fine stage effect.

At that moment in comes Don Riccardo, the royal esquire, and kneels before the King, thereby disclosing his real rank. Great astonishment on all sides and near-collapse of Silva, to the secret amusement of the King, who seeks hospitality for the night in a stupendous ensemble.

With a great show of trusting him, the King then informs Silva that his illustrious grandfather has died, leaving the succession to the Holy Roman Empire open. He demands Silva's loyalty, support and advice. While announcing his intention to stay the night (a king does not wait to be invited), he orders Ernani to leave instantly, saying aside to him, 'Vo' salvarti' (I wish to save you).

There are no directions on the score and the reason for this determined rescue is entirely doubtful. Silva's sense of hospitality is a byword, so Ernani is really quite safe. One can only hazard a guess that the King prefers to keep him alive for his own vengeance. Anyway, it is not a phrase to neglect, and in my view should be pronounced clearly, though with gritted teeth and an ominous accent. A pretty nasty comment, in fact, meriting Ernani's ironical answering comment on this concession.

In the finale of Act I opposing thoughts are expressed in words of love and hatred, vengeance and the invoking of freedom and glory. In this great ensemble Silva seems to share in the King's ambitions.

Act 2 – The Guest
In a few lines Piave and Verdi suggest the scene (which to my knowledge has never been realised): It is a magnificent hall in the palace of Don Ruy Gomez di Silva. Along the walls are family portraits in rich frames, surmounted by ducal crowns and gilded crests. Beside each portrait is a complete suit of armour appropriate to the period. There is a richly appointed table and a ducal chair of oak. The atmosphere is festive; everyone is eating and drinking and singing in celebration of the marriage between Elvira and Silva, which is due to take place within a matter of hours.

Silva arrives in sumptuous attire. He learns that a pilgrim is at the gate seeking hospitality and, true to what he regards as his most sacred duty – hospitality – orders that he shall be admitted. Enter, of course, Ernani disguised as a pilgrim, but as soon as he sees Elvira dressed as a bride he immediately flings off his disguise and reveals his true identity. In furious tones he declares himself against the King, his host and pretty well everyone else, offering his head to more or less anyone prepared to relieve him of it.

He is not the only one claiming a personal obsession, however. Silva, riding his own hobbyhorse of hospitality, refuses Ernani's plea to be exterminated and, on the contrary, hastens off to arm the castle against the pursuing King.

Left alone for a few precious minutes Elvira and Ernani exchange pledges of love and, inevitably, Silva returns to find them in each other's arms. Contemptuous and furious, he vows to part them. Meanwhile the King is at the castle gates demanding entrance. Silva has no choice but to open the gates but, true to his vow of hospitality, he has already hidden Ernani in a secret place.

Entering in a fury, the King demands Ernani, promising torture and death all round if he is thwarted. He has the place searched but in vain and his anger grows minute by minute. Elvira throws herself at his feet, imploring mercy; Silva, in tears, protests his love for Elvira and begs the King to leave her with him. But the King is adamant and offers the cruel choice – Ernani be surrendered or he will take Elvira away with him.

Nothing however will induce Silva to betray a guest and so the King, having first sung a beautiful promise of bliss to Elvira, 'Vieni meco, sol di rose intrecciar ti vo' la vita' (Come with me, I will make your life a garland of roses), departs with his army – and the weeping Elvira.

The old hatred, magnified by fresh insult, flares up in Silva's heart. He swears vengeance on the King. Then, recalling an even more pressing injury, he lets out Ernani and challenges him to come and fight outside the castle (where presumably the laws of hospitality do not operate).

Ernani, however, reveals that the King is the rival of both of them, being himself in love with Elvira. So they agree to postpone their quarrel in order to join forces against the common enemy. As guarantee of his sincerity Ernani hands over to Silva his hunting horn, promising that, once they have opposed the King together, he will be prepared to forfeit his own life should Silva, by sounding the horn, demand this.

Act 3 – The Emperor's Mercy

The third act transports us to Aquisgrana (Aix la Chapelle), now known as Aachen. We are before the tomb of the Emperor Charlemagne. Within, the Electors from the various states are in conference to choose the new Emperor of the Holy Roman Empire. The King (Carlo) enters with his esquire and sings the nostalgic aria: 'Oh, de' verd' anni miei' (Oh, my green years . . .) and disappears within the gates of the tomb to meditate. Well, he is only nineteen!

In the adjacent caves a band of conspirators, headed by Silva and Ernani, are plotting together to kill the King. Passwords are exchanged, oaths sworn, lots drawn for the one who shall accomplish the assassination and a yearning for freedom expressed. All this is encompassed in yet another of the exciting choruses which, during the Risorgimento, swept all Italy and animated every true Italian against the oppressor. 'Si ridesti il Leon di Castiglia' (Let the Lion of Castille reawaken).

Suddenly a cannon is fired three times, the sign that the election is over. The doors of the tomb are thrown wide and the Electors announce Charles V as Emperor of the Holy Roman Empire. In the first moment of emotion, the splendour of lights and the magnificence of the scene, the spectators believe the appearance of the Emperor to be the ghost of the great Charlemagne himself. But the stern and angry voice of the new Emperor threatening death to all traitors calls them back to reality: 'Carlo Vo . . . ? Oh Traditor'.

Prompt as ever with his tendency to offer his head, Ernani steps forth and, asking death for himself, declares his full identity, reciting his titles – Count and Duke of Segorbia, of Cardona, the exiled Don Juan of Aragon. Defeated now, unable to vindicate his injured father's name, and deprived of Elvira's love, he feels death to be the only choice.

Quick though the new Emperor is to accept this, Elvira, good girl, is quicker. Emerging from the crowd of ladies who seem to accompany the King everywhere, she throws herself into the thick of the conflict and implores the new Emperor to crown his election by an act of clemency. The young Emperor had not really thought of this, but catches on to the noble idea at once, realising that it would make a splendid opening to his reign. He pardons everyone and leaves Ernani and Elvira free to be married with his blessing.

The crowd, instantly converted to his favour, cry, 'Glory and honour to Charles the Fifth.' The act ends with yet another splendid chorus, which tends to have every Italian in the audience on his feet, and in Verdi's day helped to swell the enthusiastic movement which finally united Italy and helped to drive the foreign invader from the beloved country. 'Viva V E R D I' meant: 'Viva Vittorio Emanuele Re d'Italia!'

The only person left unsatisfied is the inexorable Silva, who plays with Ernani's hunting horn – and waits.

Act 4 – The Masque

The wedding of Elvira and Ernani (now revealed as Don Giovanni d'Aragona) takes place in his castle in Saragozza. All is joy and festivity in a colourful masquerade. The reception is ending with dances and happy music, the guests preparing to leave, still singing of the bliss of the newly married couple.

A masked figure in a black domino is seen, moving in and out among the revellers; and although the people remark on him, he slips away into the garden with threatening gestures.

Finally left alone, Ernani and Elvira have scarcely time to rejoice in their newfound happiness before the sound of the hunting horn, blown by Silva, recalls the fatal pact.

Silva makes his doom-laden entry, and although Ernani pleads for mercy it is in vain. Silva merely offers him the choice between poison or a dagger. Elvira adds her impassioned pleas, but to no avail. At last, true to his oath, Ernani seizes a dagger and stabs himself, finally silencing the inexorable Silva, and Elvira falls senseless on the corpse.

★

All the characters, unpredictable and a little mad, are not easy to present. They are constantly surrounded by the chorus, from which their singing emerges like a stupendous flower.

It is difficult to convince a tenor that, in spite of armour, heroic phrases and grand titles, Ernani is pretty unbalanced. Quick to respond to sudden impulses and ideas that he cannot control, he is afflicted by an almost epileptic masochism, which makes him burst into wild scenes like one demented.

The King – at this period – is presumably in the same age group as Ernani and Elvira. Therefore all three must emphasise, vocally and dramatically, their sudden quick changes of temper and their impulsive decisions.

In sharp contrast, Silva is immovable as a rock, absurdly obstinate in his blind pride, and deaf to any argument which does not accord with the principles he has himself established.

In spite of all the ranting about honour, hospitality and so on (not to mention vengeance and pride), and allowing for the hot Spanish blood seething in all of them, love does not seem in itself to be sufficient justification for such tenacious hostility between the three men.

Elivira, struggling with the three suitors in turn, snatching daggers from the King, Silva and Ernani, a prey to so many emotions, has the only touching phrases in the opera when she sings, in tears, 'Non son rea quanto tu sei crudel' (I am not so guilty as you are cruel). These drops of pure gold, though deeply penetrating the hearts of the audience, fail however to calm the temptuous sea of passion around her.

Again she has some beautiful music in the last scene, as she fruitlessly implores the old man's mercy with, 'I also am a Silva'. She is a constant figure of tragedy, and in my production I thought it only natural for her to kill herself with the weapon Ernani used to stab himself, as I felt she had nothing left to live for.

In the opera there is a whole population of ladies and cavaliers, pages, soldiers and dignitaries of the three warring factions, swirling around and swept away by the storm of absurd passions indulged in by the principal men. Not much gaiety for anyone. The hatred which consumes Silva in his monumental pride darkens and veils with sadness even the very few lighter moments.

So at the end, after the suicide of the two lovers, I had the chorus come back on to the stage like a slow pageant of suffering souls and desolate shadows. They all raise their eyes and arms to heaven, as though begging for peace and mercy, with a desperate gesture towards the lifeless bodies of the unhappy lovers.

The music is very beautiful and all the leading roles call for great vocal ability. They require true bel canto and cabaletta virtuosity, combined with dramatic power. Elvira's famous aria, 'Ernani, Ernani involami' (fly with me) is full of youthful impetuosity and is followed by a cabaletta requiring an excellent coloratura technique.

Ernani himself has a bel canto aria in the very first scene. Thereafter he is continually shouting and struggling with a difficult tessitura. Silva has a marvellous part, being called upon to sing, weep and curse with great energy and virtuosity.

But I think it is the King-Emperor who has the most beautiful music, for which he can use all the vocal colours at his command. The smooth *mezza voce* for 'Vieni meco, sol di rose', the hardly contained disdain in 'Lo vedremo, veglio audace', the meditative tones for 'Grand Dio' uttered among the tombs, which then opens out into the triumphant conclusion of the great aria 'E vincitor del secoli' . . . It is a truly magnificent role!

In Naples, among the variety of difficulties with which I had to contend, was a tenor with a good voice but absolutely devoid of any acting power. Even when he attempted to follow my suggestions he did so with an awkwardness which made me shudder. The basso was excellent and so was the baritone, both having not only good voices but real presence.

As for the Elvira, she was tall, slender and beautiful, doing full justice to Scandella's wonderful costumes. But unfortunately she suddenly took herself off without a word of explanation just a week before the opening night. Bereft of an Elvira at this late hour – and knowing of course that this is not a role in the general repertoire – we started a frantic search and were fortunate enough to find another Elvira.

The voice was really magnificent, but the figure was – stout, shall we say? Even worse, the owner of the voice was also the owner of a remarkably bad temper, which did not make things easier for anyone. Poor Scandella had never, of course, imagined that he would have to make the costumes all over again, but so it was. And the lady was perpetually dissatisfied.

For the first night, however, everyone collected all their energies and it was a real triumph. With a sigh of relief we relaxed for the second night, which was to be filmed for television. But, needless to say, we had drawn breath too soon. Elvira was busy having a row with her husband and missed the bell summoning her to the stage, with the result that the Emperor was left singing his impassioned address to a blank space.

Finally he lost patience and exclaimed, 'It's too ridiculous!' and the performance came to a halt. But at this point Elvira rejoined us, very red in the face and wearing, not her gala costume, but an ordinary house dress.

By then we were all in hysterics. But the performance picked up after that, and we finally went to bed at the crack of dawn after discussing, quarrelling, calming down and drinking a much needed glass of wine.

From first to last that production of *Ernani* was quite an experience, and I suppose it can best be summed up in the expressive English phrase, 'There was never a dull moment.'

8

Rigoletto

Vocally, the role of Rigoletto is one of the hardest in the repertoire, requiring a tremendous amount of dramatic power to be superimposed on the tender, almost sacred feelings of a father. The music is by turns impetuous, brilliant and moving, describing in a masterly way all the contrasting emotions of a human soul. Every bit of physical as well as vocal strength is called for. I shall never forget how, absolutely drained by the demanding scene of 'Cortigiani' and almost panting with agony, I would plunge into the pure bliss of 'Piangi, fanciulla' and then warm up again into the madness and triumph of 'Si, vendetta!'

As for the text, to know the value of every word and the cause and origin of each character's every action is the least that is required. On the subject of this vital 'marriage' of word and action I should like to emphasise that one of the most important things for a singer to remember (not only in *Rigoletto*) is that the legato of singing will be better expressed if it is accompanied by legato of action. The identical timing of the two will often be difficult of course, and then it may be necessary, as it were, to stretch the one to accommodate the other.

If, for instance, a short musical phrase requires a smile and a gesture of the hand to add significance to its expression it may be advisable to allow that smile to dawn and that hand to start rising fractionally before the accompanying sound. Equally, if the musical phrase is a long one it may well be most effective to start the accompanying gesture fractionally later, adding point and significance to the conclusion of the phrase. Admittedly this is a difficult thing to learn and to make an instinctive part of one's art but, once perfected, it will add to the whole presentation of a role a smooth oneness which will transform it.

One word of warning, however, to anyone adding these refinements to his or her presentation: if any of these moments is missed or bungled, never look back on it until the performance is over. The moment has gone and can never be recalled. To dwell on it will only increase a sense of confusion which can quickly lead to disaster. To let even part of your mind be preoccupied with what has happened is like tossing the stone which starts the avalanche.

When I first approached the role of Rigoletto I had little knowledge of the work, apart from having lent my young voice to a few items in a film of it with Michel Simon. But I had an overwhelming desire to study it and as at that time – 1936 – I had a modest scholarship at the Scala which entitled me to attend all stage rehearsals, to a rehearsal I went. However – with shame I confess it – something made me laugh so loudly that I was ignominiously sent out of the house.

Next I listened to a vicious discussion between so-called connoisseurs dissecting the characters in a way that made me feel sick. Then, just as I was about to abandon my attempt to penetrate the great masterpiece, Maestro Luigi Ricci (inspired coach and teacher that he was) took me in hand and guided my uncertain steps to a better understanding of how to approach such a monumental task.

First he asked me to make a thorough study of the libretto and the characters, followed by an equally thorough study of the period and the setting of the action. Then I collected all the criticisms and write-ups I could find, in which task I was ably assisted by my wife, Tilde. She rummaged through the riches in the library of her father, Raffaello de Rensis, the illustrious musicologist and critic. Last of all came the approach to the music and singing with Ricci.

By now my interest was at fever pitch and, regardless of Ricci's warnings, I plunged into the task with such enthusiasm that after four lessons I was ordered complete silence for two weeks. My vocal cords were inflamed, my throat swollen and my ears aching. I was ordered inhalations, throat sprays and so on. Finally a dish of hot spaghetti with red peppers completed the treatment and I was ready for the battlefield once more. But I now resumed work cautiously though with passionate commitment.

I began to work out the Jester's appearance and his way of walking, the left knee bent in order to emphasise the right shoulder raised by the hump. (That damned hump! never for one moment to be forgotten.) I trained myself to keep my neck distorted so that I was forced to look upward, peering at people in a mocking sideways manner. The hands prehensile and articulate.

Finally I felt it was time to attend a performance in order to check my own conception of the part. So I went to the Teatro Adriano, where a well-praised production was taking place; and received the shock of my young life. The end of each act was greeted with enthusiastic applause – but it had no resemblance at all to *my* idea of *Rigoletto*.

Undoubtedly some of this was partly due to my youthful conviction that I knew all there was to know about the masterpiece. But in retrospect – and in justice to myself – I must say that the acting was sadly old-fashioned, the costumes garish, the make-up crude and the movements stilted. Worst of all was the careless singing, the vulgarity of unfocused sound, the inartistic bawling.

How then was one to explain the applause? Had I myself been doing everything wrong? I went home, my confidence shaken and I myself utterly confused. After a night's sleep, however, and a soothing talk with my ever encouraging Tilde, I made a great and comforting discovery. That applause had been for Verdi, whose wonderful work even badly performed is, quite simply, indestructible.

All this, as I have said, happened about 1936/37. The chance finally to perform the role came nearly ten years later, in Turin. But in no sense were those wasted years, for every bit of one's development, both musical and dramatic, is called upon when one essays this tremendous role. I gave all that I knew – or believed that I knew – to that first performance, and I did well. But I realised then how much I still would have to study and work in order to be a Rigoletto who would not offend the shade of Giuseppe Verdi.

Soon after this I had the attractive offer to appear in a film of the opera. It was to be made on the stage of what was then the Teatro Reale dell'Opera and – supreme stroke of good fortune – the conductor was to be Maestro Tullio Serafin.

He looked me up and down and said: 'Your legs are right, and so is the make-up, with the nose and mouth drooping on the right side, indicating congenital malformation or partial paralysis. But why use your right arm so much? It is supposed to be almost useless. Act more with your left arm, with weak gestures which strive desperately to be imposing. You will get a stronger dramatic effect that way.'

So much for my own beginnings. Now let us consider *Rigoletto* from the point of view of everyone who is going to take part, for there are *no* unimportant roles in a great work. It is partly through the so-called minor characters – their thoughts, judgments, relationships and reactions – that the main characters become able to dominate the drama. We shall start, then, with a character who has no more than three short sentences to sing, but who moves the plot with those phrases at a moment of great crisis. This is:

The Page to the Duchess. Although the Duchess never appears on the stage her influence is felt. In the second act, when Rigoletto is desperately trying to discover what has happened to his Gilda, the Page enters with the words, 'Al suo sposo parlar vuol a Duchessa' (The Duchess wishes to speak with her husband).

He (or rather she, for the Page is a soprano) moves boldly among the courtiers. But after a few joking, ironical words and some laughter she is hustled from the scene; not, however, before Rigoletto has realised that they are concealing the fact that the Duke is with some woman other than the Duchess.

Through those short, laughing utterances he learns the tragic truth of Gilda's abduction and, by his own frantic reaction, discloses the secret of his life. Callously indifferent though they usually are, even the courtiers react with astonishment to the knowledge that Gilda is his daughter. It is one of the greatest moments in all opera – precipitated by a 'minor' character.

★

Now for someone with even less to sing, but whose largely silent co-operation can enhance – or spoil – the scene. This is the *Court Usher.* In the second act he precedes the Count of Monterone, who, flanked by halberdiers, is being escorted to prison. At the gate he calls to the guards to open, and I suggest he should reach his place in good time, enabling him to sing his five bars with a good, clear voice. Having waited for Monterone to sing his tirade in peace (no sign of impatience, please!) he watches him enter the prison and then withdraws unobtrusively through the nearest wing. He should *not* recross the stage just as Rigoletto requires the whole scene for: 'No, vecchio t'inganni!' (No, old man, you are wrong!) It will not be out of character for the usher to show a certain respectful sympathy towards his prisoner. Not everyone at Court approves of the Duke's conduct.

The people who make up the Court of Mantua are by no means uniform. They are individuals, and it is important that those playing these small roles should be aware of the character and situation which distinguishes them.

The Countess Ceprano is a lovely young woman with a jealous, not very agreeable husband. She crosses the big hall almost as the curtain rises, surrounded by elegant ladies and young courtiers. The ladies laugh at the compliments of their beaux and stop to listen during the second half of the Duke's aria: 'La constanza . . .' Then, his aria finished, the Duke approaches the Countess and invites her to open the dance with him. They move to the proscenium, dancing and singing the first phrases, followed by other couples. This delightful dancing duet calls for a lively tone as there is no serious meaning nor hidden passion in it. At the end the Duke gallantly offers her his arm and they walk away together followed by her angry husband, who does not, however, venture to make a public scene.

This concludes the role of the Countess Ceprano. But even this brief appearance calls for meticulous timing and careful stage co-ordination. I remember one spectacular production in which ballet and chorus were beautifully organised, the choreography so exactly timed that the Duke and the Countess were always at the front of the stage when they had to sing, the other couples harmoniously making room for them – until one evening when there was a last minute substitution for the tenor: the Duke did not meet his Countess until they were actually onstage. The result was that he addressed his phrases to a very beautiful ballerina, who frantically tried to indicate that he had got the wrong lady. The stage pattern was hopelessly disrupted and the Duke was left singing to the miming ballerina while the poor Countess made her replies from a distant corner.

Another hazard in this opening scene is the temptation to overload it with stage effects. When I was still the wide-eyed young man from the country, studying singing in Rome, I had the good fortune to attend a performance under Maestro Tullio Serafin with a cast that included Basiola, Gigli, Toti dal Monte and Autori. But when the curtain went up I was totally dazzled by the splendour of the decor; the immense hall, the great staircases, statues, columns, balustrades and windows. I was particularly intrigued by a gilded putto (child) on the ceiling and was still gazing at it when suddenly the house curtain swept down and the scene was over. Certainly, unsophisticated as I was, I had allowed my attention to wander, but what can be said of a production which smothered music and drama with visual magnificence?

The Count Ceprano is a rather ill-natured lordling, reserved, very conscious of his rank, and with no sense of humour whatever. Naturally Rigoletto's mockery infuriates him, though his pride enables him to treat the Jester with disdain, until the impudent suggestion that the Duke might cut off his head. With an imprecation, Ceprano loses his self-control and draws his sword. The courtiers comment on this outburst, suggesting this is an unusual reaction from him.

He is a curious character, having little in common with the lightweight courtiers. But for the sake of vengeance he joins them, and we meet him again at the end of the scene outside Rigoletto's house, in company with Gilda's abductors. In Act 2 he rejoices openly as he and the courtiers bring the news of Gilda's abduction to the Duke and, along with the others, plays his part in describing the details. When the distraught Rigoletto comes looking for his daughter, Ceprano is among those who mock his anguished pleas for help. He makes his final exit with the courtiers he despises – altogether not a likeable fellow.

Matteo Borsa is the Duke's favourite courtier, his companion in all manner of debaucheries. Elegant, something of a dandy and rather effeminate looking, he is a leader in all the odious mischief of the Court. If I seem severe in my judgment of these courtiers I must plead that, as Rigoletto, I have suffered much at their hands, and cannot help despising these servile puppets who, to please their master, go to much more despicable lengths than Rigoletto himself.

Marullo is a courtier rather similar to Borsa, elegant and frivolous, but he has some good in his heart and some sympathy for the unhappy Jester, who thinks he is a friend. Indeed it is he that Rigoletto recognises on the night of the abduction, and he who tells Rigoletto that they are in fact abducting Ceprano's wife. So in the scene when Rigoletto implores the courtiers to help him recover his daughter he clutches at Marullo's hand, saying, 'Marullo . . . to ch'hai l'alma gentil come il core,' (. . . you who are as kind as you are noble) and Marullo obviously finds it difficult to reject this piteous plea from the desperate father. He has not the courage to look him in the eye and is the first to show the way out to the courtiers chased by the Jester.

The Count of Monterone is a true nobleman, whose daughter has been the latest victim of the Duke's lust. In the first scene he should not enter in chains or accompanied by guards, as is sometimes seen. At this point he is a free man, demanding his right to speak to his lord, and no one so far really knows why. A powerful figure, he thrusts his way through the crowd and reaches the indifferent Duke. He is disgusted by Rigoletto's interruptions and his efforts to amuse his bored master, while Rigoletto, on his part, forgetting his own vulnerable position as the father of an adored daughter, stoops to savage mockery of Monterone in his distress.

The reaction is tremendous. Monterone calls down the curse of an injured father on Duke and Jester – the curse which is the central theme of the drama, already powerfully announced in the *andante sostenuto* at the beginning of the opera. All are struck with terror, except the Duke, who merely withdraws from a tiresome scene. Monterone, pushing aside the guards who come to arrest him, stands there, the dominating figure on the stage, while Rigoletto falls at his feet in superstitious terror as the curtain descends.

Monterone's appearance in Act 2 is brief but telling. Escorted by guards and preceded by the Court Usher (previously mentioned) he halts before the Duke's portrait and sings his phrases of bitter resignation since his curse appears to have failed. Then with proud bearing he enters the prison, unaware that he has prompted Rigoletto's terrible vow of vengeance.

*

Apart from the tragic heroine, there are two female characters in the opera – neither of them, it must be said, particularly admirable. The first of these is:

Giovanna, in whose care Rigoletto leaves his beloved daughter. With a smiling face she falsely promises to protect the girl, of whom she is perhaps really fond. But for money she is prepared to abandon her to a virtually unknown man. An unlikeable role, but interesting to play, with moderate gestures but telling facial expression, especially when she hides the young man. She must convey that she half believes she is acting in the girl's best interests. Perhaps she does even think that the father's strictness is spoiling the daughter's chances of romance.

Maddalena, a gypsy, is sister to Sparafucile, a professional assassin. Beautiful in a showy way, she dances in the street, attracting young men to the dilapidated tavern outside the city walls where she lives with her brother. What happens after that is his business. I like the note on the score, 'Sparafucile rientra con una bottiglia di vino e due bicchieri che posa sulla tavola. Quindi batte col pomo della sua lunga spada due colpi al soffitto.' (Sparafucile returns with a bottle and two glasses which he puts on the table. Then he knocks twice on the ceiling with his long sword.) The scene is obviously set – and few producers could improve on it! Down trips the smiling Maddalena from the upstairs room, and out goes Sparafucile to talk with Rigoletto, leaving her to entertain the young man – the Duke in disguise – who enters by another door.

She avoids any suggestion of haste lest he should think her a vulgar prostitute – which she is, of course, but must not advertise the fact too soon. Both words and music suggest pleasant skirmishes without great results. He embraces her boldly and pays her exaggerated compliments, referring to her somewhat grubby hand as 'La bella mano candida' (Your beautiful white hand). She laughs and calls him a fool, but regards the off-white hand with some satisfaction. At the same time aristocratic irony must be heard in the Duke's singing of the mock courting 'Bella figlia dell'amore' (Beautiful daughter of love), sounding like a question mark slightly extended, which gives the duet a joking, laughing tone.

She does not dislike the Duke's liberties but indicates that she is a girl who expects something more permanent, hoping of course that embraces and drinks will warm up the atmosphere while Sparafucile negotiates outside with Rigoletto. But presently she pretends to fear her brother's severity and breaks off the dalliance. The adventure has no future and the Duke, now bored, consigns Sparafucile to hell on his return and retires for a short rest, preferring not to go out into the obviously rising storm. Knowing her brother's murderous intentions, Maddalena tries – but unsuccessfully – to persuade the engaging young man to depart.

When the Duke has retired to the upstairs room she pleads with her brother, but he is adamant. He has promised to hand over the corpse to the hunchback when Rigoletto returns with the second part of the price, and he is a man of his word. Her suggestion that he should kill the hunchback on his return instead outrages him. Murder may be his trade, but he never cheats a client! However, he finally agrees that, in the unlikely event of someone seeking shelter before Rigoletto returns, that unfortunate can substitute for the corpse in the sack to be handed to Rigoletto.

This is the revealing conversation overheard by the unhappy Gilda, crouching outside the tumbledown shack and, in terror for her father and the man she still loves, she decides to be the sacrifice – and knocks. The guilty couple stare at each other and exchange a few pregnant words. Then, acting in concert, they open the door, Gilda disguised as a young man rushes in and is stabbed.

The speed and terror of this scene is indescribable, the tension immeasurably heightened by the sounds of the storm now at its height. In the Serafin production all stage effects were in the masterly hands of Maestro Ricci. Lightning, thunder, torrential rain were all there, but the timing was so perfect that never once was the terrifying hurricane allowed to interfere with orchestra, principals or the off-stage male chorus reproducing a moaning wind. To the admiration of performers and audience, Ricci produced a storm of which Verdi himself would have approved.

He was again in charge of effects for the justly acclaimed film of *Rigoletto* to which I have already alluded. On this occasion I sang Rigoletto, Neri was Sparafucile, Filippeschi a splendid Duke with ringing voice and smilingly sardonic appearance, and Gilda was sung by Pagliughi and acted by Marcella Govoni. The entire film was shot on the stage of the Teatro dell'Opera in the space of fourteen days! I am not making comparisons or criticisms, but should just like to underline the stupendous organisation involved and the spirit and enthusiasm which led us all the time. The dignity, the pride and the love for one's work! I am glad I was part of the operatic scene then.

Sparafucile is a killer, a man without heart, pretending to some sort of professional dignity by calling himself 'un uomo di spada' (a swordsman) as, with arrogant assurance, he offers his services to eliminate a rival or enemy. At his first appearance in Scene 2, he emerges from the shadows, and to the shadows he returns. His movements are slow, few but alert. He is obsequious to a prospective client, curt with Maddalena, and brisk when transacting business with Rigoletto in the last act. An interesting character to play, drawn with great clarity; it is only necessary to study the music, text and score to have the whole before one. The appearance is of course very important, and the manner and costume should characterise him from the outset.

To me Giulio Neri was *the* Sparafucile, and it was my good fortune to have this honest, simple-hearted giant as my colleague on many memorable occasions. It was a unique voice, noble and grand, guided by a precise and fascinating instinct which is hard to describe. His characterisation of Sparafucile remains unsurpassed in operatic history, as does his Inquisitor in *Don Carlo*, Basilio in *The Barber of Seville*, Mefistofeles, Fiesco in *Simone Boccanegra* and so on – right through to his Gualtiero in *William Tell* when, weak from mortal illness, he still gave of his best with heroic *élan*, and then leaned on me to ask how he was doing and if his voice was still good.

Gilda is a creature of sweetness and love. Kept in seclusion by her anxious father, she does not rebel but she longs to know something of his life, of which she is totally ignorant. She sees him for a short while each evening, lonely and sad, but has no inkling of the fact that he is jester to the dissolute Duke of Mantua. This makes it of great importance that his costume should not include the exaggerated hump when he visits his home. At that time it was customary for the deformity of a jester to be exaggerated by an artificial hump when he is on duty, which explains why Gilda has no reason to guess what her father really does for a living.

Not unnaturally, this lovely, over-protected girl has been deeply affected by the admiring glances of what she takes to be a handsome young student in church, and when the faithless Giovanna secretly introduces him into the garden it seems almost like a miracle to her. She listens to his bold, sweet words and dreams that this 'Gualtier Malde' indeed represents love. 'Ah, dei miei verginei sogni son queste, le voce tenere si care a me,' she sings. (Ah, sweet words of my virginal dreams, so dear to me).

At this point Giovanna returns to interrupt the love scene. Gilda, though feeling guilty when she thinks of her father, is reassured by the romantic boldness of the young man, the fast tempo of the music mirroring the excitement of their promises and adieux.

Left alone, she takes a candle – usually rendered unnecessary by brilliant moonlight which incidentally makes nonsense of Rigoletto's later observation on the darkness of the night – and nostalgically sings her famous and beautiful aria 'Caro nome'. Then slowly she mounts the stairs, while the courtiers gather on the other side of the garden wall to organise the abduction.

It is not unusual for a mere super to deputise for Gilda when she is carried away by the abductors. But comedy rather than tragedy results if Gilda's cry for help comes palpably from the wings. The victim must be carried with care. I once witnessed a literally stunning performance when the unfortunate girl slipped from her abductors' grasp and hit the stage with a yelp of chilling reality.

In the Court Scene in Act 2, when Gilda makes her swift entrance, I do beg conductors to resist any attempt to start at full speed the *allegro assai vivo ed agitato* before she has had time to realise that the weeping bundle on the floor is *her father* grovelling at the feet of the men who abducted her.

Her cry of 'Mio padre!' is not just a plea for Daddy to comfort her. It is a horrified recognition of the appalling truth from which he has sheltered her all her life. In the avalance of emotion which engulfs her she even forgets her own disgrace. Running from the Duke's room, she stops dead, paralysed by the horror of the revelation.

And he, still desperately trying to reassure her, actually pretends it is all some sort of joke. 'Fu scherzo,' he babbles. 'Non e' vero?' appealing to the others. 'Io che pur piansi or rido.' (It was a joke, wasn't it? I was pretending to cry, but now I'm laughing.) Fully understood, and played with the right feeling, the moment is heartbreaking.

She clutches desperately at him and stammers, 'All'onta, Padre mio.' (I am dishonoured, Father.) And with the one idea of protecting his poor child, he rises to heights of paternal dignity and, with an authority unsuspected in the weeping Jester, chases the courtiers from the scene.

Gilda stands motionless, incapable of reaction. Then, in desolate *recitativo col canto* (singing recitative) he says, 'Parla . . . siam soli.' (Speak . . . we are alone.) Three words that describe a world in ruins, a life and a dream for ever destroyed.

When Verdi writes *'recitativo col canto'* he wishes to give the singer a certain freedom of expression according to his or her personality and feeling. Ninety per cent of singers may sing their arias well and with some success, but I would say that only ten per cent sing the recitatives with real dramatic sense and plastic expression, enhancing the story and using the pauses correctly. That is what is meant by *Teatro in musica.* (Too often, of course, singers are at the mercy of insensitive conductors obsessed with strict tempo, with the idea of being 'modern'.)

During the introduction to the following *andantino* Rigoletto sinks into the great chair and, on the 8th bar (*allargando*) opens his arms to the girl, who takes refuge in them. As she tells the story of the amorous glances in church, the secret meeting the previous evening and then *dolcissimo* (sweetly, as Verdi says): 'Partí . . . partí' (He left me), the poor father can scarcely control his tears as he strokes her fair hair. Her emotion and terror when she recalls the abduction make him break out in fury, and then, as they cling together for mutual comfort, Monterone (that other father of an abused daughter) enters on his way to prison.

Monterone's imprecations to the portrait of the Duke prompt Rigoletto's final outburst of fury, terrifying in its intensity. Gilda moves very little, only imploring mercy for the man she still loves, finally falling on her knees to grasp at her father at the end of the splendid 'Vendetta!' its rhythm so vehement that it seems hardly possible for a human voice to encompass it.

By the opening of Act 3, Gilda has been crushed by the weight of her disillusionment. In a cruelly short space of time she has discovered that her romantic student is the libertine Duke, and her father the Jester at the Duke's corrupt court. Stupefied by these bitter truths, she drags herself along like an automaton, answering her father's anxious questions in monosyllables. No longer the innocent girl, she is now a woman, tasting the bitterness of grief and man's wickedness. She looks through a crack in the wall of Sparafucile's hovel and sees her philandering lover with Maddalena. Like one dead, from this moment until the end she seems to have lost her mental balance.

Rigoletto persuades her to go home, change into man's clothing and leave for Verona ahead of him. He will follow the next day. Already the rumble of thunder and the rising wind presage the approaching storm, as Gilda goes to obey her father. But she is irresistibly drawn back to the gloomy scene, the hut where the Duke sleeps upstairs while Sparafucile and Maddalena plot together.

Gilda, dressed now as a boy, with high boots and a cloak and hood, hesitantly approaches the house and through the crack in the wall overhears the plan to kill Rigoletto when he returns with the money and let the handsome young man go free. She even feels some sort of gratitude to the conscienceless Maddalena for wanting to save the young man. 'Oh, buona figliola!' (Oh, the good girl!) she exclaims. But since the rescue of her lover will mean the murder of her father, she decides to sacrifice herself as the necessary victim of the determined brother and sister.

In the great trio – sung against the almost rhythmical accompaniment of the storm – she expresses her over-burdened soul, the dramatic crescendo culminating with her offering herself to the assassin's blade. The cry which she utters in that moment marks her sacrifice and, as though placated, the tempest dies away.

Inside the hut Gilda will be slipped into the sack already prepared, and Sparafucile will carry her on his shoulders to the impatiently waiting Rigoletto. Again hauling the heroine about the stage can prove a hazard, as on one occasion when the adorable but well-nourished Pagliughi was too much for the unfortunate Sparafucile to raise from the floor. However, he was a man of resource. Taking his assassin's sword, he slit the bottom of the sack, and on that occasion my Gilda reached me safely trotting on her own two feet.

The reverse of that story was when a specially slender Gilda was hoisted with great ease on to the shoulder of the robust basso but deposited by him, in a moment of absent-mindedness, head downwards on the floor.

In this last scene Gilda is propped against a rock and it is the desperate voice of her father which brings her back to consciousness. She no longer shows fatigue or pain, for she has passed beyond all human passions and, believing that angels are awaiting her, she herself sings in an angelic voice until the end, wafted on the wings of Verdi's heavenly music.

When we come to the *Duke of Mantua*, strange as it may seem I am tempted to break a lance (a small lance perhaps) on his behalf. Of course he is a libertine. But then he is also the product of his period and position. Young, handsome, gay (in the true sense of the word), with unlimited power, he is naturally totally spoilt. The women are mad about him, the courtiers fawn on him in every new excess or debauch. He is like a young stallion running free. Noblewoman, street woman, naïve young girl – it is all the same to him as he roams at night in search of fresh adventure.

As I see him he has a soft beard framing his handsome, laughing face, with brilliant eyes and a pleasant expression. He must be richly dressed, preferably in white and gold when in his palazzo. There is nothing he does not know about pleasing a woman, and he spreads a sort of enchantment as he goes, walking proudly but with arresting charm. He is ruthless, of course – completely unaffected by the discovery that his latest conquest is actually the daughter of his Jester. But, as a small plea in his defence, may I put forward his lovely aria in Act 2, in which he excitedly admits to a strange, sweet hitherto unknown emotion. There is almost a breath of innocence in his reaction, caught perhaps from his encounter with the totally innocent Gilda.

When the chorus enter with Borsa, Marullo and Ceprano, he listens at first with surprise and some anxiety, but this changes to joy at the tale of the abduction. The following cabaletta with chorus is sometimes cut, which is perhaps a pity as it does shed a small redeeming ray on our hero's way of thinking. But not perhaps enough to warrant a strong defence of him.

Exhibitionist he certainly is, telling everyone his theories about love and adventure in the famous 'Questa o quella' (This one or that one, to me 'tis the same). As a good swordsman he is indifferent to danger and, although one must admit that he has his mean side, there is one aspect which dominates the whole, making him a tempting character to play. That is his irrepressible gaiety. He should be agile, active and not too affected, for he is neither effeminate nor pompous. In fact, he moves around his palace, Rigoletto's garden, the house of Sparafucile, all with the same ease and freedom of movement, always ready to laugh with – or at –

anyone and everything, regardless, it must be said, of other people's feelings.

My tenor colleagues have my sympathy for, try as I will, I find little else to say in the Duke's favour. The role, however, is dramatically interesting and musically difficult but rewarding. So – face the task with naturalness and merriment. Vocally you have beautiful arias and a rich display of top notes. The whole role is a pleasant contrast to the dominant feeling of tragedy.

And now I must speak of *Rigoletto* himself – the tragic jester with a heart rich in humanity. True, his faults are easy to number, but his power to love is as great as the agonies which punctuate his pitiless destiny.

His entrance in the first act must have a tremendous impact. It is 'free', no music keeping a strict rhythm, and it is up to the interpreter to make the entrance totally arresting. He should burst on to the scene, thrusting his way among the courtiers with a great laugh which descends from the top notes of irony to the lower 'fat' ones, quick and cracking like a whip, and immediately followed by the insulting question: 'In testa che avete, Signor di Ceprano?' (What have you got on your head, my Lord Ceprano?)

Rigoletto is a desperate man and desperately defends his job, however ignoble and dangerously offensive he may be. He relies on the protection of his master and, in any case, this job of his is the only means he has of keeping his daughter in comfort and safely cared for. She is the only creature in the world who matters to him, and for her he destroys himself.

His sole importance at Court is to amuse the Duke and drive away boredom. He has already exhausted his resources and de-scends to insult instead of wit, putting on a show – a sort of mock trial. Then he ruthlessly wounds the feelings of Monterone, an injured father and a victim of the Duke, going to unforgivable lengths to amuse the courtiers, who will, for their part, be willing to turn on him later and rend him. When he has finally provoked a father's curse from Monterone, he is overcome by superstitious dread. From this moment the Jester disappears, to be replaced by the frantic and terrified father.

Because of the two levels on which Rigoletto lives his life, his appearance and his costumes are of special importance. His 'home' costume should be dark and sober, with a small hump almost hidden by the collar. He should wear dark tights and shoes, the latter with short points, a long dark cloak with slits for the sleeves of his jacket to pass through, and at his belt he has a purse. On his head is a close-fitting hood, pointed on the forehead and covering the back of his neck. This is also, of course, the costume he wears for the last act.

The second costume is the jester's: rich, vividly coloured, the sleeves very large and pointed, the doublet tight and very low in the waist. The hump is bigger and taller than his natural one, giving prominence to the big stomach, like a baboon. The neck is sunk on the right shoulder, forcing him to peer upwards, the protruding chin accentuated by a goatee. Aquiline nose, distorted as though broken at some time. There is a quiff of grey hair in symmetry with the goatee, and the rest of the wig is long and thick over the neck. I give these elements in detail because they add greatly to the whole stage impression.

I used to pad my left ankle and tie it to the knee under the multicoloured tights, so that the left leg was bent and the foot turned inwards. Very uncomfortable! – but the physical pain added to the character, and I was content to have reduced my rather tall stature so that I became a deformed man with the characteristics of a jester – like Punch or the Jack in a pack of cards.

The 'folly' which Rigoletto carries is a puppet in *papier maché* that reproduces the features of Rigoletto himself; partly costumed and with coloured ribbons, it is mounted on a little stick. He carries it always when playing his jester's role and sometimes addresses it when playing his most outrageous tricks.

I made my own 'folly' which was very attractive but proved too hard. It cost me quite a lot of money eventually, for in Cairo, in the dramatic scene with the courtiers, I was so carried away that I flung it violently at them and hit one of the chorus, who ended up in the hospital with a bruised leg. Though not exactly on the danger list, he made such a tragedy of the whole thing in order to claim damages that I gave way, paid him what he wanted – and changed my 'folly' stick for a rubber one. Now my 'folly' sits in a splendid room in the Museum of Bassano del Grappa (my home town) along with all my stage costumes.

To return to the drama – after the terrifying scene at Court Rigoletto rushes home to his daughter, almost literally panting with terror, and outside his house meets Sparafucile. It is then that the professional assassin offers his services as a useful man for eliminating an enemy at a fairly reasonable price. Rigoletto tries to repulse him but cannot help listening to his proposal, for, who knows, might he not have his uses if a nightmare danger threatened? He asks Sparafucile where he can be found, just in case . . . 'E dove all'occasione?' Then he thrusts him away with the repeated, 'Va, va, va.' (Go, go, go.)

I remember the revelation about this duet imparted to me in

Stockholm in 1947 by the great conductor, Antonio Guarnieri. The excellent Sparafucile, Cesare Siepi, and I were at our first rehearsal and thought we were doing pretty well when, at the end of this duet, we were overwhelmed by a storm of abuse and invective from the conductor. – What did we think we were? Were we half asleep on the stage? This duet must be sung *pianissimo*, with a tone of mystery, and a sense of fear on the part of Rigoletto. The double-basses play a beautiful melody at this moment and our voices, he informed us, must be barely audible, creating an atmosphere of secrecy.

Cesare and I were stunned, but we sensed a new window opening on the world of interpretation. We tried again, striving to put into practice what the Maestro had explained, and the duet sounded so beautifully different that the orchestra applauded the conductor.

After the departure of Sparafucile, Rigoletto, in the great solo beginning, 'Pari siamo' (We are alike), is introspectively realistic about himself. He admits that he is no better than the assassin, for his tongue is as sharp and destructive as the other man's sword.

But, as he enters his own home by the garden gate, bitterness falls from him and he is a loving human being again, in the little paradise which houses the one person on whom he lavishes all his affection. As he says to her, 'Culto, famiglia, la patria, il mio universo e' in te'. (Faith, family and country, all my universe is in you.)

As always, he evades her questions about his life and her background, but is deeply moved when he speaks of his dead wife and the love she bore him.

'Deh, non parlare al misero' (Speak not of one whose loss to me). It is a difficult page to sing, with *mezza voce* and breath strongly sustained. Worried as he is, Rigoletto sometimes answers even Gilda sharply but, finally, after warning her to stay safely indoors, he calls the faithless Giovanna and commits his 'puro fiore' (tender flower) to her care. 'Veglia, o donna' (Be watchful, woman) also requires very exacting singing, high up in the register, where the soprano joins in this tender duet. *Allegro moderato assai* is an important injunction, (without slowing down too much).

Almost reassured, poor Rigoletto prepares to leave, little guessing that the Duke is about to enter the house, while the courtiers outside are preparing their own joke against him. Convinced that it is his mistress he is visiting, they are planning to abduct her for the enjoyment of the Duke, their master.

Rigoletto leaves – but, with a foreboding of something wrong, returns, to find the courtiers in the street. In answer to his sharp enquiries they tell him they have come to abduct Ceprano's wife – an enterprise in which he does not scruple to join, only too thankful that his daughter is safe. He leads them as far as possible from his own house, and submits to being masked like the others and finally blindfolded. They spin him round, destroying his sense of direction, then get him to hold the ladder which is propped against the wall. Only when they have stolen away with Gilda does he find that he himself has helped in the abduction of his beloved child.

Frantic with horror he rushes in and up the stairs, crying aloud for Gilda in the sounds of a wounded animal. Then, as he re-emerges, he falls, stricken by the recollection of Monterone's curse. In my young days, fascinated by the idea of a really spectacular fall, I practised on (of all things) a short marble staircase at home. Many were the bruises – and the family protests. But finally I succeeded in perfecting my fall in time for the dress rehearsal when, without preparing anyone for my great achievement, I gave my despairing cry of, 'Ah, la maledizione!' (the curse!) and precipitated myself down the full stage flight, to my colleagues' horrified cries. Only Maestro Serafin remained unimpressed, as he said, 'Very interesting for Barnum's Circus, but too much for Verdi,' and decreed that I should fall only the last few steps on to the stage.

Rigoletto, one assumes, rushes through the streets that night searching fruitlessly for his lost daughter. Then in the early morning he comes to the palace where, in the dwarfs' quarters, he changes into his jester's costume and, collecting all his remaining strength, goes to the apartment of the courtiers in the hope of hearing some news of his Gilda.

The 'La, ra, la, ra' which heralds his approach is sung in a tired, disorientated way (*allegro assai moderato*). There is nothing of the jester now; the sound is one of lamentation. With gritted teeth he answers the ironical salute of the courtiers and bitterly reproaches Marullo. Then, when the Page enters – and the short exchanges between him and the courtiers give him the clue to what has really happened – Rigoletto loses all control.

'If you've lost your mistress you must seek elsewhere,' say the courtiers, at which he breaks out in wild despair: 'Io vo'mia figlia!' (I want my daughter!) and hurls himself against the courtiers in a terrible uneven fight. He is thrown back on the floor, then clings imploringly to Marullo, whom he believes to be a little kinder than the others – but no one has an answer for him.

Before the universal silence he has nothing left but his tears. And as he weeps at their feet Gilda comes running on to the scene, recognises her father and stops, petrified, at the realisation of who and what he is. This is the peak of the tragedy.

I have been through this scene of anguish so many times, and I must warn the interpreter that, while expressing all the pain and confused feelings, he must somehow dissociate these from that part of him which is required to provide the tremendous, authoritative outburst with which he chases the courtiers from the scene. And after that passionate excitement he must be ready to find a feeble voice, full of tears, for the heart-wringing, 'Parla . . . siam soli.'

It is difficult to restrain one's feelings in scenes like this, but control must always be there – especially in view of the continued *crescendo*, culminating in the 'Vendetta', which will be demanded later in the scene. Also there will be needed the sheer vigour for the frequent outbursts of fury and grief, the changes of feeling so immediate and placed in such a masterly way by Verdi. The secret lies in a very clear pronunciation and a vocal expression rich in nuances and varied colouring. It is the quality rather than the quantity of the sound which makes this role less tiring vocally and gives a better human and dramatic effect.

I doubt if it happens much nowadays, but in my time the audience's enthusiasm often demanded an encore of the 'Vendetta'. In Parma, which prides itself (rightly or wrongly) on being the super-critical, best informed audience in the world, that 'Vendetta' moment is the crux of the matter. I remember how during the whole of the performance there we had had quite a cool, measured reception, and my nerves were beginning to feel the strain. Then at the end of the 'Vendetta' I thought an earthquake had hit the theatre. Later most of the audience followed me to the restaurant and spent the rest of the night chatting knowledgeably. They also confessed they had been stingy with their early applause because they had wanted to see how I would stay the course and whether I would get to the end with enough strength left!

Now destiny hangs heavily over the lives of our characters. The first nine bars of the *adagio* which open the last act are desolate in their simplicity and dramatic expression. The dialogue between Rigoletto and Gilda is slow and without any spontaneity, without light or hope. They walk almost as though drugged, their steps dragging with fatigue in the deserted landscape, the marshes of Mantua, under a leaden sky which seems to crush the soul and stifle any power of reaction.

Rigoletto is still seeking revenge but has no longer any satisfaction in the search. His phrases have the descending tone of resignation and an enormous weariness pervades him. In his short exchanges with Sparafucile he sounds more determined, but he is dead inside. Father and daughter sink slowly in a fatal and inevitable destiny.

Verdi has imagined, described and sung everything. It is for the singer only to shed the light of devoted interpretation upon those treasures entrusted to him. Some of the short actions, both musical and scenic, which are scattered through the work are of vital importance in the progress of the drama and the development of the characters. All the aspects of Rigoletto are real and believable. Look only for the human reason, following the thoughts which change and develop in his mind; live and suffer with him during the immense tragedy – and you will make your audience extend their power to live and suffer too.

In that last scene I always felt the need to slow down over 'Qual mistero . . . che fu . . . sei tu ferita?' (What mystery . . . what happened . . . are you hurt?) so as to have the opportunity of almost hammering out 'Chi t'ha colpita?' (Who has wounded you?) uttered in extreme rebellion against God and man. After that, the singing with his dying child in his arms is just a beautiful melody accompanying her to heaven. Then, during the ascending chromatic scale I used to rise to my feet, silhouetting my deformity against the light of dawn, and with all the breath I had left, sing: 'Ah, la maledizione!' and suddenly drop dead over Gilda's body. It is not written that Rigoletto dies, but I have always thought that the last thing one could wish the poor Jester is that he should live to tear his hair fruitlessly. Better death – and our compassion.

9

La Traviata

Some twenty-five years ago I sang in forty-two performances of *Traviata* in one season – in different opera houses and with a great variety of Violettas. Indeed from my own experience I can testify to the perennial popularity of this work and the frequency with which fresh audiences demand to hear it.

During my career there were naturally many Violettas of distinction, each subtly different from the others, each standing out in her own right. I think immediately of Claudia Muzio, Maria Caniglia, Margherita Carosio, Mercedes Capsir, the brilliant Renata Tebaldi, Magda Olivero – and so on, leading up to the incomparable Maria Callas. On the other side of the Atlantic there was the enchanting Bidu Sayao, Beverly Sills followed by the young Anna Moffo and many others. The list is endless, for Violetta remains an ever fascinating creature, one of the most interesting of all female roles. Each interpreter can use her own personality and sensitivity while still remaining faithful to the score.

Looking back, I cannot believe that anyone else in the whole history of *Traviata* ever sang that first act as Maria Callas sang it in the very early 1950s. Later perhaps she looked the part more convincingly, later she may have added certain refinements to her characterisation of the role, but I find it impossible to describe the electrifying brilliance of the coloratura, the beauty, the sheer magic of that sound which she poured out then. And with it – perfect diction, colour, inflection and above all feeling. It was something one hears only once in a lifetime. Indeed, one is fortunate to hear it once!

I think of Maria – and I venture to believe that she thought of me too – as a friend as well as colleague; and, so far as one can say one understands a fellow-artist. I came to understand something of her. First and foremost she was a diva, in the sense that she was set apart: not just in the top rank but beyond even that – something unique. This meant that people demanded the impossible of her, so that she for ever carried the burden of having to reaffirm her supremacy or else be regarded (by herself as well as by others) as in some sense failing. Such a unique position creates a great loneliness and a sense of responsibility so crushing in its weight that it is almost more than a human being can bear.

For a singer this striving for eternal perfection is particularly cruel, for the singer – unlike every other musical performer – is his or her own instrument. If the singer is sick, so is the voice. If the singer is under a great strain, so is the voice. If the singer is shaking with terror, only the most reliable technique will save the voice from doing the same.

Self-appointed critics tend to say: 'If you have a good, well-trained voice you should be able to sing well.' But it really is not as simple as that. There are so many other factors, particularly in the case of an opera singer who has to act as well as sing. And it is not acting in the sense of straight stage acting. All must be contained within the musical form. You cannot pause on a word for added dramatic effect. The music does not allow you to declaim, 'To be' – pause for effect with hand on brow – 'or not to be.' The integration of acting and singing must be absolute. In Callas this integration became nothing short of miraculous. Her musical and dramatic instincts were faultless, and her dedication to her art was total. In consequence she did not suffer fools gladly, particularly in her earlier, less patient days, and I am bound to say – why should she? For she never demanded from anyone else a standard for which she was not herself prepared to strive.

It would be absurd to pretend there were not times when she behaved badly – when she was, as people loved to say of her, highly temperamental. Sometimes she was undoubtedly in the wrong, sometimes the stories were complete invention, and sometimes she was fully justified in her reaction – as on the much-publicised and photographed occasion in Chicago when some fellow without even the manners to take off his hat tried to serve a writ on her as she came from the stage. She was perfectly justified in thrusting him from her path with words of furious contempt. How dared this oaf lay a hand on someone who had just given ninety-nine per cent of everything she had and was in her effort to serve her art and her public? Suppose she did owe money – the matter could have waited for a couple of hours. To attack any artist at such a time is contemptible.

My own single serious brush with Maria also occurred in Chicago, in 1954, and perhaps deserves a full account since I can personally vouch for the truth of it. I also give it as an illustration of what sometimes happened in the highly charged atmosphere in which this controversial figure moved. It was during a performance of *Traviata*. The second act, with its superb duets between Violetta and the elder Germont, had gone splendidly; she had left the stage, the short scene between Alfredo and me had taken place, and I had sung 'Di Provenza' which practically closes the act. Then, as the curtain fell, something went wrong with the mechanism so that one half of the curtain came down while the other remained up and then vice versa, all to the amusement of the audience. As the technicians struggled to sort things out people backstage were saying desperately: 'Go out and take another call, Mr Gobbi, until we get this damned thing right.'

I looked around, enquiring once or twice for Maria and the tenor to join me, but was forced to take several solo calls – to considerable applause. Out of the corner of my eye I saw Maria's husband, Battista Meneghini, go off in the direction of her dressing-room and presently she joined me for the last call and, the curtain having decided to behave by now, we went off to our respective dressing-rooms.

As the interval lengthened out extraordinarily someone came to me to tell me that Madame Callas was very angry with me and wanted to see me in her dressing-room. I went along there, passing Meneghini in the doorway.

'They tell me you are angry with me, Maria,' I said. 'What is the matter?'

'Shut the door,' she ordered, as though I were a servant. And then: 'You must understand that I will not allow anyone to interfere with the success of *my Traviata*. If you ever do such a thing again I will ruin your career.'

As will be imagined, I took a deep breath at this. Then I replied very calmly: 'You were right to suggest that we close the door. Now – first I have always understood that it was Verdi's *Traviata*. As for what happened with the curtain, I did what seemed best at the time, with no thought of harming my colleagues. Your saying you will ruin my career is just a piece of nonsense. It is true you are a power in the opera world, but I also have some power and don't forget that I arrived on the scene ten years before you did. I give you three minutes now to go on the stage and continue the performance. Otherwise I go out and explain to the audience exactly what has happened – and you know I will do it.'

I left her then. Two minutes later she passed my door on her way to the stage.

The third act went beautifully and just before the last act I went onto the stage to check the lay-out, as I usually do. Only the work light was on and suddenly from the shadowed bed a rather subdued voice said in Venetian dialect: 'Tito, s'i tu rabià?' (Tito, are you angry with me?)

'Oh, Maria,' I replied. 'Are you already there?'

'Yes. Are you still angry with me?'

'No, Maria, I'm not angry,' I said more or less truthfully, for there was something so silly and childlike and touching about this tentatively offered little olive branch that it would have taken a harder man than I am to reject it. 'We all have our nervous explosions at times. Now forget about it.'

I never had any real trouble with her again, and in later years there were times when she would not take on certain engagements unless she had my support.

This is a rather extreme case of temperamental behaviour, but when I told her that we all have our nervous explosions it was true. I can myself recall a few times when I kicked things around the dressing-room. I hope those occasions will never be chronicled but, if they are, may they be recorded with a little charity.

On the subject of Maria's total dedication to her art, of which I have spoken, there were some interesting personal results, none more so than the dramatic change she made in what might be called her public image. It was, I remember, during the 1953 recording of *Lucia* in Florence, when we were all lunching together, that Maestro Serafin ventured to tell Maria she ate too much and was allowing her weight to become a problem. She protested that when she ate well she sang well and, anyway, she was not *so* heavy.

With a lack of gallantry which surprises me now, I remarked that there was a weighing machine just outside the restaurant door and suggested she should put the matter to the test. We went there together and, after the shock of reading what the machine recorded, she gave me her handbag and her coat and kicked off her shoes. All the palliatives that most of us have tried in our time! The result was still somewhat dismaying, and she became rather silent. In one's middle twenties – which was all she was then – it is not pleasant to have to face the hard facts of excessive overweight.

I saw her only briefly later that year, when we recorded *Tosca*. In the following year, when we were to record again, I was coming from the theatre one morning when a voice called: 'Tito!' And I turned to see a lovely, tall young woman in a long coat. She flung open the coat and demanded: 'What do you think of me now?' And I realised that it was Maria, completely transformed.

'Maria,' I said with all my heart, 'you – look – beautiful.'

At which she gave me a smiling, sidelong glance from those lovely long eyes of hers and said, with an enchanting touch of coquetry: 'Tito, are you courting me?'

'Of course!' I replied. 'May I join the queue, Maria?'

To myself I said: 'She is really awakened now; she knows she is a woman and a beautiful one at that.'

I think it was her absolute determination to channel everything into becoming a world star which had induced her to make that dramatic change, and for good or ill it made her a world figure overnight. Now she was not only supremely gifted both musically and dramatically – she was a beauty too. And her awareness of this invested with fresh magic every role she undertook. What it eventually did to her vocal and nervous stamina I am not prepared to say. I only assert that she blossomed into an artist unique in her generation and outstanding in the whole range of vocal history.

★

At the risk of being accused of boring repetition, I must reiterate that the task of penetrating deeply into the psychology of a character is arguably the most interesting aspect of our job. Added to which, of course, it is infinitely easier to perform your recitatives and arias if you know your character in depth.

With the elder Germont, for instance, I always enjoyed portraying him in a slightly different way at each performance, putting in some new accent, adding different shades to his famous aria, 'Di Provenza il mare, il suol' (From fair Provence's sea and soil).

Too many young singers are like racehorses. They cannot wait to be off at full gallop as soon as they are on the course, in a frenzy to reach the famous phrases, the celebrated arias. Thus they skim over the score, neglecting to study the text, ignoring stage directions or

suggestions, sometimes making mistakes, or just singing the melodies without grasping the meaning. If you plead guilty to this – go
back to the beginning and start all over again.

Any recollections of my own prowess in *La Traviata* are rather
few, but I do recall in my early days at the Scala being instructed by
the producer to have a good look at the scene for Act 2. With the
assurance of a young man who knew all, I flatly refused, arguing
that Papa Germont had never visited Violetta's house before and I
did not want to lose the spontaneity of *my* first visit there. Not bad
in theory, of course – but what I had forgotten was that although
theatre is fiction representing fact, it is very necessary to know the
'lay-out' of that fact beforehand.

Another time, also at the Scala, I unwittingly created a small
sensation for, as I put down my hat and stick on a chair in Violetta's
room, the stick rolled away right down to the prompter's box. I
went after it, picked it up and calmly restored it to the chair. But oh,
dear! that was all wrong and I was severely scolded, though it
seemed to me (and still does) no more than the natural way to deal
with a small emergency. After all, such a minor accident can happen
to anyone, either Papa Germont or another. Just as, if you drop
your handkerchief or whatever in the course of a scene, surely it is
more natural to pick it up than leave it there for the chorus to tramp
over. I chalk that up as one of my first moments of revolution in
favour of commonsense.

In *Traviata* it is important to keep in mind that everything
happens within the space of seven months, for this explains and
highlights the feverish anxiety and thirst for life which animates
Violetta from the first moment she appears in her own reception
room. A room, incidentally, which should *not* be presented with a
richness and grandeur suggestive of Versailles. It is just one of the
many Parisian drawing-rooms of the period where discontented
gentlemen went to enjoy something they could not easily find at
home.

To make the scene even more unnatural those enormous reception rooms are at intervals crossed and recrossed by liveried servants bearing champagne and richly garnished dishes, while in and
out among the gambling tables pass a crowd of masqueraders
reminiscent of the carnival of Rio di Janeiro. It is all quite illogical,
and makes it difficult to calculate how the fortune which supported
these scenes of luxury could be dissipated in a matter of three
months, making it necessary for Violetta to sell horses and carriages
and all that she owns: another case where a dash of commonsense
would give a more satisfactory appearance to the production.

For Flora's home the score does suggest 'a palace richly decorated

. . .' but even here some moderation might well restrain the excessive scenagraphic ambitions frequently indulged. A more intelligent note is struck in Franco Zeffirelli's Christmas card, which lies before me on my desk. It shows a picture from his film of *Traviata*. The guests are seen from above, some standing and some sitting at the round table. Everything is colourful and brilliant in an harmonious composition, evoking the music of the 'Brindisi' (the toast): 'Libiamo, libiamo' (Let us drink). Sight and sound are obviously most beautifully balanced at this moment.

At the beginning of the opera Violetta is still convalescent from one of her frequent attacks of illness. She receives her friends and guests with slightly languid graciousness, but seems to gather some strength as she gallantly replies to Alfredo's toast.

The conversation ebbs and flows and a sort of careless gaiety animates the scene. Nothing is really important, the guests finding amusement and love without anxiety, as noblemen and *nouveaux riches* mingle and exchange nonsense in an atmosphere enlivened by champagne and complacent ladies. There should not be too much movement among this group of 'viveurs'. They just amuse themselves in their own way, forming the right background to Violetta's declared happiness as she thinks of what her destiny might be.

She has a personality all her own, subtly different from those around her. Set aside by her good taste and her transparent beauty, she seems to walk the world in which she lives without being contaminated by it. Eager to please, graceful and romantic, appreciating riches and the beautiful things they can provide, she has her dreams. They are normal and very human dreams – but they will never come true.

For Violetta is well aware that her health is undermined by an incurable illness, which she fights with almost frenetic determination, passing from pleasure to pleasure in a whirlwind of desperate gaiety.

Throughout Act I her liveliness is forced, as though in the life she leads she is seeking some support against her fear of the future. But one sincere expression of love, one phrase recalling her girlish dreams, will make her doubt. While she debates uncertainly with herself the idea of 'un serio amore' (a real love) is already planted in her heart: 'Amore è palpito . . . croce e delizia al cor' (Love is a throb of the heart . . . both torture and delight). It is with this exquisite and deservedly popular melody that Alfredo penetrates the heart of Violetta, deeply troubling her.

She does not want to listen; she rejects this love at first. She wants to live freely, to pass from one fancy to another; and the glorious aria which ends Act I expresses in a masterly way all her varied emotions. The pensive recitative encompasses so many shades of vocal colouring as she wonders, 'Saria per me sventura un serio amore?' (Would a real love be a misfortune for me?) But the utter sincerity of the young man has deeply impressed her, and she then asks herself whether she would be right to reject such an attachment in exchange for her brilliant but arid life, alone among the crowd.

'Ah fors' è lui . . .' (Perhaps he is . . .) she dreams, singing with the lightness of a fluttering butterfly's wings. It is a meditation which merges into a hymn: 'Di quell'amor ch'è palpito dell'-universo intero' (Love, a heartbeat of the whole universe). Her assurance is wavering, but Alfredo's serenade spurs her on to fresh rebellion. With magical trills, laughing cascades of notes, she breaks into, 'Sempre libera degg'io' (I want to be ever free), and this indescribable outburst of lyric élan brings Act I to a close.

Act 2 opens in a cottage in the country near Paris. It is January, though this fact, stated by Verdi, is frequently ignored and we are treated to a set disclosing a large verandah opening out upon a beautiful sunny park, Violetta making her entrance with an armful of freshly gathered flowers.

I cannot deny that I prefer spring to winter. But in this case I should like to see misted windows, the fireplace with burning logs, naked trees in the park outside, and a general impression of prevailing cold which oppresses the soul and slows down action.

Alfredo is content to have detached Violetta from her world and, having conquered her heart, he feels more of a man. He goes hunting and lives in the clouds of his golden dreams. Unaware of – or ignoring – the fact that it is very expensive to live in the country, he comes down to reality only when Annina, the devoted maid, returning from Paris, reveals that she had gone there to sell the horses and carriage in order to raise a thousand louis.

Ashamed, Alfredo promises to provide the sum required, and it is a pity that the cabaletta which would lend him some respectability used often to be cut. 'Oh, mio rimorso, oh, infamia' (Oh, remorse, oh, shame) he sings, as he promises to make amends.

I have a certain fellow-feeling with Alfredo and Violetta in their devotion to their country paradise, for when I was a young and successful baritone I built a lovely house with a large garden by the sea. It was near Civitavecchia and we used to spend all our free time there. We presumed to call it 'Il Riposo' (Repose), but that soon became more of a joke than a reality, for it was permanently crowded by ever-welcome family, friends and colleagues. They came from every corner of the world so that as for repose – there was never a moment of it.

Seeing everyone and feeling at the same time so very much at home was, however, intoxicating. We sang, painted, read and played every kind of game. We walked to the beach, swam, fished or went boating. We cooked at night on a barbecue. We made fantastic plans, dismantled our cars and put them together again, played cards or darts in endless sequence, and when we out-numbered the eighteen beds – why couches and sofas did very well for the overflow. A perfectly marvellous time in a crazy way. I thought of it because I believe Violetta had also dreamed of a place in the country to enjoy with Alfredo, but in her villa as in my 'Riposo' all of a sudden the quiet life was transformed into a very busy one.

★

For her, however, the dream was to be rudely shattered, and in Act 2 there is a very busy day, with people coming and going and presenting her with insoluble human problems.

First she has to worry about financial affairs – which have never troubled her before. She keeps the facts from Alfredo, but she is waiting for the visit of 'a man of business' – probably a usurer to whom she will sell some of her jewels. Then comes the gardener, followed by the postman, who brings a letter from Flora. She has discovered the address of Violetta's retreat and invites her to a party that evening. Laughing a little, Violetta brushes off the very idea of Paris meaning anything to her now. And then – quite unex-pectedly, the much feared father of Alfredo arrives, and with him comes the tragic break-up of the lovely, fragile world of Violetta's happiness.

In Act 1 the interpretation of Violetta must reflect her state of mind and her way of living. She must be light in voice and action, gracefully elegant and fleetingly frivolous. She pays kindly but superficial attention to the conversation, which does not particular-ly interest her, but she knows how to give emphasis to what really strikes her attention. Her personality is quite distinct from that of the other women in the drawing-room. She is herself aware of that and is good-humouredly amused about it.

Although she smiles, she thanks the Viscount quite sincerely for the precious gift of a new and devoted friend in Alfredo Germont. But at the young man's declaration of his love she laughs teasingly. 'Si grande amore dimenticato avea' she says. (I had forgotten such a great love could exist), and she brushes aside the serious moment in the brilliant final waltz.

By Act 2, however, she is a different creature. The graceful elegance of manner and bearing is still there, but the careless gaiety has disappeared, her gravity enhanced by the necessity of having had to learn to deal with the difficulties of life.

She restrains her surprise at the appearance of Germont Père, but reacts promptly and with dignity to his offensive insinuations. 'Donna son io, Signore, ed in mia casa.' (I am a woman, Sir, and in my own home.) A reaction which impresses her visitor and slightly changes his way of approach.

It is a very difficult meeting, totally different from anything she could have dreamed. Hoping to make it clear that she is not exploiting his son, she shows him some deeds of property she is about to sell. With eager assurances she is prepared to discard her past; it no longer exists for her. She has sincerely repented and God will forgive her, she claims.

The old man is adamant, however. He has come to this visit well prepared to defend his family honour, taking his stand firmly on the somewhat hypocritical moral standards of the period. Standards which were specially important to the bourgeoisie, and so obstinately maintained that the fiancé of Alfredo's sister has actually refused to go on with the marriage unless Alfredo abandons his disgraceful relationship with Violetta.

The music clothes the father's plea with so touching a melody that Violetta gradually prepares herself for a short separation from her beloved. But this, it seems, is not enough. The elder Germont makes it perfectly clear that she must leave his son for ever. He forecasts her inevitable future in hard and bitter words although, prepared as he was to meet a vulgar, grasping woman, he is deeply impressed by her natural dignity.

In vain she pleads her failing health and her loneliness. The dialogue does become more human and sympathetic, but the old man cannot and will not relinquish his absolute aim – the complete separation of Violetta from Alfredo. His heart is truly touched by her despair and her sincerity, but he will not give in.

They both fight with everything they have and, in the touching and dramatic climax in which she discloses that she is fatally ill, he does not withhold his sincere pity. But she knows now that it is hopeless to continue the fight against convention and her destiny. She is a fallen woman and can never recover in the eyes of the world – and of men.

'Dite alla giovine si bella a pura . . .' she sings at last in accents of indescribable pathos (Tell to that girl so beautiful and pure . . .) And she also begs that Alfredo be told of her immense sacrifice – a sacrifice which makes of her a noble woman admired and loved by all, even by Georges Germont.

As Violetta weeps she must make others weep, not only with her eyes but with her voice, which expresses the growing anguish of her soul. She sees all her dreams collapse and that life is slipping from her day by day.

The elder Germont, a country gentleman, had never expected to meet such a sensitive and pure-hearted woman. A man of authority and immovable conventional morality, he had gone to the interview with reluctance. He achieves his purpose, but he leaves humiliated and deeply moved by Violetta's innate nobility. They embrace with genuine affection and in taking leave of her he respectfully kisses her hand.

Alone, Violetta presses the kissed hand against her cheek in a gesture of tenderness. Then she rapidly scribbles a few lines, calls Annina and asks the surprised maid to see it is delivered in Paris. As the maid goes out she turns to the much more agonising task of writing to Alfredo.

'Ed or si scriva a lui? Che gli dirò? – Chi men darà coraggio?' (What can I write to him? What shall I say? – Who will give me the courage?) The sound of the violins is heart-wringing. There is nothing left of the Violetta we have previously known. Utter tragedy has fallen upon her, destroying her. She quickly writes a few words to Alfredo, but hides the note hastily at his sudden appearance.

He is upset by her agitation. More upset than she is, it would seem. But then it is the woman always who has the strength to hide her pain. She has promised – she has made her decision to leave Alfredo and go back to her old life, but she cannot bear to think of it. She pretends to smile – and then suddenly bursts into frantic tears. In a paroxysm of sobs and wild words, with a crescendo of voice and emotion, she implores him to love her always – always, as she loves him. Her agonised 'Amami, Alfredo, amami quanto io t'amo –' has transported every audience in the world, in every decade since it was written.

Though puzzled and disquieted, Alfredo lets her go, sure that Annina will now prevent any ruinous sale of her possessions. But hardly has Violetta gone when a note is brought to him. He tears it open with a sense of foreboding and reads her few lines of farewell. She has left him for ever, presumably to return to the Baron Duphol.

His few wild words of anger and horror are interrupted by his father, who re-enters from the garden, hoping to comfort his son and persuade him to return home. In vain he makes his plea with his beautiful aria 'Di Provenza il mare, il suol.' Briefly the younger man keeps himself in check, listening with some sort of respect. But then excitement and rage engulf him and he thrusts away the offered consolation and, in almost childish rage and desire for vengeance, rushes off in pursuit of Violetta.

Scene 2 opens with the truly grand reception at Flora's home. Troups of gypsies and picadors are dancing and telling fortunes. The great room is full of guests, who comment curiously on the arrival of Alfredo – alone. With apparent coolness he sits down at the gaming table, and then presently Violetta arrives, on the arm of Baron Duphol. Distraught at the sight of Alfredo, she endeavours to remain calm, while the Baron abruptly orders her not to speak to him.

From the torn heart of Violetta rises the stupendous phrase, like an ascending prayer, which is repeated three times. In it she regrets having come and appeals to God to sustain her in this agonising situation: 'Ah, perchè venni incauta, pietà gran Dio di me.'

Flora is kind and attentive, but during the ensuing scene the atmosphere becomes more and more tense. Alfredo, winning heavily, spitefully throws off offensive remarks obviously directed at Violetta. The young man is evidently thirsting to provoke a scene, and presently from a dispute at the gaming table a challenge to a duel develops.

With Flora's help Violetta seeks a brief talk with Alfredo. The scene becomes violent and she begs him to leave, but he will do so only on condition that she follows him. Bound by her sacred oath she cannot either agree or explain, and the disillusioned (and one must say caddish) young man loses all self control. Calling in the others from the adjoining supper room, he insults Violetta publicly. Flinging money at her, he requests them to bear witness that he has paid her for her services. His father enters, stern and overwhelming, 'Disprezzo degno . . .'

The guests are horrified and Alfredo, already regretting his actions, exclaims, 'Ah, si che feci, ne sento orrore, gelosa smania, deluso amore.' (What did I do? I am horrified! My mad jealousy – my disappointed love.)

At the height of the great musical ensemble the tragic voice of Violetta floats over everything, still protesting her undying love for him.

In Act 3 Paris is at the height of carnival, the joyous shouts of the people in the street filtering through the half open windows into the shaded room where Violetta is dying. Her voice when she speaks is weak and tired. No trace of vanity or levity is left as she reads the letter of Georges Germont in which he describes how the duel took place, the Baron was wounded but is recovering, and Alfredo has gone away abroad.

He will, however, be returning to seek her forgiveness now that his father has told him the whole truth of her cruel sacrifice. 'Curatevi', (You deserve a happier future). Tears choke her, and she exclaims despairingly, 'It is late! He cannot come in time.' Death is already there waiting to receive her – and she knows it.

She is alone, having sent Annina on some errand, and in desolate tones she bids farewell to the past and its lovely dreams . . . Everything, everything is over. 'Addio del passato bei sogni ridenti . . .' A sublime page in its bare simplicity, it tells the passion and the pain of the poor resigned soul. The cruelty of a frivolous and censorious world has condemned this gentle creature with inhuman indifference.

Then Annina returns full of excitement: Alfredo is back! He is coming in this very moment!

Violetta rises from her chair, staggers a few steps towards him and falls into his arms, the music rising with the immense uprush of her frantic joy and emotion as they embrace. Her face, her voice, everything about her is irradiated by new strength, new hope, as feverishly they make fresh plans for their future, their momentary hope of happiness. But the flame is of short duration, and as it begins to flicker towards extinction Violetta implores God to keep her alive now that the joy of her life is back.

The elder Germont arrives, deeply remorseful for his share in the tragedy, her devoted doctor who has striven to cure her is also at her side. She looks round and says with infinite pathos, 'Tra le braccia io spiro di quanti cari ho al mondo.' (I die in the arms of the people dearest to me.)

In angelic but ever weakening tones she speaks to Alfredo, giving him a miniature of herself for the girl he will one day marry. Then suddenly she is aware that all pain has gone, new life is flowing back into her. Smiling and radiant, she rises to her feet – and falls dead in the arms of Alfredo.

Since the end of Act 1 this is her only truly happy smile.

There is little to suggest to the interpreter who approaches this complex, infinitely human, beautifully feminine role. Just bring all your compassionate understanding to the part and, with total conviction, identify yourself with the tragic Violetta so that you and she become one.

All light-minded gaiety must be left behind after the end of Act 1; the remaining three acts are lived in pain and anguish to the end. The theatrical illusion must come from a reality so deeply felt that it appears – indeed becomes – the truth.

Once you have overcome the formidable difficulties of the vocal score, give yourself wholly to the intepretation. Let your heart go free, and revel in impersonating this marvellous role. It is a precious gift from Verdi and God.

All the characters are well drawn and worthy of careful study, but Violetta is the absolute protagonist. It is her evening or it is nothing.

IO

Simone Boccanegra

The opera *Simone Boccanegra* by Giuseppe Verdi takes place in Genoa during the fourteenth century, and the action is set against a background of continual factional strife between aristocrats and commoners. The libretto – taken from Antonio Garcia Gutierrez's drama – was originally by Piave, but was later altered and improved by Arrigo Boito. We can actually pinpoint the date of the opening scene as 23 September 1339, for on this day the real Simone Boccanegra did indeed become first Doge of Genoa by popular acclaim.

According to the libretto, before the work opens Simone has led an adventurous life as a corsair, fighting to free Genoa from the threat of African pirates, and his exploits have won him considerable fame. In the Prologue we see him returning to his native Genoa, summoned by Paolo Albiani, who has been rousing the populace on his behalf. An equally pressing reason for his return is that he is seeking Maria Fiesco, now virtually a prisoner in the family mansion of her aristocratic father Jacopo Fiesco.

Simone and Maria have had a daughter out of wedlock and the child – left in Simone's custody – has disappeared in mysterious circumstances. It is Paolo who has suggested to Simone that, should he become Doge of Genoa, even Fiesco would not dare to deny him his beloved Maria.

The two men meet outside the palace and Simone humbles himself to Fiesco, asking pardon for his offence against the family honour. The vengeful old man replies that his only hope of pardon is to return the child and, when Simone explains that his little daughter has disappeared, Fiesco thrusts him contemptuously aside and goes on his way. Alone before the strangely silent house, Simone determines to make his own investigations. He enters the place, only to find Maria lying dead.

As he staggers out again, overwhelmed by horror and grief, the populace, roused and encouraged by Paolo and the lesser conspirator Pietro, surge on to the scene. At the moment of his deepest despair, Simone is acclaimed as Doge, the music magically contrasting personal tragedy and public triumph.

Twenty-five years pass between the Prologue and the drama. My opinion, after some acrobatic calculations is: on the day of his election (1339) Simone is twenty-three years old, the late Maria Fiesco was twenty and the lost child, Maria, three.

Simone is now Doge and the plebeian party is in power. Fiesco, under the name of Andrea, lives quietly in the house of the great Grimaldi family, his beloved companion being the young Amelia Grimaldi adopted as a child by the Grimaldis in place of a daughter who died. Amelia is in fact the long-lost Maria, child of Simone and the dead Maria Fiesco, though her true identity is unknown even to herself. She loves, and is deeply loved by, the young nobleman Gabriele Adorno.

One morning, the Doge, visiting the Grimaldi castle in order to arrange the marriage of his henchman Paolo to Amelia, discovers with supreme joy that they are daughter and father. He therefore forbids Paolo to marry Amelia–Maria, and then Paolo tries to abduct her.

During the course of the action Maria will twice shield the Doge with her body as he is attacked by the bold-spirited Adorno. But, finally aware of the fact that she is the daughter of Simone, Adorno pledges his loyalty to him. Their wedding takes place while Simone, poisoned by Paolo, faces Fiesco and discloses to him the whole truth, ending in a beautiful reconciliation.

Simone blesses the couple and dies with the name of 'his Maria' on his lips.

★

Let us now go back and consider first some of the lesser characters who people the scene. I shall start with one who does not sing at all, but has quite an important acting role. This is the *Captain of Arms* and I regard him as my personal discovery! Improbable though it may seem, I discovered him in California – in an old history book, dated 1579, which I found in the famous Frank de Bellis Collection. The writer, Petro Sentinati, describes in detail the duties of the Captain of Arms at that time.

He carried the keys of the city and the insignia of government, and would have done this when the representatives of the city meet Simone as newly elected Doge of Genoa in the Prologue. He will remain always near the Doge, carrying the ducal sword, representing military order. In the Council Chamber he will stand near the throne. In Simone's study he will come running with his guards at the moment of crisis. And at the death of the Doge it will be his duty to lower the flag over the body.

★

Among the members of the Plebeian Party we have the relatively minor character of *Pietro*. Boccanegra would not have been his choice for leader but, influenced by Paolo, with his superior intelligence and ambition, Pietro joins the insurrection, making himself useful rousing sailors, workmen, fishermen, and so on. In the Prologue he moves busily among the crowd, inciting them to rebellion and persuading them to vote for Simone.

Later he obviously has some sort of a career, sitting in the Council, enjoying the honours and riches promised him by Paolo, but remaining subordinate to the stronger personality of the other man. He does not give orders; he carries them out. It is under Paolo's instructions that he attempts to abduct Amelia, and, in the Council Chamber Scene, it is he who first takes fright and says to Paolo, 'Fuggi, o sei colto!' (Flee or you will be caught!)

At his final appearance (the scene in the Doge's study) he is still taking orders when Paolo sends him to bring the imprisoned Adorno and Fiesco. Having delivered up the two men, he withdraws and is not seen again. I doubt if he involved himself further when the actual fighting took place. More likely – if I may give a pointer to the kind of man he was – he retired to the country with his accumulated wealth, perhaps to grow flowers.

In *Amelia's personal attendant* we have quite a charming little female role and, since it was fashionable at that time for the nobility to have Circassian slaves, I gave Amelia a Circassian attendant in

my first production of the work. She added a welcome touch of
exotic colour to the sombre architecture and costumes of the
period.

The girl should move with grace and good timing. Thus, on her
first appearance (in the Garden Scene) she should bring the light
wrap and put it round her mistress's shoulders *before* Amelia begins
her important first aria, 'Come in quest'ora bruna.' In her second
brief appearance, to announce the arrival of the Doge's messenger,
she must pronounce her words clearly and slowly. I suggest she
enters in good time before singing, waits for Amelia to note her
presence, and then sings her phrase. She does not bow to the
messenger (really Pietro) but gestures to him to approach. Only
when Amelia answers, 'Il puote' (He may enter) does she withdraw, accompanying the departing messenger.

Paolo, the villain of the piece, is of very different stuff from Pietro,
and of great importance. When I had my first opportunity to
produce *Simone Boccanegra* (at the Lyric Theatre in Chicago in 1965)
I remember hurrying to Maestro Serafin for his approval and
suggestions. And when he had congratulated me his first question
was, 'Who is going to be your Paolo? You must make sure he has a
good voice but, above all, that he is an intelligent actor. It is of
primary importance.'

Paolo Albiani is a goldsmith and a leading figure among the
Plebeians. Verdi himself, in a letter to Boito, fixes the size and
character of him. 'It is a pity,' he wrote, 'to have such powerful
verses in the mouth of a common rogue . . . I have, therefore,
decided that this one shall be no petty villain.'

He is ambitious, ruthless and truly wicked. Loving the gold in
which he works and deals, he will undoubtedly – as soon as his
position allows – dress richly, in defiance of Genoa's austere taste at
the time. As Chancellor he can venture to ignore the rules of
austerity established by the Doge, for has he not himself set him on
the throne? The more splendid his attire, the more theatrically
effective will be his eventual downfall.

Already in the Prologue we see his skill in manipulating public
opinion as, apparently without effort, he draws the people on his
side. But he is capable of switching his allegiance to suit his own
ends and, incidentally, it was Boito who suggested to Verdi that:
'Paolo should take an active part in the later uprising of the Guelphs
to betray and dethrone the Doge. He will be caught, imprisoned
and condemned to death. Thus we shall at last see the Doge put
someone to death!'

Paolo's fortunes begin to decline after the Grimaldi Garden

Scene. Simone, having discovered that 'Amelia Grimaldi' is, in fact, his lost daughter, refuses Paolo's claim to marry her with brutal curtness and, in his hatred and disappointment, Paolo plans her abduction.

Later, in the Council Chamber Scene, when he sees Amelia enter with the crowd, he realises that his plot has failed and he tries to slip away. But the Doge stops him and, before everyone, questions him closely and finally orders him to pronounce a curse on whoever was responsible for the attempted abduction.

There are no words to describe the drama of this scene, which gives the singer a superb opportunity to show himself an actor. Paralysed by superstitious terror, he must not resort to superficial grimaces. His actions tense, his gestures spare, his expression controlled, he must convey the bitterness of his realisation that he has brought about his own ruin, the collapse of his ambitious dreams. He does not know where to turn for escape from the curse which the whole crowd insist he shall pronounce. The Doge, with a flash of the old corsair temper, contemptuously seizes him and throws him to the ground, crying 'e tu ripeti il giuro' (and you pronounce the curse). Paolo's desperate full-voiced 'sia maledetto' (may he be accursed) is succeeded by the crowd's terrified whisper 'sia maledetto, sia maledetto', which freezes the blood.

It is a scene of immense power, requiring, as Serafin so truly said, two actors of great intelligence.

By the following scene (the Doge's study) Paolo has regained some measure of his arrogance. He first puts poison into the jug of water standing on the Doge's desk, then he tries to incite the two prisoners, Fiesco and Adorno, to murder the Doge. Fiesco scornfully refuses to sink to such low treachery and is sent back to prison. Adorno, however, Paolo inflames to jealous passion by assuring him that Amelia has become the mistress of the Doge. Then he withdraws, leaving him locked in the room.

By Act 3 his treachery has been discovered. In chains, crushed by the catastrophe, he resists restraint, spits out fresh words of venom and, in a final outburst, reveals that he has poisoned the Doge.

'Ei forse gia'mi precede nell'avel!' he cries. (Perhaps he will now precede me to death.) In my view this should not be uttered with a triumphant sneer but rather in horror of his approaching end. Plots and poison are the tools of a coward at heart, and I think he is suddenly overwhelmed by terror when death is near.

Gabriele Adorno is basically a fine and generous man, but with violent passions. His love for Amelia is a jealous love and he falls an easy victim to unjust suspicions against the Doge. In addition, we must remember that he is influenced by Andrea (Fiesco) whose hatred of Simone has never abated with the years.

In the Grimaldi Garden Scene he announces himself off-stage with two beautiful strophes – almost a troubadour song, with the rhythm of a barcarolle and the accompaniment of a harp. He will get his most beautiful effect by following Verdi's exact instructions, singing the first part from afar – *ben lontano* and the second nearer at hand – *piu vicino*.

It should be noted that this is one of the many moments in the opera when one is made keenly – and ravishingly – aware of the nearness of the sea, with a great sense of space. Indeed, the sea is in a sense the protagonist of the work – Boccanegra's life and almost his last thought before death. I, myself, when producing this opera insist on even the Prologue taking place beside the sea.

The love duet between Adorno and Amelia unfolds with nobility and I recommend few embraces but a quiet elegance in their movements and attitudes. He listens with Amelia when the message is brought that the Doge is coming, and accepts joyfully her brave suggestion that, in order to avoid the marriage plans which the Doge may have for her, they should hasten their own wedding.

She retires to prepare for the Doge's coming and, on the entry of Fiesco (Andrea), Adorno asks for his blessing on their plans. In honour bound, Fiesco then discloses that Amelia is not truly a Grimaldi but an adopted child of unknown origin. Adorno declares that this in no way affects his wish to marry her and, in strains of almost religious beauty and nobility, Fiesco gives his blessing.

In the Council Chamber Scene Simone, looking from the great window, recognises Adorno (but not Fiesco) fighting among the Guelphs. Both men are brought into his presence during the tumultuous entry of the crowd and, furious and panting, the younger man rushes upon the Doge with drawn sword – only to be stopped by the sudden appearance of Amelia, stepping before her father to shield him.

She then tells the story of her attempted abduction, at which point nobles and commoners, each blaming the other, fall upon one another with drawn swords. They are stopped by the stupendous oration of Simone as he appeals for peace between the two warring factions and, at the end of the great ensemble, Adorno, with dignity, surrenders his sword to the Doge. Simone, appreciating his valour, refuses it and, eye to eye, the men take the full measure of each other. There is quite a long pause, which is immensely effective and allows Adorno to withdraw flanked by guards and Simone to return to the throne without haste.

These complicated scenes with close timing are of course particularly prone to unexpected crises. I remember once, when I was singing Simone at the San Carlos in Lisbon, the tenor, having raised his sword against me on the words, 'Pel cielo! Uom possente sei tu' (By heaven! You are the man in power) just continued to stare at me in such wide-eyed horror that I thought the place must be on fire. Then, drawing near me, he whispered hoarsely, 'I've lost my voice.'

Grasping the situation, I cast a terrible glance upon him and, with an authoritative gesture, indicated to the guards that they should remove him. Amelia's aria, my plea for peace – all continued without a tenor. But at the beginning of the grand finale I saw, to my amazement, an Adorno with a different face and heard the beautiful phrase, 'Amelia e salva, e m'ama!' (Amelia is safe and loves me) soar triumphantly to the roof.

Carlo Cossuta, the famous tenor, happened to be in the house and, realising what had happened, promptly offered to replace his ailing colleague, now in tears in his dressing-room. Cossuta did not know the sets and, moreover, had never sung the role on-stage. But with glances and occasional nods the producer and I managed to steer him through the ordeal in safety.

Adorno's role has no psychological problems and is theatrically easy to perform. Passionate, loyal, enthusiastic and full of *élan*, he should act elegantly and with expressive gestures. Once he has learned the true relationship between his Amelia and the Doge he gives Simone his full admiration and support. At the end he will kneel by his dead body and pray for him, *not* puff himself up pompously when created the new Doge of Genoa.

Jacopo Fiesco is a proud nobleman and an inflexible enemy of Simone, withholding his forgiveness until the very end, when he learns the whole truth from his dying enemy.

In my experience only once did those two men act in concert from the beginning, and their action had nothing to do with the plot. On the opening night, and during the first conversation between Simone and Fiesco (played on this occasion by Andrea Mongelli), I became aware of a small forest of bamboo canes sprouting all round the proscenium, each one carrying its little pirate microphone. Without pausing in our stage conversation I drew my Fiesco's attention to them and, with one accord, we charged.

The astonished audience were then treated to the extraordinary spectacle of Mongelli's powerful figure pursuing the excited Simone as we trampled upon and smashed one microphone after another, Simone never pausing in the tale of his sad destiny which he was unfolding to an unsympathetic Fiesco.

Of course a battle followed – and still continues, for it is difficult to bring to justice those dishonest people who poach on our artistic preserves.

But let us return to Jacopo Fiesco. In spite of intensive research I have failed to unearth any historical reference to the man himself, but he came of an ancient and distinguished family in Genoa. One member, the Duke of Livorno, held important political posts and had great influence on the life of the city, and the family gave no fewer than two Popes and seventy-two Cardinals to the Church. In addition the Fiescos, in competition with other great families like the Dorias and the Spinolas, produced a long line of prelates, generals, admirals and ambassadors.

Our Jacopo emerges in the Prologue from the palace where his erring daughter lies dead. We are not told in what circumstances she returned home; only that she was kept in seclusion there in order to stifle the scandal of her association with Boccanegra. In the gloomy mansion the poor creature dies without singing a note!

Verdi is very precise about the impression he wishes Fiesco to make. Writing to Ricordi, he says: 'For Fiesco I need a deep voice with something inexorable, inflexible, prophetic and sepulchral in it. Give me a low F and a voice of steel.'

When he wrote that I think Verdi had particularly in mind the first violent clash with Simone – where a voice of steel and a heart of stone combine to express fanatical pride and desire for revenge. In my view Fiesco should be intensely aristocratic in demeanour; even his manifestations of hatred and anger must have dignity and an almost regal authority. The difference between this man of high rank and what he regards as a mere plebeian must be felt in the way he addresses his adversary simply as 'Simone' while the other says 'Fiesco'.

The patrician still has no respect for Simone even when he has been Doge for many years, and in the Council Chamber Scene he laments, in most beautiful sonorous phrases: 'O patria a qual mi serba vergogna il mio sperar! Sta la città superba nel pugno d'un corsar!' (O my country, what shame for you! This proud city in the hands of a corsair!)

There is nothing ignoble about him, and there are moments when he displays real human feelings. First in the beautiful 'Il lacerato spirito' of the Prologue, sung against the off-stage chorus's heartrending 'E'morta' (She is dead). Then, also, in the Grimaldi Garden Scene when (as Andrea) he blesses the proposed union of Amelia and Adorno. This short duet with the tenor has an almost mystical quality and sounds like a spontaneous prayer.

At the end, still confronting Boccanegra with inflexible hatred, still vengeful for the wrong done to his family honour, he suddenly collapses at Simone's revelation of the truth. Realising his lifelong mistake, he throws himself into his enemy's arms in one of the most touching duets of the whole Verdi repertoire. Then, almost shouting the words in order to hide his grief, he announces to the people the death of the Doge. These last fifteen bars, with free tempo, emotional pauses and very clear pronounciation over the *pianissimo* of the orchestra, should seem to waft everything heavenward – the hopes, the promises, the noble soul of the Doge.

Amelia Grimaldi (otherwise Maria Boccanegra) is very much a woman of her period. Feminine but courageous, chaste and a little melancholy, she has accepted exile as the Grimaldi daughter, but is well aware of the political struggles around her, knows of the plotting of the exiled conspirators and fears for her beloved Adorno who is involved in them. She dreams sometimes of her childhood, recalling the cottage by the sea near Pisa, and contrasting this with her present life in the proud castle of a proud race. The music of her first aria, as she awaits her lover, recalls the undulatory movement of the waves. That sea which is never far from Verdi's musical imagery in this beautiful opera.

When the Doge arrives Amelia greets him coldly for, as the protégée of a Grimaldi, she will regard him as a tyrant and an enemy. She does not bow immediately over the *andante mosso*, but waits until the hammering of the small crescendo on the fourth or fifth bar. I interpret this as a command in the fiery glance of the Doge, demanding respect for what he represents. At her deep, if belated, curtsey, he relaxes and addresses her in free tempo: 'Favella il Doge ad Amelia Grimaldi?' (Is the Doge addressing Amelia Grimaldi?)

'Così chiamata io sono,' she replies (So they call me), her tone equivocal, almost hostile.

The reaction in the orchestra underlines the severe answer: 'E gli esuli fratelli tuoi non punge desio di patria?' (Do not your exiled brothers wish to return to their country?) Then he hands her a parchment and watches as she reads with amazement that the Grimaldi brothers are pardoned.

Irresistibly drawn to this great man she is meeting for the first time, Amelia finds herself telling him something of her story. She is certainly no longer a child, but it is almost as though she were as she confides to him what she remembers of her early days and how, on the death of her nurse, she wandered away and was lost. As she recalls the circumstances with almost dramatic fervour she moves around the stage. In her touching recollections again we have the unmistakable suggestion of the sea, as well as the rising hope and excitement in the heart of Boccanegra. Insensibly they approach each other, their feelings merging in a strange emotion, conveyed by the music.

They start the *allegro moderato* hesitantly, almost breathlessly. Then, as they compare the miniatures, gradually the tempo quickens and the crescendo grows until, swept by a great wave of feeling, they tenderly embrace. It is of great importance to have every musical detail right. For the *allegro giusto con espressione* mark carefully and precisely the quavers and semi-quavers; slow down slightly to keep your mezza voce safe; the *dolcissimo* must be truly sweet – and then come the small crescendos. Allow yourself a little histrionic freedom, remembering that here Verdi is singing with the soul of a father, ever sadly mindful of his own lost children.

This exquisite duet is extremely difficult, particularly for the baritone, who has to sing with the softest mezza voce high up in the stratosphere! Once you are safely past that it is pure paradise, where only the heart needs to speak: 'Figlia, a tal nome palpito.' (Daughter, I tremble at that word.) When they part it is with great tenderness, the Doge exclaiming ecstatically 'Figlia!' on a top F, which is deeply moving and effective.

It was my good fortune to do much of my work at a time when, although rehearsals were under the absolute authority of the conductor, he was usually willing to give intelligent consideration to the singers' ideas. 'Give me your reasons,' Maestro Serafin would say. 'If they are good we will see what we can do.' Consequently, I was always allowed to end the sublime Garden Scene on that top F, the curtain descending while I stood there ecstatic and motionless. The effect is both vocally and scenically breathtaking, and never fails to transport the audience.

I am aware that today few have the courage or taste to take the responsibility of making an artistic cut. (Indeed, in the name of 'fidelity to the original' some would almost perform the cover of the score.) This cut at the end of the Garden Scene has caused controversy, but I am myself in favour of it. After all, Amelia herself tells the story of her attempted abduction, with great clarity, in the next scene. This is all that is required. To have Paolo and Pietro muttering away over questionable music at the end of the Garden Scene adds nothing much to our understanding and spoils a magnificent 'curtain'.

Amelia's arrival in the Council Chamber Scene must be carefully prepared and scenically obvious, as – with an almost heroic atmosphere about her – she steps in front of her father to protect him from her lover. The recitatives which follow must be handled freely according to the situation; with great authority or soaring declamation, and every word is clear. It is with sweetness and almost childlike supplication that Amelia turns for the first time to her father, imploring mercy for the man she secretly loves. And he in his turn answers with paternal emotion, singing *legato*, *rallantando*, *dolcissimo* until the long pause. '. . . al suon del suo dolore tutta l'anima mia parla d'amore.' (. . . at the sound of her grief, my inner soul overflows with love.)

I think that when Amelia sings her aria, 'Nell'ora soave' (in that sweet hour) the absolute necessity is not so much for feminine emotion as clarity of pronunciation, for on this depends the reaction of the people siding with her. Again, she needs absolute purity of tone for the heavenly 'Pace! pace!' which soars above the conclusion of the Doge's passionate appeal for peace: 'E vo'gridando pace, e vo'gridando amor!'

In the following scene, in the Doge's study, Amelia again reveals her passion and courage when she finds Adorno in her father's apartments. Weighed down by the secret she cannot yet disclose, she still prevails on her lover to withhold his jealous anger and to hide as he hears the Doge approaching.

Her father enters in thoughtful mood, but when she asks, 'Sì afflitto, padre mio?' (So sad, my father?) there is no need to adopt a plaintive tone; the semi-quavers are enough to indicate her agitation. Questioned by her father, she firmly declares and defends her love for Adorno. Her vehemence shocks and moves the Doge, who wearily bids her leave him. Then he drinks the water which Paolo has poisoned.

As Amelia goes she exclaims, 'Gran Dio! Come salvarlo?' (Dear God, how can I save him?) Her anxiety can be much emphasised if, in her exit, she suddenly changes direction and hides in a place from which she can observe and protect her father from Adorno. We sometimes neglect these little subtleties which guide the understanding of the audience.

The short duet between Adorno and Amelia is excitedly sung *sotto voce* while the Doge sleeps. But when Simone awakes and raises his sword against Adorno she unhesitatingly drops on her knees, shielding her lover with outstretched arms. Not until Simone's revealing exclamation of, 'la mia figlia!' does she rise to his paternal embrace and remain in his arms to the end of the trio. Then, over the off-stage chorus, Adorno swears loyalty to the Doge, receives his pardon and his sword, and goes out with the Captain of Arms.

In the last scene Amelia, a radiant bride, will notice her father's dying condition only at his words, 'Tutto finisce, o figlia!' (All is ended, daughter.) The couple should emerge from the chapel well before, 'Chi veggio?' (Whom do I see?), which is uttered as she notices Fiesco with her father. The music here suggests their happiness; and joyful reactions at first will give all the greater effect to the sudden grief and alarm as, realising the situation, the young couple approach the Doge for his blessing. As always – listen to the music; it is ever our best guide and support.

★

So, beginning with the unnamed Captain of Arms, we have now in some degree come to know Simone through the actions and reactions of enemies, followers and loved ones. Let us then see how his creator – how Verdi – who knew him best, describes him.

Writing to Guilio Ricordi in 1880, he declares:

> Either the opera is for the singers or the singers for the opera. It is an old axiom no impresario ever understands, but without which there is no possible success in the theatre. You have made a good cast for the Scala but not for Simone Boccanegra. Your baritone [Maurel] is probably a young man. He will have all the voice, talent and feeling one could wish – but he will never have the quiet composure, the visual authority, so important for the role of Simone. It is a role as tiring as Rigoletto, but a thousand times more difficult. In Rigoletto the role is already there, and with the requisite amount of voice and feeling one can get away with it quite well. In Boccanegra voice and feeling are not enough. Boccanegra lacks theatricality. The role has to be made. So – great actors before all. A passionate, ardent, fiery soul with an outward dignified calm (so difficult to achieve) that is what is required for Boccanegra.

Another view of this unique figure has been provided by Emilio Radius:

> Simone Boccanegra has the role of a lion – but an old, tired lion, oppressed by enemies. A lover of peace in a country and a period stained with blood. Simone Boccanegra is also a manifestation of Verdi's deep love for Genoa, Liguria and the sea. As an old man he loved to spend the winter in Genoa and, with careful listening, one can continually hear the echo of the billows from the beginning to the ending of the work. Verdi's sea is powerful and naïve – seen from the shore with admiration, fear and a childlike enthusasm.

Simone is not only the first Doge of Genoa but, in Verdi's mind, represents the Italy of the Risorgimento, with which his sentiments were so closely involved. Simone's very wording recalls the letter written by Francesco Petrarca to the various Italian Communi and Signoria, urging them to cease fighting each other; the first one to plead for unity of the country: 'Adria e Ligura hanno patria comune.'

Boccanegra represents an ideal government, operating with justice, honesty and love. His humanity is immense, embracing as it does fatherly love, love of country and an abiding love of the sea. He is generous in pardoning an injury, and he proclaims his belief in Almighty God. To Him he turns in his last moments, forgetful of the assassin who has brought him to his death. Serene at the end, he entrusts to Fiesco the child of his love, of the Maria whose name he invokes with his last breath.

By any standard Simone is a giant, both physically and in character. He cannot be performed by a small man. The statue on his sarcophagus attests to the physical fact and Verdi invests him with the moral stature.

I cannot describe the joy, the respect, the sheer love with which I have tried to serve this great work, both as a protagonist and producer. Conceit as a performer, trendy gimmicks as a producer, are to me unforgivable sins. For in the realisation of an opera we are only the interpreters and not creators, and our duty is to transmit in the best way possible the ideas of the composer, not to add extravagant conceits of our own. What we must contribute is our own sensitivity, thus giving subtle individuality to the interpretation of a well-known role.

The so-called 'inner meanings' invented by some producers in order to show off their preposterous claims to penetrate the real intention of the composer are usually beneath contempt. There is no need to indulge in perverted analysis of the libretto and psychology of the characters. We have only to walk the same way that the composer did before he wrote the first notes. That way will be easier and nearer to the truth.

If Leonardo da Vinci could have known one half of what has been 'explained' about his Gioconda, he would never have begun to paint her!

There are, I fear, in both music and painting, all too many pigmies 'interpreting' the great in terms of their own resentful mediocrity. But let us, with relief, return to the great figure of Simone Boccanegra – literally to the figure of him on his tomb in the Museum of Ligurian Sculpture and Architecture in the Church of St Augustine in Genoa.

As I have said, the figure is of a tall, imposing man; which brings me to the very important matter of the physical appearance of the role. Indeed, of *any* role! I strongly advise any artist considering an operatic repertoire to remember that the stage appearance must have credibility. It is not a question of what you would like to sing. It is not even a question of what is suitable for your voice, although naturally this is of first-class importance. A short Simone Boccanegra is simply not to be thought of – any more than one could entertain the idea of a frail, spindly-legged Otello. Handsome or not, one must be credible, and a small sacrifice of ambition shows respect to oneself and one's art.

I remember, when I was young, meeting in the home of my maestro Giulio Crimi, the baritone Carmelo Maugeri. He had a large voice, ringing and sonorous, and a laugh like a thunderbolt, but he was stout and on the short side. With great intelligence, however, he had chosen a repertoire suitable to his physical appearance, and in this he was highly successful. In particular, he was unsurpassed as Gianciotto in Zandonai's *Francesca da Rimini*. It was a classic example of disciplining one's ambition to the demands of theatrical credibility.

In the Prologue Simone is still the agile, impulsive corsair. By the opening of the opera proper, years later, he has become the noble leader. He should then show a certain age, his hair and beard grey, but his bearing strong and erect, his manner calm and infinitely distinguished, his gestures controlled. Bitter experience and grief have drawn deep lines around his eyes and on his face, adding nobility to his countenance. His walk is poised and assured.

There is nothing ostentatious about him. It is the strength and nobility of the inner man which makes the effect, and he should be in harmony with his surroundings. When I produced *Simone Boccanegra* in London I used the bare architecture of white and grey stone to mark the Genoese austerity, which also abolished jewels, furs or anything suggestive of gaudy riches. The London critics disapproved on the whole. But the following year (perhaps having done further research on their own) they had considerable praise for 'those beautiful bare stone walls'.

The scene in the Grimaldi garden, ending with his discovery that Amelia is his own daughter, requires great depth of feeling but, also, great control of the emotions. Tears are fatal when it comes to singing! and one must not identify too emotionally with the character. I remember once, when I was singing abroad – feeling lonely, missing my family and thinking of my own beloved child Cecilia, I had to try hard not to be overcome. Apparently, however,

I did not quite hide my emotion, and dear, warm-hearted Maria Caniglia saw the glitter in my eyes. Instead of leaving the stage, she ran back to me, burst into tears and flung her arms around me. There she remained in a close embrace until the end of the scene, while I strove to sing my top F mezza voce. Not quite what was intended, but very effective!

In the Council Chamber Scene every director indulges himself in pageantry and movement, and I was no exception. Yielding to the temptation to use the few bars before the rise of the curtain, I had the curtain up right away, the Doge sitting on his throne and all the counsellors on their feet.

My old friend the Captain of Arms introduced the delegation from the King of Tartary, bringing rich gifts, including a golden sword which a splendid ambassador placed in my hands as a token of peace. It was an impressive sight. But I must add that, even after having been Simone hundreds of times, I still seek better ways of presenting that scene. Detailed instructions for the development of the great scene are unnecessary – even presumptuous – for both Verdi and Boito have supplied these very clearly. To 'improve on them' would be to insult both composer and interpreter.

After the conversation with Amelia in the study scene, and her withdrawal, Simone leans back in his chair with increasing fatigue and thinks (the beautiful recitatives are his thoughts) with weary sadness of the burden of government, culminating in the miraculous phrase, 'Perfin l'acqua del fonte è amara al labbro dell'uom che regna.' (Even fresh water is bitter on the lips of the man who reigns.) After a performance in Lisbon, the late King Umberto came to my room and told me how deeply he was moved by those words, set to such wonderful music.

Verdi's dynamics always give a rapid conclusion to dramatic situations and unexpected changes. So we pass quickly from the almost angelic phrases sung by Simone half in his sleep to the drawing of his sword against Adorno, the threat of torture, Adorno's noble decision to serve the Doge on learning his true relationship to Amelia, and the appointment of Adorno as messenger of the Doge to stop the fighting – all set against the splendid rhythmic chorus off-stage.

The final scene has a shape, strength and colour all its own. Simone enters with dragging footsteps, his pain and weakness underlined by the lamenting chords in the orchestra. Clutching at the walls and columns for support, he gains the window and reaches out his arms towards the beloved sea. 'Oh refrigerio! La marina brezza! – il mare! . . . il mare . . .' Comforted by the breezes, he is totally unaware of the approach of Fiesco, whom he has long believed dead, until a strangely familiar harsh voice recalls him to reality.

Struggling through the mists of increasing weakness, Simone tries to identify the voice. Then, with a great cry of mingled joy and sorrow, 'Fiesco . . .' he recognises his old enemy and thanks God for the gift of reunion before he dies. To music of heart-searching beauty, the two old men, who have wasted a lifetime in useless resentment, meet at the very end to share a little consolation in the happiness of the young couple they both love. Here again it is the heart of Verdi mourning over the remembrance of his own past sorrow.

When the two men finally embrace, the tempo must slow down from 'Ella vien!' (She is coming) to the end, giving full development and breadth to the cadenza which concludes the miraculous duet, 'Vo' benedirla . . .'

As the flame of his life flickers to extinction the Doge staggers to his feet, supported by his erstwhile enemy, and blesses the kneeling couple – singing with an almost unearthly *pianissimo* the short but difficult prayer, 'Gran Dio, li benedici . . .' Then he slowly collapses on his throne, where he remains throughout the finale.

In the *pausa lunga* he recovers some strength and, with great authority in the enunciation of his words, he names Adorno the new Doge and entrusts to Fiesco the task of enforcing this order. Then he raises his arms to heaven, to the Maria who was taken from him but whose likeness he has always worn on his heart and, with her name on his lips, he drops dead on the ground, as Amelia and Adorno utter the word, 'Padre, Padre!'

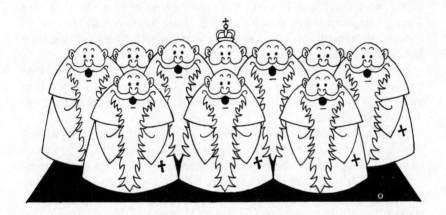

11

Don Carlo

In order to give a convincing portrayal of characters in a work based
on history it is vitally necessary to search between the lines of the
libretto, to check dates and references, and even to seek among tales
of fantasy and romantic adventure.

Certainly you will find inaccuracies, but most of these have been
deliberate on the part of the librettist, the better to heighten the
drama and add stimulus to the composer. In Verdi's *Don Carlo* the
whole family background is of importance, and both understanding and enjoyment will be enhanced if it is realised that:

Charles V, Emperor of the Holy Roman Empire, was born at
Ghent in 1500, abdicated in 1556 and retired to a monastery at
Estremadura, where he is believed to have died in 1558.

His son, Philip II of Spain was born in 1527 and married – as his
third wife – Elizabeth of Valois in 1559, one year after the alleged
death of Charles V. (Incidentally, Philip's second wife was the
English Queen Mary Tudor.) Philip himself died in 1598 at the age

of seventy-one, but at the time of Verdi's opera – which takes place around 1560 – he is no more than thirty-three: not tottering angrily to his grave, as he is sometimes portrayed.

Don Carlo, who gives his name to the work, was born at Valladolid in 1545, son of Philip II and his first wife, Marie of Portugal, who died soon after his birth. In 1554 came Philip's brief marriage to Mary Tudor, Queen of England, which ended with her unlamented death in 1558, leaving him free to make overtures for Elizabeth of Valois in 1559. At the time of Philip's third marriage Carlo was therefore fifteen and, even allowing for the fact that young men developed much earlier in those days, one has to stretch a point to accept the instantaneous love which flares up between him and his young stepmother.

His ultimate fate, historically speaking, was a sad one. Imprisoned in the fortress of Alcazar, he died mysteriously in 1568 (ten years after the death of his grandfather and thirty years before the death of his father).

In the complicated development of plot and situation the characters do in fact move with great dignity and clarity, compelling us to identify closely with their fate and emotions. Most of all, turning from the real characters of history, I offer my personal thanks to Schiller, upon whose play the opera is based, for creating the almost ideal man in the person of Rodrigo, Marquis of Posa. He did not exist in historical fact, but he stakes a claim to be the most human character in the whole drama.

For my part, I take it in my stride that Don Carlo, historically speaking both mentally and physically weak, begins even at fifteen to make the kind of trouble which will eventually bring him to early imprisonment and death. I accept all that Verdi suggests – even that Carlo sees in the mysterious penitent monk none other than the great Emperor Charles V, whose retirement to the monastery is established but whose death date remains uncertain. I am not a stickler for cast-iron facts when it comes to a good libretto!

'Ei voleva regnare sul mondo . . . Grande è Dio sol . . . è grande ei sol' (He wanted to rule the whole world . . . Only God is great.) This beautiful chant, which floats solemnly over the chorus of monks, opens the four-act version of the opera which Verdi prepared for the Scala in January 1884. The first performance of the original version, in French and in five acts, had taken place seventeen years earlier in Paris.

In the original version the first scene takes place in the Forest of Fontainebleau on the outskirts of Paris. Don Carlo has concealed himself among the retinue of the Spanish ambassador and secretly observes the daughter of the French King Henry II who is to become his bride. At the first sight of the beautiful creature he feels his heart leap with joy, and presently he contrives to introduce himself to her as a simple Spanish gentleman wishing to offer the portrait of her fiancé. Elizabeth realises his true identity, and it is love at first sight between them. They exchange vows of devotion and, for a tragically short time, they are supremely happy.

But then the Spanish ambassador, Count Lerna, enters followed by courtiers and dignitaries. He salutes Elizabeth as Queen of Spain, wife designate to Philip II, for it has now been decided that she is a suitable wife for the King himself rather than the Prince.

Utter wretchedness falls on the two young people, their brief dream of happiness torn from them. But there is no gainsaying a decision made for state reasons. For the sake of her father, the French King, and the good of her country she complies. It was a fate not uncommon for royal princesses at that time, of course. She leaves the stage with the ambassador and his train while Carlo remains alone, overwhelmed and unable to accept his cruel destiny.

We find him in the following scene back in Spain, wandering among the tombs in the cloisters of Saint Giusto. He watches the procession of monks and then, when they have withdrawn, collapses over the tomb of Charles V, lamenting his lost Elizabeth, now the bride of his father. In the solitary monk he presently sees wandering in the cloisters he thinks he recognises his grandfather Charles V, whose ghost is said to haunt the place.

Dispirited and crushed by disaster, his weak young mind fragile and insecure, he is an easy prey to despair and enthusiasm alike. The interpreter must immediately make clear this lack of balance and growing insecurity, not only in his acting but in the colouring of the voice, with touching inflexions and deep sadness in the singing. He will thus have full understanding from the audience, though not perhaps their deep sympathy or favour.

While lying on his grandfather's grave the Prince is discovered by Rodrigo, Marquis of Posa, his faithful friend and support. They meet with warm affection, and Carlo immediately confides to Rodrigo his terrible story and the anguish he is suffering.

At this moment the chapel door opens and Philip enters, accompanied by his young wife, both having come to pay their respects to the tomb of his father. Carlo is powerfully affected by the sudden appearance of his beloved Elizabeth, whom he must now regard as his 'mother'. But when the procession has departed Rodrigo comforts him and strongly encourages Carlo to devote his strength and his deepest feelings to fighting for the freedom of Flanders, now lying in dire distress under the cruel yoke of Spain.

The two friends are carried away by enthusiasm and brotherly love and join in a solemn oath of eternal friendship: 'Dio che nell'alma infondere amor' (God who inspires our souls with love and hope). This beautiful music will return throughout the opera to mark their friendship.

In the second scene of Act 1 Court ladies are discovered playing and singing outside the monastery while they await the Queen who is within. Chief among them is the Princess Eboli, who sings the Song of the Saracen, a playful, amusing number but with a story which is largely lost and impossible to understand. It must be sung brilliantly, with marked agility, and also mimed with comic grace – a feat in which Giulietta Simionato was supreme.

The Queen arrives, her beautiful face as always shadowed by sadness. She seats herself and a page announces the Marquis of Posa. He enters, walking with elegance and assurance among the admiring murmurs of the laides . . . At least, I thought that was what I heard! With a deep bow he salutes the Queen.

It is a beautiful entry for the performer prepared to take advantage of it: only four bars of music, a few well calculated steps and a bow controlled by the rhythm. Here he comes, the most important man in Spain at that time, created by the impassioned mind of a poet to be a giant on the stage. Fiction – but a beautiful fiction, symbol of loyalty, unselfishness and faith in the rights of man. He loves freedom and, as an outspoken idealist, he dares to challenge the wrath of the absolute monarch, pleading for freedom and peace for an oppressed people – and an oppressed young prince.

The Marquis is slightly vain and refinedly elegant in movement and speech. During the short duet with the Princess Eboli he flirts aimiably, indulging her coquetry in order to give the Queen a chance to read the message from Carlo which Posa has cleverly concealed in the letter from the French Queen Mother to her daughter.

'Carlo ch'è sol il nostro amor' (Carlo who is our beloved) is an aria which must be sung with heart, for to look only for vocal effect will give no result. The enthusiasm, the thrust of noble human feeling make Posa a great and lovable character from his very first appearance. He is a consummate diplomat and understands very well the possessive temper of Princess Eboli. In the aria pleading for Carlo he subtly seems to talk in turn to the Queen and the Princess, so that Eboli repeatedly asks herself if it is she herself whom Carlo loves. 'Amor avria, avria per me?' (Could he possibly love me?) These Spanish beauties seem to take fire very easily.

Anyway, Carlo is received by the Queen and, on his knees, he begs her support and help with the King. He cannot live here, he

With Tito Schipa. *The Barber of Seville* at Rome Opera House.

With Renata Tebaldi, Anna Maria Canali and Giulietta Simionato. *Falstaff* at the Lyric Opera of Chicago.

With Mirella Freni. *The Marriage of Figaro* at the Royal Opera House, Covent Garden.

With Geraint Evans. *Don Giovanni* at the Lyric Opera of Chicago.

With Maria Callas. *Tosca* at the Royal Opera
House, Covent Garden.

With Mario del Monaco. *Otello* at the Royal Opera House, Covent Garden.

With Renato Cioni, Orianna Santunione and John Shaw. *Simone Boccanegra* in rehearsal. My production at Covent Garden.

With Boris Christoff. *Don Carlo* at the Royal Opera House, Covent Garden.

With Placido Domingo and Ileana Cotrubas. Recording
Gianni Schicchi for C.B.S.

 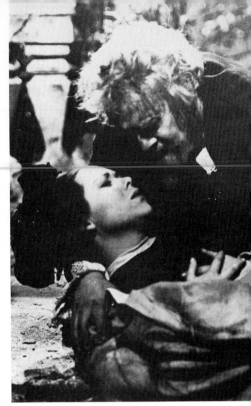

With Marie Collier in *Il Tabarro;* Renata Scotto in *Rigoletto;* and Elizabeth Robson and cast in *Gianni Schicchi*. Patricia Foy's films made for B.B.C. Television.

wants to be sent away as Governor of Flanders. The dialogue becomes more and more tense and Carlo cannot control his passion. Waves of memory of the past brief love overwhelm him and in his dream he loses consciousness, to the desperation of Elizabeth.

When he comes round he is still powerfully excited, but with a supreme effort Elizabeth recalls him to reason, asking him bitterly what he supposes he can do? Kill his father and then take to the altar – his mother? Horrified, Carlo rushes away, crying out that he is accursed.

Elizabeth is still on her knees, thanking God for an end to the scene, when the King suddenly enters. Finding the Queen alone and quite unattended, he summarily expels from the Court her lady in waiting, the French noblewoman, the Countess of Aremberg, her only friend and beloved companion. As he orders her to return to France in disgrace the whole Court is taken aback at his brutal behaviour to the Queen.

It is a superb occasion for a superb aria, depicting Elizabeth's farewell to her one friend. Everyone prepares to leave, including Posa, who, shocked by the King's behaviour, has not yet paid his homage to him. Philip, ill-humoured and a little perplexed, imperiously recalls him: 'Restate!' (Stay here!)

The Marquis turns and walks back haughtily to the King. But at the overwhelming regard of the monarch, demanding the respect due to what he represents, he drops on his knees and removes his feathered hat, to the accompaniment of a powerful crescendo which only Verdi can impose with such dynamic conciseness.

The Marquis of Posa speaks frankly to King Philip in a collision of wills which discloses noble greatness on both sides. Hard reality fights with equal arms against the yearnings of a dreamer, whose loyalty the King appreciates in spite of all. He opens his heart to this man, confessing suspicions, pain and misery in his family life. He gives his full confidence to the true man he has finally found.

What an unforgettable time it was when the cold, hawklike eyes of my brother-in-law, Boris Christoff, met mine – serene and fearless. The enjoyment started from that moment, and we were both transported until the end of the act. We were deeply aware of the subject we were discussing – one which is still debatable to this day. In the artistic tension we loyally measured swords, supporting each other, the audience scarcely breathing during the performance as they shared with us the joy of living through those moments of sublime inspiration.

During one of our first performances together, after my phrase (passionately but not hastily uttered) 'Orrenda, orrenda pace, la pace è dei sepolcri!' (Horrible peace . . . the peace of the grave) I saw him lunge at me, his stick raised to strike me, his face frightening in its proud ferocity. I did not move, and we stood there eye to eye. Then slowly, softly, on a note of outrage and reproach, I breathed the words, 'Oh Re, non abbia mai di voi l'istoria a dir: ei fu Neron.' (Oh, King, may history never say: he was another Nero.) I took the liberty of uttering this phrase slowly, against the suggestion of the score.

It was a terribly moving and dramatic effect, a superb theatrical friction which we repeated in all our subsequent performances. Notwithstanding the direction on the score, conductors invariably agreed with us, allowing the pause in order to support our interpretation.

The text is rich and powerful, a real political debate, and the music supports with supreme fidelity. We were able to underline every single emotion, enjoying a rapturous excitement which only we who have lived through it can appreciate and know.

Inevitably at this point I recall the stupendous, most beautiful of all productions – the one performed at the Royal Opera House Covent Garden in 1958, when the General Manager was the incomparable David Webster. Carlo Maria Giulini conducted, and the cast included Gre Browenstijn, Jon Vickers, Fedora Barbieri, Boris Christoff and myself. The sets and costumes were of rare beauty, magnificent to the last detail, and the whole was directed and illumined by the extraordinary genius of Luchino Visconti.

With a magically light hand he welded us all into a complete unit – an organic whole – so that days and weeks passed quickly by without our even noticing the strain of rehearsals and preparation. We were all so deeply imbued with the feeling that we were about to create something highly artistic and of exceptional beauty that there was no time left for any other reflection . . . Not only were we ourselves in this fever of enthusiasm, but the whole opera company became involved: in the rehearsal rooms, on the stage – where dear Stella Chitty (as stage manager), soft voiced but ever present, was invariably ready to give us her affectionate assistance. The fervour with which everyone worked is certainly inscribed in the golden pages of operatic history.

We had of course our problems. The most worrying – and rather funny – was the business of the dogs. Luchino had selected two magnificent creatures (Scottish or Irish – I forget which now). They were huge, with rich coats of silver hair, so strong that they almost broke the wrists of the young man who held their leash.

They made their entrance among the retinue of King Philip, under Boris's tolerant glance. But during a rehearsal in costume Boris had hardly uttered his angry, 'Perchè sola è la Regina?' (Why is the Queen alone?) when the bigger of the dogs regarded him with curiosity and, bending his head, replied, 'Woof! Woof!'

Consternation! The dogs were muzzled and confined further upstage, where every night they clowned dangerously. So in the end it was decided to cut their performance to a single passage before the King's arrival – and fortunately before our duet.

The encounter between Posa and the despotic King, dreaded by everyone else as a tyrant, concludes the act, and they take leave of each other with moving words. The King, having opened his heart, trusting the honour of his family into the loyal hands of the Marquis, warns him personally of the Grand Inquisitor. Then he abruptly extends his hand which Posa kneels to kiss.

Both Boris and I needed a few minutes respite to relax after these demanding nineteen pages of music – both demanding and exhilarating I should say. Then we were ready to face the enthusiastic audience. One of the great artistic moments in our lives!

A short prelude opens Act 2 – in the Queen's Garden. The night is clear and Carlo waits impatiently near the fountain, for he has received a note which he believes to be from the Queen, in which a rendezvous is made. Presumably the moon then goes behind a cloud because when a lady appears to keep the assignation he has no hesitation in embracing her, declaring his undying love, not realising until she lifts her veil that she is in fact not the Queen but the Princess Eboli.

A normal mature man so caught out would undoubtedly laugh the whole thing off – and so would we. But the beautiful expressions of love and passion, the wavering mind of the adoring young Prince, demand at least our tender comprehension of his dilemma.

Dear tenor colleagues, do not puff out your chests in heroic attitudes at this point, nor react with exaggeration. Carlo is a feeble youth, sick and with an inferiority complex. No one at Court pays him any attention, and he is bitterly wounded by the indifference of his father. In this moment he has reason to doubt even his only friend.

Posa, always alert to protect Carlo, arrives at this moment and tries to calm the furiously disillusioned Eboli. She seeks vengeance and threatens to report the intrigue to the King. Posa, aware of Carlo's dangerous position, asks him to hand over to him a somewhat compromising document which he knows Carlo has with him. At first Carlo resists. 'A te, all'intimo del Re?' (To you? the intimate friend of the King?) he says, doubtfully and with hesitation.

Rodrigo, deeply hurt, asks sadly how he can doubt him, and the

Prince, immediately repentant, hands over the incriminating paper. The friendship theme of Act 1 accompanies their exit. This agitated little dialogue must indeed be very touching, and requires a lot of varied colouring: distrust, surprise, disillusionment . . . and finally friendship again.

The second scene of Act 2 opens in the big Square of Nostra Donna D'Atocha, where, I am afraid, the 'Draculism' of stage directors gives free reign to spectacular displays of bloodshed and horror. The Auto da Fé, the stakes for the heretics, fanatics torturing their own flesh, all instigated by the monks of the Inquisition – and whatever else you like to add. The supers are the protagonists, but for heaven's sake may there be a certain degree of moderation in order to avoid the ridiculous and a personal feeling of nausea.

I often ask myself – as I suppose all reasonably intelligent and decent people must do – how on earth women and children of the time, led by the monarch himself, could stomach such abominable and revolting scenes without fainting or being sick. But then the frightful cruelty of man has been common to all ages – and today we have the television training us even in our own homes.

The King has come out of the cathedral to join the procession when a Flemish deputation fall at his feet begging mercy for their unhappy country, in the most beautiful melody sung by six male voices. They are guided by Don Carlo, who rebels against the King's refusal to intervene, protesting: 'Sire, egli e tempo ch'io viva, stanco son di seguire un'esistenza oscura.' (Sire, it is time for me to live! I am tired of my useless existence.)

This is enough to set the King's eyes blazing. But worse is to follow, for the excited Carlo draws his sword, proclaiming himself the defender of the Flemish people.

There is general commotion. 'L'acciar innanzi al Re! L'Infante è fuor di se!' (A sword drawn before the King! The Prince is out of his mind!)

It is unheard of rebellion. But no one dares to interfere and Philip himself unsheathes his sword to disarm his son. It is a terrific moment, and I still see Boris, as the King, meeting the uplifted sword of the young and handsome Corelli (playing Carlo), and the fierce blows they exchanged before I, Rodrigo, stepped hastily forward to prevent quite a serious accident. Recalling this tempestuous rehearsal, I cannot help asking myself whether some magic from the scenic suggestion affected them or some private grudge provoked this realistic encounter.

Well, these are small incidents which pass over like thunder clouds in summer. Posa restores calm with four well-placed E flats – tremendous and very effective. Then he quietly disarms the Prince, for which service the King creates him a duke. But alas, Posa loses his friend, who fails to realise that Rodrigo was saving him.

The friendship theme is heard softly in a minor key while, slow to understand, the Prince walks away bewildered and resentful. At the same time the Voice from Heaven accompanies with pure melody the poor condemned wretches passing to their fate, wending their way through the crowds gathered there to exalt the King.

In the following act the King is discovered in his study absorbed in melancholy reflection. To govern has become more and more difficult, particularly now that the liberal ideas of Posa are beginning to infiltrate the thoughts of men – and perhaps the King's own heart. He is tormented by doubts of his son's destiny and bitterness over his loveless marriage; and in the famous aria 'Ella giammai m'amo' (She never loved me) he expresses his anxieties and anguish, looking forward to his eventual death as something almost of relief.

A great deal of *mezza voce* is required to underline the intimate and painful thoughts of the King. Also there must be a good use of *legato*, giving the voice the possibility of expanding with intensity in the famous *andante mosso cantabile*, in the long phrases between expressive pauses, and in the excited *stringendo*. Be watchful for the triplets at the beginning of the aria 'Ella giammai m'amo' – one seldom hears them. In all it is a great and most beautiful inspiration, an aria which everyone would like to sing but which very few can do well.

Philip is alone in his large study, severely and barely furnished. Two candles are slowly expiring as dawn whitens the balcony outside, heralding another demanding day. Suddenly his meditations are interrupted. Count Lerna announces the Grand Inquisitor, whom the king has summoned there. The ninety-year-old prelate walks in supported by the two brethren. He is blind but, stopping on the threshold, he sends away his assistants. Lerna also retires. Then the Inquisitor, striking the floor with his stick, advances into the room, imposing and menacing like his reputation.

'Son io dinanzi al Re?' (Am I in front of the King?) he demands. And then they begin one of the most tremendous and spectacular duets ever written. The collision of two terrible forces is overwhelming.

The King asks advice about the public rebellion of his own son. Death or exile? And if death – would the Church absolve him?

The Inquisitor is for death, and will absolve the Christian father, since God Himself sacrificed His own Son to redeem the world. It is a law enforced everywhere as it was on Calvary. (A very peculiar piece of religious interpretation, I must say!)

The King meekly assents. But the talk is not yet over. The Inquisitor rises after a long pause and, in a thundering voice, firmly accuses Rodrigo, Marquis of Posa, the King's closest friend, who is doing damage to the Church by his liberal ideas. *His* betrayal, in fact, makes Carlo's look like a futile bit of play.

Philip denies this with all his strength, claiming that in Rodrigo he has found the one man of true worth in all his court. 'Non piu, Frate!' (Enough, friar!) he cries.

But the terrible old man threatens to drag the King himself before the Inquisition tribunal and ruthlessly states, 'A te chiedo il Signor di Posa.' (I demand the head of Posa from you.)

Once again the King is forced to obey, even to the extent of begging the Inquisitor to overlook their bitter argument. And when the old man has finally taken his leave, Philip exclaims, 'Ah, dunque il trono piegar dovria sempre all'altare!' (So as ever the throne must bow to the altar!)

It is not a good day for the King. No sooner has the Grand Inquisitor gone than the Queen enters, panting and in great agitation. Her precious jewel case, with her dearest souvenirs, has been stolen. And then she suddenly sees it is on the King's desk. Despite her refusal to open it, he breaks it open himself – and discovers a portrait of Carlo inside.

Useless for Elizabeth to try to defend herself. Furious, the King threatens her and violently abuses her, at which she collapses unconscious. Baffled, the King calls for help, 'Soccorso alla Regina!' (Help for the Queen!)

The first person to arrive is Eboli, who instantly recognises a situation which she herself has precipitated. Then Rodrigo enters and, with unhesitating integrity, reproaches the King for his lack of self control. The Queen, partially reviving, joins in the beautiful quartet which depicts the varying emotions of the four people concerned and weaves a magical weft and web of intertwining melodies. This is one of the precious games of harmony so dear to Verdi and so challenging for a well balanced performance. It must not of course be in any way a contest between the four voices. On the contrary, each singer must listen to the other voices and balance with them.

The Queen, recovering her senses, laments her isolation in a foreign country. Eboli, fiercely but in low tones, regrets her guilt. The King reproaches himself for his loss of control. And Posa dreams of giving his life for Spain and liberating oppressed people, his voice soft and high soaring over the quartet.

Posa follows the King from the room, determined to hand over to him the incriminating papers he persuaded Carlo to give up while taking full responsibility for them himself. Thus, in accusing himself he will save his friend the Prince.

Eboli remains and, the moment she and the Queen are alone together, she throws herself at the Queen's feet, confesses that it was she who stole the jewel casket, and admits that she loves Carlo and was driven to the deed by jealousy. For full measure, she also confesses to having been the King's mistress.

Overwhelmed though she is, Elizabeth retains her senses. Following the suggestion of the orchestra, she passes from three *pianos* to six, using very little breath, just enough to murmur the hard, firm punishment: 'Rendetemi la croce . . . Tra l'esilio ed il vel sceglier potrete.' (Give me back your cross . . . You can choose between exile or the convent.) I am wholly in favour of little action in this scene, but great and sober dignity in the vocal and dramatic interpretation.

Left alone, Eboli sings her famous aria, 'O don fatale.' The direction on the score is *allegro con disperazione*, which might seem a slightly amusing contradiction in terms, but of course *allegro* refers to the tempo and *disperazione* to the interpretation. Also this is the point at which I take the liberty of reminding 'whom it may concern' that the 'don fatale' is *not* Don Carlo, but the gift of her fatal beauty which Eboli curses.

The aria, which starts with an outburst of desperation, is very beautiful, very difficult, but highly successful when brought off well. The mezzo is put to a hard test, but has the advantage of ending the scene on her own, thus gathering the immediate reaction and applause of the audience.

★

Before embarking on the last act, which draws together all the threads of the drama and settles the ultimate fate of the main characters, let us have a little look at these characters – both the minor and the principal ones. (Though perhaps 'look' is not quite the right word for the first one in the list, since she remains a disembodied creature.) This is *La Voce del Cielo* (Voice from Heaven). The soprano is, as I have said, unseen but her voice is completely exposed and must be clear and distinct in pronunciation, as befits the voice of an angel. I remember a struggling rehearsal with a very meticulous but not very experienced conductor. He chose to torment the poor soprano, who, perched on one of the lofty bridges of the stage, had to sing seven or eight times the extremely demanding high phrase.

The Maestro was still not satisfied with the celestial effect, and asked to hear the Angel again. At which the dark bass voice of

Giulio Neri was heard to say: 'One more time and she will be hoarse enough to sing the Grand Inquisitor.'

The defence was successful!

The *Royal Herald* also has a brief phrase that is really formidable and merciless. He is alone in the middle of a crowded stage, and sings without orchestral support the implacable phrase. There is no way out. It either comes – or it doesn't. It is a question of pitch and vocal technique, too hard for young singers. There was an excellent *comprimario* at the Rome Opera who sang this phrase with unfailing pitch and good line. At the end he used to turn to the chorus and say exultantly, 'Nice little voice it is still, isn't it?'

The Count of Lerma should be pompously elegant, not to be mistaken for a page.

A Page, Tebaldo (Soprano), on the other hand, is an elegant page, not to be mistaken for a Count.

The Countess of Aremberg is a super. Though she does not sing she must act gracefully and naturally like a gentlewoman. She must react to and enhance the farewell song of the Queen.

Princess Eboli (Mezzo) is a dangerous beauty, haughty and very sure of herself, but untrustworthy. In her view she is superior to the Queen, an inexperienced foreigner, a weak person, out of place at the Spanish Court. Eboli feels that *she* is the first lady, the King's favourite. But her thirst for power and her unrestrained jealousy would have enabled her to pass easily from the father to the son – from the King to the Prince – had the latter not revealed his love for the Queen, stepmother though she is. In her mad jealousy she steals the Queen's jewel case, hoping to recapture her place with the King by discrediting the Queen. Like many women of her kind, she becomes the victim of her own passions and plotting. On an unexpectedly generous impulse she eventually confesses her guilt . . . but too late.

Eboli is beautiful, richly dressed, affected and rather provocative. Sometimes she wears a black patch over one eye, worn like a decoration. Legend has it that she once was wounded saving the King from an attacker. I don't know if the story is true – but I do know that the patch is rather uncomfortable for the singer portraying her.

Hers is a complex character to depict, changeable and unpredictable. In each act she has new attitudes, new actions requiring varied vocal colouring to go with these alterations of mood. The Saracen Song is brilliant and sightly ironic, and needs to be sung with a light, smiling voice. In the next scene her voice will become dramatic, passion gradually overcoming it until the end of her big aria.

She was created a Princess of Eboli (a province in the south of Italy) by the grace and favour of the King. I am unaware of her origin but like to think of her as a rather bourgeois social climber, dangerously controlled in her behaviour, but underneath ——?

Elizabeth of Valois, daughter of the French King Henry II, is married to Philip II of Spain for state reasons – at the horribly early age of fourteen, according to strict historical truth. Sweet, gentle and bewildered at first by the harshness of the Spanish Court, she soon comes to learn grief and sadness. She also learns how to react and express her own opinions, even challenging the severity of her royal husband.

She has the strength to receive the distraught Carlo and she publicly consoles the exiled Countess of Aremberg. She also shows unexpected pride when rejecting the offensive accusations of the King: 'Ben lo sapete un di promessa al figlio vostro fu la mia man; or v'appartengo e a Dio sommessa ma immaculata qual giglio io son. Si dubita di me e chi mi offende è il Re.' (You know well that I was betrothed to your son but now I belong to you and, submitting to God's will, I am immaculate as a lily. Doubts are expressed about me and it is the King himself who insults me.)

At the end of this painful scene with her husband she dares to tell him with sad disdain, 'Pietà mi fate' (I pity you). The lovely innocent girl has become a woman, sharing the throne with a husband she does not love and who does not know how to love her.

A Friar (Ghost of Charles V) needs very little action, but his movements must be slow and authoritative. His resolute gaze is fixed as he looks directly ahead of him. His voice should be mysterious but powerful, with well supported *legato*.

As for *The Grand Inquisitor* – to have seen Giulio Neri in the role is to have witnessed the definitive interpretation. He had everything which is required: the deep, dark voice, great presence, and a terrifying emanation of ruthless power.

Immensely tall, he was skeletonlike in his costume, and the eyes were covered with a little gauze to make them without colour, empty of all expression. He was almost hairless, pale of features and with crooked, bony hands emerging from the sleeves of his Domincan robe to grasp the ivory stick on which he leaned. From the wide collar rose the skinny neck of the nonagenarian with proud arrogance.

The Inquisitor keeps himself upright by an iron will which is stronger than life. The appearance must be spectral and imposing and should be matched by the dark and threatening colour of the voice. The right voice is of prime importance. It is not a case where any good bass voice will do – it is a question of all or nothing. For this terrible old man represents and expresses all the horror of the Inquisition.

Some years ago James Levine offered me this role at the Metropolitan. I had sufficient regard for the young Maestro's judgment – and gratification at his making the suggestion – to ask for a little time to think it over, and try it out on my own.

The role is short and of great effect, and the offer was tempting. I started work. But the more I was attracted by the role the more my knees trembled. Maestro Levine was insistent but prepared to be patient while waiting for my decision. I confess it was not an easy one to make.

The vivid memory of Neri haunted me, making me feel insecure and inferior. Never could I be as he was. Even if I could rely on my qualities as an actor, as a singer I did not want to distort my baritone voice – which, honestly, I found not suited to the role.

What would Neri himself have advised? I asked myself. And, as I thought deeply, it seemed to me that I could hear his dark, honest voice telling me: 'Tito – let it go. This role is not for you.'

So I relinquished it . . . And I think I was right.

Rodrigo, Marquis of Posa – handsome, rich and totally trustworthy, with his pure faith in human ideals. He is elegant, intelligent and a gallant soldier, openly professing his love for these virtues; and without doubt he is the most vital and indeed the most lovable character in this drama. Warm and intense in his attitudes, with brilliant eyes and a smiling countenance, he has the clear and noble voice of a man who despises meanness. That's all.

Don Carlo – a young, unhappy Prince, whose state inheritance and family health weigh heavily on him, working havoc with his not very strong mind. A victim of adverse fortune, he is perpetually in doubt, hesitating to take any decision. He is easily depressed and, equally, easily elated, but it is a most attractive role to play, with beautiful music to sing. The ecstatic melodies, recitatives and phrases which Verdi offers him are a precious gift for the willing interpreter.

Philip II – severe, haughty and hard-hearted, at least to all appearances, is convinced that his is the right way to govern his vast empire. At thirty-two or three he is already feeling his age and regrets his 'crin bianco' (white hairs), while as a father and a husband he is both miserable and suspicious. Certainly he has few reasons to be happy. In addition to his family worries he is tormented by gout, and leans on a stick, which gives importance to his aspect and walk. His capacity to smile was lost in the cradle.

★

Now that we know the characters a little better, let us return to the drama – to the second scene of Act 4, which takes place in the prison where Don Carlo is incarcerated.

In Chicago, when (as Rodrigo) I left my dressing-room for the stage at the beginning of this scene I often ran into my friend and mentor, Pino Donati. He used to rub his hands and say, 'Well, well, now I really go to the opera!' So much did he love the scene of Rodrigo's death.

Donati, who was the husband of the great soprano Maria Caniglia, was a very fine musician and, after having been Superintendent at the Communale in Bologna, the Communale in Florence, the Arena of Verona and the San Carlo in Lisbon, was at that time Artistic Director of the Lyric Opera in Chicago.

In the *andante* which begins this Prison Scene with sad, heavy chords, I never wanted officers or guards. Each bar of this music weighs on Rodrigo's heart like the suffocating thought of death. I slowly descended the steps and from there I said, 'Son io, mio Carlo' (It is I, Carlo).

Ignoring the painful irony of his reply, 'Ti son ben grato di venir di Carlo all prigion' (I am grateful that you come to Carlo's prison), I embraced him, and presently my words of comfort banish all feelings of unease between us.

Silent and surprised, Carlo listens to my 'Per me giunto è il di supremo' (My last day has arrived). Then violently he reacts, refusing to believe his friend's sad premonition. But Rodrigo tells him that the compromising papers found on him mean death. This had been his intention when he insisted on taking the papers himself – to save the beloved prince and friend, happy to die for him, for Spain and Flanders.

Suddenly the sinister shadow of an armed man is seen on the wall – tool of the inexorable Inquisition. A shot is fired and Rodrigo, mortally wounded, collapses into the arms of the horrified Carlo. He consoles the young prince with his last breath, singing the marvellous farewell aria 'O, Carlo, ascolta' (Carlo, listen to me.)

I have already given an account in my book *My Life* of how this aria won me my first artistic battle. Maestro Serafin wanted me to sing with full, beautiful voice to the end, while I pleaded for a little verismo. Having sung plenty of full melodious notes during the evening, I was all for a realistic death rattle choking my voice at the end. I won my point – and heart-warming applause. And Serafin was great enough to concede that this innovation was right, thereby confirming my ambition to be a singer-actor.

Sometimes we used to have the curtain descend on Rodrigo's death and, egotistically, I confess I loved it! But the arrival of the King, Carlo's display of some courage and strength before fleeing, the rebellion of the populace demanding his death, the imposing intervention of the Grand Inquisitor and the final Hosannah do all add up to a marvellous ending to the scene, it must be admitted.

The last scene of the opera takes place in the cloisters of Saint Giusto. Elizabeth lies prostrate before the tomb of the Emperor Charles V as she prays: 'Tu che la vanità conoscesti del mondo –' (You who have known the vanity of this world –) With infinite sadness she recalls her own beloved country, the Forest of Fontainebleau and her first happy meeting with Carlo. Then she bids farewell to the golden dreams and illusions with the touching words: 'Se ancor si piange in cielo si pianga sul mio dolore che offro ai piedi del Signore.' (If they still weep in Heaven then weep for my pain, which I lay at the feet of God.)

She has come to meet Carlo for the last time. The lovely music recalls their previous meetings, and she reminds him of his promise to Rodrigo to help the Flemish people and bring peace and happiness to their tormented country.

The great soprano aria is very demanding and comes at the end of a long performance. The duet is no less difficult, full of infinite longing and the struggle of the two young people to stifle their love and comply with their duty. They seem unable to part, and he says, 'Or che tutto fini e la mano io ritiro dalla tua man . . . tu piangi.' (Now that all is over and I relinquish your hand you weep.)

Conflicting emotions trouble their souls and test their strength. It is a duet which requires each singer to think just as much of his partner's words and feelings as his own. But duty does conquer: 'Si lassù, ci vedrem in un mondo migliore'. (Yes, we shall meet in heaven, in a better world.)

At this point the Grand Inquisitor and the King appear, united by an absurd thirst for vengeance. They order the officers of the Inquisition to arrest the Queen and the Prince. 'I will do my duty!' shout Philip and the Inquisitor in unison. (Not to mention the will of the Holy Office, of course.)

Carlo draws his sword in defence, when suddenly the revered Emperor Charles V, whom all believe to be dead, appears, embraces his grandson and takes him inside the monastery.

A wonderful *coup de théâtre à la Verdi* – who as usual resolves a difficult situation with his dynamics, translating reality into the realms of mystery and conjecture.

Many scholars, musicians and producers have suggested changing this finale, substituting for it that of the Schiller play. But, quite apart from the musicial difficulties this would present, I myself don't believe one has a right to profane a work of art to bring it in line with the ideas of others, however respectable they may be.

It would be like straightening the eye of Venus and taking away from her that slight, enchanting squint.

12

Otello

I cannot remember a time when there was not discussion about 'the crisis in opera'. Books and letters dating back many years also contain the same phrase. And, for my part, I am convinced that the crisis in opera was born with opera itself.

In early times everything was in the hands of some wealthy patron or nobleman, for whom opera was a personal indulgence. He opened his purse and enjoyed playing the role of Maecenas. Then on to the scene came the impressario, a better organised gentleman because he was at least a professional, but with scant regard for the performers, who usually led a dog's life as little more than strolling players. Presently emerged the era of fantastic scenic apparatus, which added greatly to the stage spectacle but usually at the expense of the composer.

By now the private Court theatres were being opened to the public and fresh ones were built. Men of influence invaded the scene, often people who had risen by way of intrigue or politics.

Varied interests insinuated themselves into both opera and performances, and the position of manager of an opera company –
carrying with it the opportunity to have important contacts at the
centre of events – became a coveted prize. Those who had failed to
make the grade retaliated by complaining that opera was going to
the dogs, crumbling daily, sliding down a slippery slope. Voices
were raised in argument, offering innumerable plans for improving
the situation – though seldom was a singer invited to give his
opinion on the subject.

Accusations, propositions, urgent decisions, protests and com-
plaints (particularly about lack of money) were, like sharp knives,
thrust with rhythmic regularity into the flesh of opera, but somehow without killing it. On the contrary, like some kind of magical
acupuncture, they have made it immortal. For the truth is that no
one can take away music and the sound of singing from mankind.
Music is there in the air, in the soul, in the silence. As Pope Pius XII
said to me: 'music is the favourite daughter of God.'

Early in the century two or three people were enough to manage
an opera company. Today hundreds, if not thousands, live on it and
exploit it – though still without killing it. In the modern world
'progress' goes on, ruthlessly pushing poor confused humanity out
of the way. Individual man no longer has much value, for all is now
'mass' reaction. Mass politics, mass stage direction, mass media.
Which last means, I take it, that certain groups speak the same
phrases as if they had only one brain between them. The compulsion to accept without question someone else's ideas and suggestions leads inevitably to a deathly mediocrity. Which is why art
hardly exists today. It has become just an organised job.

And the reason for all this? Well, my answer would be, quite
simply: *greed*.

For the increasing greed of humanity has become a sort of
epidemic from which few are immune. To get ahead, regardless of
the means by which it is done, has become a way of life. And with
that urge has come a sort of shameless 'poaching'. Someone who is
no genius will attach himself to some work of art which is the real
thing, as though that work of art were a sort of soft clay on which he
can claim the right to leave his own arrogant and contemptible
imprint. There are so-called opera producers and directors who
hardly know a note of music, who just invent a thousand absurdi-
ties and abominations for the obedient puppets they expect the
interpreters to be.

Dripping water will eventually wear away the hardest rock, and
mankind is in danger of losing his real artistic identity if he submits
to this sort of thing. It is the artist who must come to the rescue of

his art, and face up to his principles and responsibility. This may – probably will – involve sacrifice for a time, but artistic self-respect is a precious jewel which, once lost, is hard to recover.

And what, you may ask, has all this to do with *Otello*? I have been prompted to indulge in this outburst by the recollection of an *Otello* when I myself had to stand firm, though with great regret, for what I felt to be artistically right. It was at the Metropolitan Opera House in New York many years ago, when I had been engaged to sing Iago. The producer was one I knew well and whose work I had often admired; but in this case his conception of the work – and in particular of Iago – was totally uncongenial to me. Both personally and professionally it was a wrench for me but – I withdrew from the production. And in so doing I still think I served the work more honestly than if I had forced myself into a mould which to me was wrong. *Iago was more important than Tito Gobbi*.

And so we come to the discussion of Verdi's *Otello*.

It is well-known that he thought a great deal about this opera, aware of the difficulties – and possibly hesitating to measure his own genius with that of Rossini. Boito wrote the libretto, and in 1880 Giulio Ricordi succeeded in getting Verdi to read it. He fell in love with it and bought it, but still hesitated some while before going to work on it.

Boito, a most accomplished musician, was also a true poet in his own right, and his first version was very faithful to Shakespeare. Too faithful, in fact, for operatic purposes or for the taste of Verdi, with his love of rapid action, dramatic stage effects and unexpected incidents. The theatre of music is quite different from the legitimate theatre and, though concerned for the drama and anxious to remain faithful to Shakespeare, Verdi was well aware that the action had to be simpler and clearer of purpose. So he urged Boito to adapt the drama to a more compact, more concise, more 'immediate' libretto.

Musically, the first thing to strike the observer in *Otello* is the gradual disappearing of the *forme chiuse* giving a continuity of musical discourse. This was something at which Verdi had always aimed – a flowing musical discourse without interruptions – free, logical, unexpected, like life itself. In *Otello* this is immediately arresting, and in *Falstaff* it was to find its complete realisation. It is wrong, however, to regard these two great works as totally unexpected masterpieces. They are, in fact, the logical consequence of the miraculous Verdian evolution.

Verdi had accepted melodrama in the form passed on to him by his predecessors, but not slavishly so. Even as early as *Macbeth* (1847) one instinctively feels that he is constricted by the bonds of the *forme chiuse*; and already in the earlier creations he amplified these forms, trying to bend them to a continuity of dramatic development. It is only necessary to note the structure of his operas – especially after the so-called 'romantic trilogy' – to see how he concentrated attention on the principal characters and situations.

He had inherited melodrama with its arias and recitatives, etc. They were a foregone conclusion, for to him the dramatic *expression* was first and foremost vocal. But now he began to give increasing thought to the element which revealed the dramatic *action* – the recitative.

Verdi's recitatives are extremely expressive, from the early operas onwards, for he soon realised the necessity of enobling the musical content of this element. In *Macbeth* and in *Luisa Miller* the true Verdian recitative already appears, extraordinarily flexible, capable of the most varied expression, freely mingled with aria, declamation and melodic cadence, the orchestra often supporting with simple and sober accents of great effect.

By the first operas of the romantic trilogy melodrama has changed its character in Verdi's hands, the traditional forms being solved in a fresh and individual fashion. Recitatives, arias, ensembles have now a new structure and the orchestra adds to the dramatic expression in a new way. From this moment one can easily trace the path followed by Verdi in order to transform the melodrama into the authentic music drama of *Otello*.

In moving away from the *forme chiuse*, however, Verdi by no means dispensed with them. Rather, they are 'set' or inserted into the flow of a melodic *arioso* declamation of extraordinarily plastic expression. Everyone knows Iago's Drinking Song, Credo and Dream, and the 'Ora e per sempre addio' of Otello. They are all *forme chiuse*, but they do not interrupt the flow of the musical discourse.

The characters in the drama – and especially Iago – do not reveal themselves in these lyric expressions, but rather in a number of minor episodes, insinuating phrases, inflexions of tone. The dramatic personages grow and develop and are not just sketched *alla brava* and defined in one scene.

On a first reading of the libretto it may seem that Otello's psychological passage from love to jealousy is too quick and not entirely convincing, that Cassio is too foolishly vain and Desdemona perhaps too naïve. It should be remembered, however, that for some time Verdi thought of calling his work 'Iago', and it is in fact Iago whom he makes the real protagonist. To him belongs the possibility of casting light on everyone else.

Thus Cassio's vanity acquires a certain character of its own because of his proximity to Iago; Otello's jealousy – instinctive and passionate – quivers exasperatedly into full flood under the latent perfidy of Iago; Desdemona herself appears the more pure and unhappy because of the contrast between her figure and that of Iago. Because of Iago everyone's behaviour becomes more credible. One might almost say inevitable. In the fullest sense of the term, he drives the plot – and with it the helpless human creatures involved in it.

At one point Verdi asked his friend the painter, Domenico Morelli, to do him a painting representing the moment when Otello has fallen unconscious and Iago looks at him with an infernal smile as he says, 'Work, my poison!' In answer to some suggestions of Morelli, Verdi said, 'Well, very well, very, very well. Iago with a gentlemanly countenance; you have hit it. I already see this "priest" – I mean this Iago with a priest's face.'

Two years later, however, since Morelli had not succeeded in pleasing him, Verdi expanded upon the characteristics of this Iago who obsesses him: 'If I were an actor and had to perform Iago I . . . would have his attitude nonchalant, almost indifferent to everyone and everything. He should speak both good and evil with levity and an air of not really considering what he is saying. Thus, if someone should challenge him for some infamous remark, he can reply, "Really? I didn't notice. Forget it." Such a man can deceive anyone – even his wife, to a certain extent.'

The most serious mistake any actor can make is to represent Iago as a sort of demonic creature, with a satanic sneer and a devilish glance. Such an interpreter shows that he simply does not know what this work is about. In every word he utters Iago is a man – a wicked one, but a man.

Shakespeare says he is about twenty-eight years of age. And Cinzio Giraldi, the author of the tale from which Shakespeare derived his masterpiece, says, 'An ensign of most handsome appearance, but with the most wicked nature ever seen among men.'

He must be good-looking, then. Jovial, frank and pleasant. Thus everyone believes him to be honest, which immensely strengthens his power to deceive. One of his great arts is to be different to each person: easy and jovial with Cassio; ironic with Roderigo; pleasant, respectful, devotedly subdued with Otello; brutal and menacing with Emilia; obsequious with Desdemona and Lodovico.

In comparison, the psychology of Otello himself is simple. Quick to anger and prone to suspicion, he does not look too closely for hard evidence but allows private grudges to affect his powers of reasoning. Almost with ease he becomes the pray of Iago's villainy, a villainy which is not prompted by a desire for revenge. It has nothing to do with disappointment over his thwarted ambition to become captain, or his suspicion that Otello may have had an affair with his wife. These are trifles to him. It is simply that he is the incarnation of evil – gratuitous evil – an artist in deceit who enjoys ruining people. If we try to find a logical reason for his behaviour we lose him.

Whatever reservations anyone may have about the dramatic or literary side of the libretto, it remains a splendid one, not unworthy to stand beside the original work.

★

Now for the people on whom Iago has a lasting effect, and who are one and all, the flies in the web of this spider.

Montano, Governor of Cyprus before Otello's arrival, is a true soldier with respect for his work. Not specially young, he is a good swordsman and a stern commander, loyal to the new Governor and the laws of the Serenissima. In the quarrel in Act 1 between Cassio and Roderigo he intervenes only to act as peacemaker, but becomes violently involved with the intoxicated Cassio. In trying to parry the blows of the young man he is wounded. He does not fall but leans for support on a solider, answering Otello's enquiry with a brief, 'Son ferito' (I am wounded). Then without dramatising the situation, he retires on his own.

The role of Montano requires only a few more words in Act 4.

Lodovico. A Senator of the Venetian Republic, Ambassador to Cyprus, he has the unenviable task of summoning Otello back to Venice and establishing Cassio as Governor of Cyprus in his place. Still a little young for his high position, he is grave and austere, with deep respect and sympathy for Desdemona, whom he greets with affection. A member of his retinue will take the ducal message from him and present it to Otello, who reads it with visible anger and disquiet. Offended by his dismissal, but even more by the fact that Cassio is to replace him, Otello vents his anger on Desdemona, to the extent of raising his hand against her.

The reaction of Lodovico is immediate and vehement.

'Ferma!' (Stop!) he commands, and dismay falls on everyone. Then Otello, in uncontrollable fury, throws his unhappy wife to the ground and, with a terrible gesture, holds off anyone who would come to her aid. Lodovico, however, thrusts his way through and, with Emilia, tenderly helps the stunned Desdemona, who remains on her knees.

During the ensuing great ensemble all maintain fixed places and, in dismay, sing their individual thoughts. The sole exception is Iago, who moves furtively round from one to another, weaving his terrible plot.

It should be clear from the first that, in spite of the cheers and welcoming cannonade, the arrival of the Venetian Embassy is a surprise for the Cypriots; even more so when it is disclosed that they have come to dismiss – or at least to relieve of his position – the man who has recently won such a glorious victory. The two most important men in the gathering do not at any time draw near to each other. Their greeting is formal, with nothing friendly or personal about it.

At that time excessive luxury was the fashion in Venice, and one must have the sharp contrast between the magnificence of the Venetian visitors' fine clothing and the provincial attire of the people living on a dusty, sun-baked island. The Cypriots cannot help staring at the precious brocades and silks of the distinguished Venetians, with their air of visiting a mere colony. I suggest that the Venetians come down from their galleys with measured steps, very refined and elegant in appearance, with a few perfumed handker-chiefs under some aristocratic noses and, all in all, a great air of superiority.

The appearance and demeanour of Lodovico can be of immense importance, as I once saw splendidly demonstrated. The Lodovico in the cast fell ill and I was asked to persuade my good friend, Giulio Neri, to step in. Without question he did so, and I see him now in my mind's eye, arriving on the stage, leading the delegation with slow and noble movements of indescribable authority. His large, majestic gestures reduced us all to midgets. And when he solemnly declaimed his few very beautiful phrases it was as though we faded into insignificance before the sound of his terrific voice. It was a unique presentation which blended the large beautiful voice and the truly regal presence in a surprising unity. Once more the proof of the importance of a so-called minor role. When performed like this, the few lines can raise the level of the whole scene. Equally, of course, a small role badly performed is like a false stroke on a great painting.

At the end of the great ensemble Lodovico escorts Desdemona from the stage, the chorus following.

In his brief final appearance in Act 4 he enters the room with Iago and Cassio at Emilia's cry. He imperiously demands Otello's sword of him and, after an initial refusal, Otello resignedly delivers it into his hands. Taken by surprise, Lodovico cannot prevent Otello's suicide, any more than Cassio or Montano can. He then discreetly withdraws from the tragic scene with the others.

Roderigo, a rich young Venetian, is elegant and very timid. He secretly loves Desdemona, who is completely unaware of this. Being a naïve young dreamer, he falls an easy prey to Iago and becomes a docile instrument in his hands, unwittingly helping him in his ignoble plotting.

During the Drinking Song, Iago pushes him around, prompting him to excite the people, pouring wine for them from a big jar. Roderigo complies with uneasiness and little spontaneity; one sees he takes part without enthusiasm, always under Iago's feet and getting brutally pushed out of the way. At the end of the Drinking Song, however, he is quite ready to start fighting, but Iago restrains him, encouraging him instead to shout with all his might, 'Sommossa!' (Riot!) to create disorder and bring Otello on the scene.

During Act 3, in the scene with the visiting Embassy, Roderigo always stands to one side, his shyness all the more obvious because of his fear of betraying his secret passion. When he sees Desdemona flung to the ground he would like to run and help her, but the ubiquitous Iago catches him by the arm and stops him, with an air of feigned caution.

These are characters who have little to sing in the opera but are nevertheless important. The participation of Montano and Roderigo in Act 1, for instance, is vital, for to them is entrusted the animation of the scene. Without running about or making exaggerated gestures, they must always be in the right place to be seen, and with the right expression. During the duel which degenerates into a fight, eyes and ears must be ever vigilant for the conductor's baton, with full attention to both music and action. The mistake of one can be the disaster of all.

Once, because of some old grudge, I remember a young and vehement Cassio clashing with a Montano who did not want to be second to anyone. They were both good swordsmen, and neither would yield. Consquently, the duel was continued beyond all reason, until a gigantic and courageous chorister grabbed one of them round the waist and lifted him out of the combat.

Cassio is an important role, one of those erroneously called minor roles which actually determine the success of the performance. Such roles are difficult and complex, not only musically. For the interpreter often has to adapt his interpretation to that of the principals (not to mention having to suffer without question the whims of producer or conductor). He must be well prepared – agile, musical, precise, and in every way more alert than is often required for a major role.

The possibility of a mistake is always there, and in a smaller role this can be fatal because there is no chance of recovery. The lack of continuity, the long pauses, sometimes of an entire act, these make for unexpected pitfalls. Yet these roles are frequently entrusted to beginners who have no stage experience. And they are the first to be reprimanded, poor things! To reprimand a so-called 'star' is difficult. To be frank, the stellar crown sometimes rests on some odd heads, and who can say how the reprimand will be taken? I once heard an illustrious performer say: 'When I step on to the stage and lift one finger I have already earned my fee; of the rest I make them a present.' And the sad thing is that he *believed* it.

But to return to Cassio. If he might be described as a *comprimario*, he is certainly a luxury *comprimario*. A Captain of the Venetian Republic, he is young in appearance and bearing, a brilliant conqueror, easily infatuated with women. He likes to joke about his love affairs, is elegant but not particularly intelligent. A good swordsman, very conscious of his honour as a military man, he is a bit of an exhibitionist and likes to be noticed. He is not really given to drinking, being aware that he has not much of a head for it. But he must be on the scene for the 'Fuoco di Gioia', drinking and enjoying the general gaiety.

At this point it should be said that the 'Fuoco di Gioia' are frequently misinterpreted. They are, in fact, fireworks and nothing to do with a jolly bonfire. Legend has it that Marco Polo brought fireworks with gunpowder to Venice some centuries earlier, and the fireworks were popular for festive celebrations or for signalling ships at sea. Coloured flames would be used, lighted greasy rag balls on sticks waved around to illuminate the night and reflect in the lagoon. In my production I had groups of youths and dancers chasing one another , carrying 'fuoco di gioia' in different colours which were tossed into the air to fall backstage into the 'sea'. It made a beautiful display, in perfect harmony with both music and words.

Amid this festive scene, and egged on by Roderigo and Iago, Cassio begins drinking – at first with some grace and elegance, but then, pressed to excess by Iago, he becomes noisy and obstreperous. Quarrels break out among the crowd and, in the ensuing uproar, Iago incites Roderigo to insult Cassio. In a tipsy rage Cassio fiercely attacks him and then Montano, his quarrelsome behaviour quelled only when the voice of Otello commands, 'Abbasso le spade!' (Down with your swords!)

As Otello's close friend, Cassio is the more crushed by the harsh reprimand and, dropping on his knees, murmurs an apology which is ignored. Then, at Otello's command, he surrenders his sword to Iago, who reassuringly presses his arm with feigned sympathy, and walks from the stage with the others.

In Act 2 Cassio is deeply depressed by his disgrace, but Iago cheers him again and suggests he should go to Desdemona and ask her to intercede with Otello on his behalf. He does so, and her willing involvement in this enterprise sows the first seed of jealousy in Otello's heart. That and the fact that the handkerchief, which has so much romantic significance for both Desdemona and Otello, passes during this scene into the possession of Iago, who knows how to use it for his own ends.

The handkerchief, with its tragic importance, deserves a few words on its own account. I have seen many versions of it in my time, naturally. Shakespeare describes it as embroidered with red strawberries by fairy hands, while in Verdi's work it becomes 'Un tessuto trapunto a fiore piu'sottil d'un velo' (a tissue as thin as a veil embroidered with flowers). For my part, as a Venetian, I prefer that it should be white and cobweb fine with delicate *Burano* lace. With that in mind I was once able to solve a handkerchief problem which was nearly a prime tragedy itself.

Actually during the performance it was found that the handkerchief was missing; the propman was frantic as he explained the crisis to me. I added a small quantity of glue to some liquid chalk, cut a square from the net curtain at the dressing-room window, and dripped a fetching design in liquid chalk on the net. It soon dried – and there was a very beautiful theatrical 'Burano' handkerchief ready to go on stage.

In Act 3 Iago's malevolent genius reaches its full height. With the listening Otello concealed behind a pillar, he leads Cassio into a gay and laughing discussion about his successes with his latest mistress. But with such skill does he choose his words and actions that, as half-heard questions and answers are wafted his way, Otello is convinced it is Desdemona whom they are discussing. As a final stroke of genius, Iago asks Cassio to show the handkerchief he found in his own home; (which Iago himself had stolen and planted in Cassio's lodging).

In this rapid scene, Cassio's manner must be nervously gay, and not quite natural. Beneath it all is the contrast of his very real inner humiliation and unhappiness. At the sound of the trumpets announcing the arrival of the Embassy from Venice, however, he leaves the stage somewhat reassured.

When he is recalled in the following scene, to be informed that he is to replace Otello as Governor of Cyprus, Otello's savage aside to Iago, 'Eccolo e'lui nell'anima lo scruta' (Here he is, search into his soul) shows plainly how well Iago's poison has worked. Cassio shows no unseemly elation at his sudden promotion, and when Lodovico moves to assist the distressed Desdemona he, quite naturally, also goes to help her and retires with them, obviously grieved at what has happened.

In the last act, when Iago's villainy is laid bare, Cassio can hardly believe it. Bewildered, he says of the handkerchief, 'I found it in my home,' and asserts frankly that it has no romantic significance for him at all. That he was ever suspected of a relationship with Desdemona is complete news to him.

As the plot becomes clear and Iago makes a quick move to escape, it is Cassio who cries, 'Afferratelo!' (Grab him!) Finally, when Otello is dying he retires upstage with Lodovico and Montano – sad, but with nothing on his conscience except the original drunken brawl which precipitated so much tragedy.

Emilia is not, I must admit, a favourite character of mine, and my dear wife tells me that I am rather too hard on her! Certainly she is afraid of Iago, and must make it plain that this is what keeps her fatally silent until it is too late to save her mistress. I completely reject the idea – sometimes put forward – that she herself had an amorous flutter with Otello. She knew her own man too well to indulge in anything of the kind. Iago would have been quick to blackmail, if he had such a weapon at hand.

She knows the full villainy of her husband – how could it be otherwise? And, in any case, this is clear from one or two things she says. So her fear of him is understandable. But she also claims to love her mistress dearly, and Desdemona is a particularly lovable person, who has probably defended Emilia from Iago's harshness more than once in the past. It is hard then to excuse her for not uttering a single word of warning at any point. She had her opportunities.

Of course, if she had done so the whole course of the drama would have been altered, and we, the audience, cheated of the final tragedy. So Emilia must remain a coward – one degree better than Giovanna in *Rigoletto* perhaps, for at least she is not taking money for her perfidy.

I would say she is rather older than Iago – unassuming and not much to look at. Possibly it was once a great thing for her that the attractive young fellow actually married her. This would partly account for her reluctance to face unpalatable facts about him, even though she knows enough to be genuinely afraid.

When she first enters, in attendance on Desdemona who is greeted by children with flowers and song, I would prefer her not to indulge in too many embraces or much sentimental handling of the children. She can leave that to Desdemona. Iago and Emilia obviously have no children and she (and we) must be thankful for the fact. An infant Iago is a gruesome thought!

Later in the scene, when she picks up Desdemona's dropped handkerchief and has it wrenched from her by Iago, she should show the quick dismay of someone who immediately guesses he will put it to some evil purpose. It is also the moment for her to show that her fear of him overrides any other consideration.

Whenever she is in attendance on her mistress she may legitimately show affection, even tenderness, because she is truly fond of Desdemona – only not enough to conquer her fears and save her. With regard to the Act 2 quartet I have a special prayer to her. Will she, for the love of God, learn her part in the quartet properly? In nine cases out of ten it goes out of time because of her.

By the last scene her fears and suspicions must be heavy upon her. She need not just go on brushing Desdemona's hair as though it is the tail of a restive horse which might kick. She can pause, indulge in a deep sigh or two. And I suggest she allows to pass through her mind the awful thought that Desdemona *might* be in danger. Don't go far enough to gather sufficient courage to save her! But allow that thought to colour your last farewell. And after the final embrace put your hands to your face and burst into desperate tears as you run from the room. Maybe it was your last chance to save her, but you didn't have the nerve, did you? Not a nice thought to have to live with. No wonder you scream out your accusations to Iago when it is too late.

Otello, the Moor of Venice. Both Moor and Venetian, 'civilised' to all appearances, a General of the Venetian Republic, of the 'Serenissima', but still with some inferiority complexes under the hard skin of the soldier. The splendid self-imposed 'varnish' covers the primitive man in whom violent emotion will erupt and shatter that protective covering. Jealousy is to be his downfall, jealousy on account of that young, beautiful, noble woman who has challenged all the traditions of her world and family, the whole might of Venice, to follow the man she loves: a Moor.

He is by nature loyal and honest, and he believes in the honesty of others to an almost naïve degree. Every thought and gesture is marked by basic goodness and a religious faith. On his initial entrance, victorious and saved from the raging sea, his first utterance, 'Esultate!' (Rejoice!) is a prayer and a thanksgiving to heaven. Then he hurries to Desdemona. His love is ecstasy, but the inborn sensuality has a purity which controls his passion and gives a sort of innocence to it.

When he returns to the scene, in anger at the outbreak of violence, he deals rapidly and harshly with the emergency. Then, as everyone else leaves the stage he stands there, *without turning* but knowing with every instinct in him that she, his beautiful white goddess, is approaching. He feels her hands on his shoulders and, in the most beautiful phrase, 'Gia'nella notte densa' (Already in the dark of night) there is a hint of apology for his previous outburst of fury.

The love duet is pure magic: sweetness, passion, yearning and desire blend slowly, driven by the music in a crescendo of voluptuous intensity. Laurence Olivier told me that, having once heard this duet at Covent Garden, he missed the music when playing that scene on the stage.

In the first act Otello is in the full pride of his physical strength and success, secure of himself and invulnerable. The greater, then, and more ingenious will Iago's machinations appear as he seeks to destroy him. At first Otello does not even notice Iago's insinuations, then he rejects them out of hand, but then he is curious to know more.

Once he has accepted the evidence, the change in the libretto is perhaps too quick. And the difficult task for the interpreter is to balance the psychological crescendo and passage through different moods with the utmost adherence to the musical expression.

As is well known, the original Otello, Tamagno, was the possessor of an immense voice, therefore there grew up the idea that a tremendous voice is essential for the part. On the other hand, Verdi himself said, 'There are long *mezza voce* phrases that Tamagno will never be able to do,' and Ricordi . . . 'In ten seconds the audience becomes used to any intensity of sound; what is really required to win the public in the right way is the energy and variety of accents.' All this can be found, not by imitating, but by using one's own personality. Imitation is never acceptable. The great singers who came before us should be good examples but never models to be slavishly copied.

In the finale of Act 1 the three kisses which Otello gives Desdemona are quick, light touches, as if he were afraid to interrupt the ecstasy. The music trembles with desire . . . What invitation, full of veiled promises, is sweeter than: 'Tarda e'la notte' (Late is the night)?

And here I see Otello open wide his arms to her: 'Vien, Venere splende' (Come, Venus is shining), Venus, the goddess of love, transfused in Desdemona, her white splendour enhanced by moonlight.

By Act 2, Otello is already a changed man as Iago instils the first poisonous drops into his soul. At first Otello is controlled and careful; then more tense and nervous, changing by rapid stages until the culmination of the final oath. He is already the prey of Iago's machinations, and in making the infernal compact with him he submits without hope of escape. The man of Act I has disappeared, except for a few rare moments. He is lost.

His shameful behaviour before the Venetian Embassy indicates a tremendous breakdown, otherwise he would be arrested. But the drama demands its tragic end, foredoomed and inevitable. Otello is the victim of a sort of blind magic which imprisons both mind and heart. It is as though he is led by a tremendous negative force right up to the moment when he kills Desdemona. Then, when the truth bursts upon him, it is as though he awakes from his tragic hypnosis to face the unbearable reality, with which he realises he cannot live. Again, he kisses her three times – the candid victim of his immense love – and, stabbing himself, he falls dead beside her. It is to be hoped without the disturbing sound of a melodramatic crash.

Desdemona, a lovely, loving creature, was born under a malevolent star. Like a Veronese fresco or a Titian portrait, with her red-gold hair and her delicately arched eyebrows, she is a true Venetian beauty. Her expression and attitude are those of one who is used to being admired, and she accepts the compliments with extreme grace.

She has opposed – and conquered – all the tradition and prejudice of her native Venice, and has married the Moor. Even though all obstacles have now been removed, there is a touch of desperation in their loving. It is a love which is suffused with poetry and under-standing, but the music suggests a very physical love, so unhoped for, so unexpected that it seems both fragile and sublime. They are almost afraid of the embraces in which they lose themselves.

On the stage this love must be shown with grace and a certain purity, as they hardly touch one another in order to postpone the supreme moment. This intensity in Act 1 diminishes in Act 2 and in Act 3 is almost gone. Desdemona's disappointment and sadness will help her to play with greater effect her incredulity as she says: 'Tu di me ti fai gioco,' (You are mocking me). She will react violently to his brutally offensive accusation: 'Ah, non son cio'che esprime quella parola orrenda!' (I am not what that outrageous word implies!) One must realise that she is totally unused to such treatment. Hitherto a light touch of her hand has been enough to get whatever she wants of him. Then when she defends herself with such energy, to my mind, one sees a flash of the girl who opposed her will to the Senate in Venice and won the right to have Otello for her man.

In the last scene she is more than resigned: 'Una gran nube turba il senno d'Otello e il mio destino.' (A great cloud troubles the senses of Otello and my destiny.) Finally, even when she realises that her husband's insane jealousy has brought her to her death, her last words are almost in defence of him. 'Al mio signor mi raccomanda . . . Muoio innocente' (Commend me to my lord . . . I die innocent.) These phrases must be uttered with extreme clarity, according to Verdi's direction.

★

I began with Iago and I shall finish with Iago, because his personality and his actions surround and encompass the actions of the other figures to a degree unique among operatic characterisations. The supreme challenge to the interpreter of Iago is to convey his full wickedness to the audience while concealing it from everyone except Emilia on the stage. And that without any significant glances at the audience, please, or secret whispers behind the hand!

To obtain the desired effect it is vital to be intensely aware of *oneself as Iago* from the beginning. Not the man who is playing the part and singing to the best of his ability, but *Iago*. You enjoy the wickedness, the ingenuity, the growing success of your deceit. The words and music supply you with most of the character development. Look to your impression of the attractive creature who is leading them all astray without anyone suspecting him. The rest will follow naturally.

Over the years I myself have gradually stripped away all unnecessary ornament from Iago's costume. He would regard such details, including medals or signs of military rank, as unworthy of his attention. They have no interest for him. (Just as he never approaches the throne, which he regards as a symbol of mock power.) The power he wields is so much more potent.

To realise how he works you only need to follow the way he starts with mock humility in his handling of Otello – 'Beware, my lord, of jealousy,' (while seeking to instil that very emotion in his heart); then progresses through carefully graded degrees of suggestion, persuasion and advice, to authoritative command: 'Restrain yourself!' when Otello is entirely in his hands.

In the opera, as distinct from the play, there is such a fascination about this terrible character that one cannot help speculating on what happened to him after the curtain went down. Was he caught and given his just deserts? Or did he slip away from Cyprus by boat, to involve himself in the destiny of some other poor wretch?

I wonder . . . But your guess is as good as mine.

13

Falstaff

Almost a hundred years before Verdi produced his *Falstaff* Antonio Salieri had tried his hand at the comedy, as also had the Irish composer Michael Balfe (who studied in Italy and in Paris with Rossini). Then came the German Otto Nicolai with his *Die Lustigen Weiber von Windsor*, which had a very good success until the arrival of Verdi's *Falstaff* and is still quite often performed, particularly in Germany. After Verdi the English composer Ralph Vaughan Williams wrote *Sir John in Love*, which had some success on the English scene.

Verdi was perfectly aware that the Falstaff of *The Merry Wives* had only the name in common with the 'true' Falstaff. Indeed, writing to Italo Pizzi, he specifically stated: 'I am not making an *opera buffa*. I am presenting a character. My Falstaff is not only the one of *The Merry Wives of Windsor*, in which he is just a buffoon made fun of by the women; he is also the Falstaff of the two Henrys.'

Arrigo Boito, the Italian poet who wrote the libretto for Verdi, followed the story of *The Merry Wives of Windsor* – the most light-hearted of the three Shakespeare plays in which Falstaff appears – but drew deeply from *Henry IV*, taking from those plays not only many phrases but the Honour Monologue, the lovely 'Quand'ero paggio' (When I was a page), and much also from the monologue in Act 3. In so doing he gave back to Falstaff many aspects of the original character lost in the comedy, offering to Verdi a libretto ingenious in its play on words, rich in jokes which depend on sound, and extravagances which give greater importance to the comic element.

With love and consummate art he wove this material into one of the finest librettos in the whole range of opera, worthy to stand beside the great original conception. The music grows out of the libretto, producing an opera freed from all previous conventions, written in a musical prose of the highest order. The work is filled with episodes involving the different characters, like a Flemish painting in which each group of figures has its own life but remains a vital part of the whole.

Every role must be drawn as clearly as the next one, with everything combining to give a living picture of minute exactness. For no performer should stand out against another or detract from the completeness of the ensemble. The figure of Sir John is certainly the dominating role, the pivot around which everything turns, but if even one minor character is feebly performed it will damage the delicate balance of the whole.

The credit for that miraculous balance belongs largely to Boito. The exquisite music in which it is clothed is pure Verdi. Together they created, as Richard Strauss said, one of the great masterpieces of all time.

Verdi had for a long time wanted to compose cheerful music for a happy story without violent emotions. Rossini himself once said that Verdi would *never* attempt an *opera buffa* – which was more than enough to tempt the indomitable octogenarian. And when *Falstaff* first appeared in February 1893 everyone cried aloud at the freshness of the masterpiece. The work of the old man showed a totally new Verdi, they exclaimed, absolutely unexpected and with a different appearance from all his previous works. But the fact is that, if *Falstaff* is different from the previous operas, Verdi is still Verdi and recognisable in everything he creates.

Speaking to a journalist in 1890, he had said, 'For forty years I have wanted to write a comic opera, and for fifty years I have known *The Merry Wives of Windsor*. . . Now Boito has made for me a comedy different from any other. I amuse myself putting it into music; no plans of any sort. I don't even know if I shall finish it.'

From this clear and simple statement it is evident that the preparation and ripening of this opera has been long with him. And one also senses the respect and devotion he felt for the English dramatist throughout his whole life.

'In writing *Falstaff*,' he said, 'I have not been thinking in terms of opera houses or singers. I have written *for my own pleasure*, and I believe that instead of its being performed at La Scala it should in fact be done at S. Agata. I am afraid the Scala is much too large for a comedy, in which the rapid flow of the dialogue and the play of facial expression are the most important parts.

It is quite clear that he wants the opera to have an intimate frame, and this *must* be ever present in both the performing and the interpretation. 'Our singers,' he said, 'know only one way of singing, "con la voce grossa", with little suppleness in the voice, no clear enunciation, lacking both breath and accent . . .'

Alas, poor us! Harsh criticism indeed.

Verdi wants actors for this opera. He does not ask for singing as the first priority, but a musical dialogue, fluent and clearly enunciated. Singing is demanded only when the music unquestionably requires it.

And so the curtain rises!

★

In the Garter Inn the celebrated Sir John has been living for some time, oblivious of the broken beams and the poor furniture. They have nothing to do with his real importance. The innkeeper is responsible for all that – and it is sheer impudence on his part to present any bill to Sir John. The honour of his presence is sufficient payment. This arrangement suffices for his needs, after all, and there he makes himself comfortable, like a big bear in the hole of a tree.

Bardolph does what might by courtesy be called the housekeeping, and Pistol keeps guard. They have no payment for their services, but get by very well all the same, cheating their master on every possible occasion. They steal his wine and meat and possibly betray him in various ways. Certainly they are all too willing to sell him to the rich Master Ford.

It is a quiet morning – everything calm. Falstaff is busy writing his two identical love letters to Mistress Ford and Mistress Page, Pistol and Bardolph are lounging comfortably, half asleep.

Suddenly the door is thrown wide open and, like a ruffled cat pursued by dogs, Dr Cajus enters, shouting accusations and protests, vowing that Falstaff's two scallywags robbed him the previous evening. For their part, they just make fun of him and consign him to the devil.

Throughout the scene Sir John preserves his Olympian calm. But it is a different matter when the innkeeper enters and presents a long list of wine and meats as yet unpaid for. Realising that he must put on an act to rid himself of this nuisance, Sir John rises to his full height and, with a great display of fury, pushes his rascally servants around, declaring that they feed on him.

This tremendous scene, with Falstaff swaying his great bulk and thundering reproaches and threats, terrifies the innkeeper, and the wretched man beats a reluctant retreat, unaware that Sir John is really amusing himself and enjoying all the excitement.

That matter disposed of, Falstaff prepares to hand over his two love letters, enjoining his rogues to take one to each of the two ladies. They, however, have the audacity to declare it is against their honour to undertake such an errand. In a glorious display of thunderous contempt Sir John then launches into the famous Honour Aria, a superbly cynical and amoral dissertation on the real meaning of honour. According to his personal philosophy and requirements, can honour fill the belly? replace a shinbone? – a foot – a hair? No. Can it live with the living? Do the dead feel it? – and so on and so on. Honour is nothing but a word – full of air!

Well, then, he can do without it. And he can do without them too! And, seizing a broom, he chases them all over the place, shouting at them, and finally drives them from the stage, a great burst of hearty laughter from him closing this short scene.

It is particularly demanding for Falstaff himself, both vocally and scenically. He has to sing all his so-called philosophy and his rascally plans and, at the same time, move his great bulk around – which is no easy matter. Nevertheless, it is, so to speak, Sir John Falstaff's visiting card and he must play it for all it is worth . . . quite apart from having to sing out a high G over a blazing orchestra!

Meanwhile, the page has been sent running with the two letters to the delightful lively Alice Ford and Meg Page. I think those two charmers were initially flattered by such beautiful letters, even if written by the portly knight. But amusement turns to fury when they discover the two to be identical. Laughing but piqued, they decide to give him a very sharp lesson. 'L'allegria d'oneste donne ogni onestà comporta.' They will teach him that a merry woman can yet be an honest one.

At the same time Pistol and Bardolph seek vengeance upon their master for having driven them away. They go to Master Ford to warn him that the fat knight is preparing to seduce his wife, using every term of abuse to which they can lay their experienced tongues.

Then, while the men and the women are pursuing their respective conspiracies, the young lovers, Nannetta and Fenton, secretly exchange kisses and promises of love, their enchanting relationship contrasting exquisitely with the irate machinations of the grown-ups. Thus, the reading and comparing of the two letters amidst gales of derisive laughter is crowned by the beautiful ascending phrase, 'E il viso tuo su me risplenderà come una stella sull'immensità.'

The women's quartet, flashing like a jewel, illumines from time to time the 'humming of the wasps and hornets' (il ronzio di vespe e d'avidi calabroni) of the plotting men, blending together in the famous nonette which expresses so many different feelings. And again the beautiful phrase of the lovers rises like the sun in splendour . . . until the whole thing ends with a burst of laughter, for is it not a comedy?

To have heard this phrase sung by Maria Caniglia or Renata Tebaldi is to have heard something never to be forgotten. The sensation has sunk so deeply into one that just to remember it is to be fascinated all over again by the sheer vocal magic of it.

As for Quickly . . . nothing can efface the characterisation of Fedora Barbieri, the Quickly *par excellence* for the richness of the voice and the intelligence of interpretation. When I produced *Falstaff* in Paris (singing the title role myself) I accepted an entirely French cast, with one exception only. I had to insist on Fedora Barbieri as Quickly. Thus, I knew I should have an infallible support and guide with the French 'Wives' when I was engaged elsewhere.

Mistress Quickly, chosen to be Cupid's messenger, is charged with the honour of conveying the answers of the two ladies to Sir John. Flattered by the speed of the response, he is ready to believe everything. The conversation between them is the most gloriously amusing scene in the whole work, the mock reverence of the scheming Quickly contrasting superbly with the condescension of the pompous Falstaff. He swallows the bait whole and on Quickly's departure can hardly wait to make his splendid preparations for the rendezvous with Alice 'dalle due alle tre' (from two to three).

With beatific smiles he intones poems of praise to his old flesh which still yields him such pleasure. His triumphant little march – the music a perfect accompaniment to the words – is simply magical: 'Va, vecchio, John . . .' he sings, as he marches to and fro, and when he reaches the words 'ancora spreme' they are significantly accentuated with a little tight C flat 'spre', almost conveying the effort required for this pleasure. Sheer genius!

But his self-congratulatory reflections are interrupted by the unexpected visit of a Master Fontana. This is, of course, the jealous Ford in disguise, coming to make some investigations of his own in order to discover just what Falstaff is up to. The visit is untimely, since it interferes with Falstaff's plans to dress himself up and generally make himself irresistible for his rendezvous. However, the visitor brings wine and money with him, and it is not long before they are on the most friendly terms.

They confide to each other their amorous adventures, Falstaff allowing the younger man to do the talking while he himself maintains the complacent air of one who knows all about it. Finally he undertakes to pass on later to Fontana his own recent conquest – none other than Ford's own wife, the charming Alice, with whom, he smugly admits, he has a rendezvous 'dalle due alle tre'.

Full of himself, and rather forgetting his status as a gentleman, he rails against the cuckolded husband in somewhat vulgar terms of abuse. Then, regaining his self-control, he becomes once more the amiable, winning gentleman who must now go and make himself beautiful.

This scene between Falstaff and Ford is inexpressibly humorous, both roles requiring considerable acting power. Ford has his enchanting monologue and Sir John a great deal of work most of the time. Much change of vocal colouring is called for, for instance after the violent tirade against the betrayed husband, when Falstaff has to produce a flutelike tone to sing, 'Vado a farmi bello' (I am going to make myself beautiful).

We are left with the horrified Ford. Stupefied by the old knight's plan of conquest, he starts to think how to do this, how to do that in order to prevent the appalling deed. He endeavours to arouse himself, as though waking from a dream to the dreadful realisation of the projected assignation. He came here to make fun of Falstaff – and now he himself is the ridiculed husband. 'Tua moglie sgarra e mette in malo assetto l'onor tuo la tua casa ed il tuo letto.' (Your wife wrongs you and disgraces your home, your honour and your bed.) In a bitter outburst he cries, 'Laudata sempre sia nel fondo del mio cor la gelosia!' (Praise be! There was always some jealousy at the bottom of my heart!)

It is a most beautiful aria, one of the few *forme chiuse* in the opera. With its mixture of drama and the grotesque it gives immense opportunity for vocal interpretation; and for more than one promising young baritone this has been the stepping-stone from minor to major roles.

Is this monologue serious or comic? From the wretched Ford's point of view it is deadly serious, of course. But this tone and expression of seriousness must be so nervously accentuated that the comic side inevitably emerges. A victim of his own trick and now desperately frightened, he loses his temper and his nerve. This is one of the few moments when one personage has the stage to himself. Enjoy dominating the scene, by all means, but without becoming the protagonist. No one must stand out too much, damaging the harmony of the ensemble.

Falstaff returns, dressed to kill in a manner reminiscent of the page he once was (quand'ero paggio del Duca di Norfolk, in fact). But alas, the clothes have not grown with him and now fit his immense frame like a sausage skin.

Regally uncaring of the slight inconvenience, he stalks proudly before the incredulous Ford. They exchange compliments, while showing their teeth, and after some rearrangement at the door they contrive to go out arm in arm. Years ago I enjoyed tremendously performing both roles for BBC television in London. It was a fortunate series on opera directed by Patricia Foy in which I appeared as Falstaff and Ford at the same time . . . arm in arm.

The opera has three distinct aspects. Humorous–ironic, lyric–idyllic, and fantastic–romantic, each relating to a particular aspect of the *commedia lirica*.

In the middle of the humorous–ironic aspects sits Falstaff, whose music reveals every facet of his being. He is supremely indifferent to everything which does not concern him personally. He is sensual, but he is also shrewd in a sprightly, biting way, which helps him to extricate himself from awkward situations. This shrewdness and an immeasurable vanity are absolute essentials to his character and are shown in the very first scene, in the two great monologues from Acts 1 and 3, and in the exquisite little *cabaletta* 'Quand'ero paggio'. This is not an air of success, but rather a slightly melancholy evocation – not without irony as he remembers the past.

The lyric-idyllic side of the comedy is in the chattering of the Wives and their plotting to punish Falstaff, and in Nannetta and Fenton's pursuit of each other (with the complicity of Mistress Quickly) and their fresh love music. Verdi wants them always in the forefront in the less highly dramatic moments.

Elsewhere we have little family episodes: the ladies, awaiting news from Mistress Quickly, attending to the usual household chores; the answering calls to each other at the end of the fifth scene as they part at sundown to organise the rendezvous at Herne's Oak; in the wood itself as the last touches are given to the masquerade after Fenton's magical aria.

The romantic-fantastic element takes in the whole last scene of the opera, announced unmistakably by the sound of the horn before

Fenton's sonnet. This scene is a great musical *fresco* to be enjoyed strictly from the musical point of view. It gives a festive conclusion in which the comedy on stage is the projection of the music – with the colour of a pastoral fairytale.

Here is what Verdi wrote to Giulio Ricordi about the interpreters:

> In the role of Ford there is not much to sing; but if in the finale of Act 2 he does not shout, jump up and run around he will have no effect.
>
> The role of Quickly is different. You need singing and acting, great scenic naturalness and the right accent on the syllable. For Alice the same qualities as Quickly, but more brilliant with great vivacity. She is the one who manoeuvres everything.

I think he wanted Meg also to be a vivacious woman, sometimes impertinent and something of a comedian. For Nannetta he wants a young woman who can sing and act well, having particularly in mind those two lively little duets with Fenton.

Quoting Verdi again:

> Fenton is a sentimental young man much in love. Caius a pedantic fool and a bore. Pistol an empty-headed, but very noisy chap and Bardolph both ignorant and malicious.

In the great monologue of Act 3 Falstaff is really himself (the Falstaff of *Henry IV*), more so than at any other stage of the story. He has no audience, nobody before whom he need make a show. He is raging from the terrible humiliation he has just suffered – 'Essere portato in un canestro e gittato al canale coi pannilini biechi come si fa coi gatti e i catellini ciechi . . . Mondo reo! Mondo rubaldo!' (To be taken in a basket and thrown into the water along with the dirty clothes – as you might drown a blind kitten! . . . Wicked world! Guilty world!)

As though in a nightmare, he sees his inflated belly floating – the only thing that supports and saves him. 'Non c'e piu virtù.' (There's no virtue left.) 'Va, vecchio John, va, va per la tua via; cammina finchè tu muoia.' (Go, old John, go on through life, go on until your death.)

In imitation of this well-known passage Verdi wrote a touching 'farewell' to the completed score, which was not brought to light until Toscanini discovered it thirty years later:

> Tutto e finito.
> Va, va, vecchio John –

Cammina per la tua via
Finchè tu puoi.
Divertente tipo di briccone
Eternamente vero sotto ogni
Tempo, in ogni luogo –
Va, va, Cammina, cammina, Addio!

[All is finished. Go, go, old John – proceed on your way as long
as you can. Diverting type of rascal that you are, eternally true, in
different guises, at every period, in every place – go, go, proceed
on your way. Farewell!]

Wet, chilly and shivering, Falstaff wraps himself in a blanket
snatched from a line of washing and indulges in black melancholy.

But suddenly he calls to the taverner to bring him a mug of wine –
hot! When it comes he seizes it and pours the drink down his willing
throat, while the murmuring strings of the orchestra echo the
comforting sensation. A feeling of relaxed well-being steals over
him and once more he becomes the bold and gallant knight. A
thousand little devils awaken in his brain and, forgetting the insults
he has suffered, he continues to drink and to laugh triumphantly.

The sudden appearance of Quickly jerks him back roughly to
reality and he begins to rage like a baited bull. He would like to cut
Quickly – and the other Wives – into little pieces, as in great
agitation he recalls the blows of the madly jealous husband, the
dirty linen, the water . . . and he ends his great scene shouting at the
top of his voice, 'Canaille!'

But his overweening vanity is again his undoing. He falls
headlong into the new trap, seduced by a few cajoleries from
Quickly and a letter from Alice imploring him to meet her at
midnight in the Royal Park, at Herne's Oak. He is to disguise
himself as Herne the Hunter, whose ghost is said to walk at that
hour.

True to his instructions Falstaff enters in the last scene, trembling
and walking in time to the twelve marvellous chords. He arrives at
the oak – to the love call of the young doe, Alice. Yet his vague fears
are amply justified, for after Nannetta's heavenly aria as the Fairy
Queen, the forest comes alive with a medley of magic people – elves
and sprites, fairies and witches, and other bizarre and unidentifiable
creatures. The jest is a far-reaching one, putting a severe strain on 'il
fianco baldo e il gran torace' – not to mention the physical stress on
Falstaff's interpreter!

Nevertheless, in his unquenchable optimism, Falstaff is destined
to rise again. He has been cruelly mocked, derided and beaten by

every sort of common person yet he is still able to state grandly: 'It is I who make you lively; my wit makes others witty.'

In *Henry IV* Falstaff gives an amusing portrait of himself: 'A handsome man, vigorous and plump, jolly and of a noble de-meanour . . . around fifty or a little more.' Take care, then, not to think him a buffoon. The mistake would be grievous. Sir John is a man very sure of himself and his attractions, and would not dream for a second that anything he does could be undignified or unaccept-able. He feels so superior to the mere townsfolk of Windsor . . . The only knight among them, a close friend – well, a close ex-friend – of the Prince of Wales, now King of England.

His glory and his physical prowess have, by his boasting, grown into a legend. It is enough for him to grumble and it will sound like a roar. The warmth of the sun brings new life to him, and the smile of a woman is the breath of spring. He is a coward at heart, but though fearing many things, he is too curious to avoid experiences . . . and of this is comedy made.

Verdi allows to Falstaff the signal for the conclusion of the work. 'Un coro e terminiam la scena' (A chorus and we finish the comedy). The actors who have represented a *divertimento*, as it used to be called in earlier days, join in.

An amusement – a *divertimento* – is the image of life, but not real life, and should never be taken too seriously.

The final chorus 'Tutto nel mondo è burla' (All in the world is a jest) is perhaps the moral of the tale, and on this phrase, written by Boito, the genius of Verdi created the masterly fugue which crowns all his work.

For years Mariano Stabile was the living example – *the* Falstaff – to whom we all looked for inspiration. Avidly I studied his make-up, his movements and gestures, those 'fat' notes full of superior vanity – and that incomparable falsetto! Try as I would to copy that, I could not achieve more than a pitiful sort of rattle which half strangled me and made me cough. So finally, on the advice of maestri and producers, it was arranged that Bardolph, with his back to the audience, should sing my phrase while I mimed it with my lips! 'Io son di Sir John Fa-al-staff.'

The trick always worked, but I could not bear being saved by a deception. I was bitterly humiliated. 'By golly – and *mondo ladro* – and all that,' I said to myself, 'enough is enough!' And, silently begging Verdi's pardon, I sang the preceding phrase, 'Al mio congiunto che parea dir . . .' with a very dark heavy voice and then, with a large 'yellow' voice, simpering like a woman in love, I sang an octave lower, 'Io son di Sir John Falstaff,' obtaining with the contrast what I could not have naturally.

How I loved the role! How much I still love it, and as I remember each stage of it my most grateful thoughts go out to Maestro Serafin – the father of us all but with, I think I may say, a special partiality for me. When he first allowed me to undertake the role of Falstaff (previously, of course, I had sung Ford) I was commuting between Rome and Naples for performances of *Don Carlo* which Maestro Serafin was conducting. By a thoughtful arrangement – although he hated fast cars – I drove us to and fro and he sat beside me with the score on his lap, patiently instructing, explaining, counselling and correcting. In the back sat his devoted housekeeper, Rosina, from time to time peeled an orange for one or the other of us to restore our dry throats. And so I made my first approach to that marvellous role.

Many times did I sing it under Maestro Serafin, and then later with de Sabata, von Karajan, Giulini, Gavazzeni, Votto and so many others. Each time the experience – and the joy – became richer with fresh collaboration.

But perhaps the most extraordinary experience of all came when I was singing the role at Covent Garden. Even now I don't know how this happened, but a report got abroad that this was to be my last Falstaff at that beloved opera house. The generous audience gave me such an ovation that even now I cannot recall it without a lump in my throat. It was all the more wonderful because to me it was completely unexpected.

Such cheering and clapping, such a demonstration of personal affection is hardly to be described. I took endless bows to cries of, 'Tito, don't go! Tito, come back! Tito, we love you!' while flowers and gifts were showered upon me. One of the gifts I specially treasure, handed to me by the conductor, was a lovely tankard with a card saying, 'It was a rare pleasure! Colin Davis.'

I4

I Pagliacci

A small company of strolling players: three men, a young woman and a donkey. They might have gone around the countryside indefinitely, playing the eternal story of love, comic betrayal and absurd frenzies of jealousy. But death entered the scene and put an end to it all.

Apparently Leoncavallo witnessed a similar tragedy as a boy, and later made a libretto out of it for the opera which brought him lasting fame. He had been embittered by several disappointments and failures before this. But finally he was touched by inspiration and produced the work which was to find a place in the repertoire of every major opera house.

He had had – and still has today – more than his share of criticism from musicians and musicologists. Even now when *Pagliacci* is under discussion there are always a few superior people to pull a sour face, turn up a disdainful nose or twitch offended ears. Some so-called great conductors seem actually to be afraid of being contaminated by contact with the work – forgetting that it was Toscanini who was the first to conduct it. But the plain fact is that if anyone could conceive and bring to birth an opera of comparable worth tomorrow, the world would be his.

I grant there is a certain amount of mould and sediment to be cleaned from the score, after nearly a century's accumulation of 'custom and tradition' in the bad sense of the terms. But what a fascinating job, surely, for someone with culture and intelligence to undertake. To establish a better reading, restoring dignity and fidelity to this ever popular, but often abused, work would be a goal worth pursuing.

Few people will need to be told that the work begins with the famous Prologue – unique in the world of opera. It is said that this was prompted by a request from the renowned baritone, Victor Maurel, who wanted an important solo in his role. Well, personal interest – and the power to press for it – can have its uses. If we indeed owe that Prologue to Maurel let us salute him gratefully. It made operatic history.

Like most aspiring young baritones I myself had Silvio for my first role in this work – at the Castello Sforzesco in Milan in 1937. I was an inexperienced youth but somewhat bold, I fear. I promptly fell in love with the beautiful Nedda, and performed my part in the love duet with such fervour that the applause of the audience slowly changed to a prolonged, 'O-o-oh . . .' mixed with appreciative laughter. Certainly I had pressed realism too far. But, looking back now as a somewhat elderly gentleman, I must say that I recall no objections from my Nedda.

Later on, of course, I sang the Prologue and Tonio.

Oh, that Prologue! There is in it an A Flat – not written in the score but always expected by the audience if one has any pretensions whatever to being a baritone of value. Especially is this so if the poor devil is a beginner. (Later on – which is just as bad – he must continue to produce it for the sake of his honour.)

I had never tried it before and fear tightened my throat at the very prospect. I had an A Flat all right . . . but one octave lower than that demanded. However, I had undertaken to sing the role at the Teatro San Carlo in Naples, and that high note was part of it so far as the Neapolitan audience were concerned. As time drew on I felt desperate, gripped by uncontrollable panic. I determinedly tried to reassure Tilde, however, with the claim, 'It will come all right at the performance, and I'll make my mark as a baritone. If not,' I added, hedging my bet, 'we'll just have to change our plans for the future and do something else.'

So I skipped the fatal note at all piano and orchestral rehearsals.

Finally the General Manager, Maestro Sampaoli, asked abruptly, 'Have you or have you not got this top note?'

'Maestro,' I replied, in what I hoped was a tone of amused protest, 'if I could not sing this A Flat, I would hardly have accepted the role. Only it seems to me pointless to make unnecessary exertions during rehearsals.'

Somewhat doubtfully he accepted my reassurance – and the day of the dress rehearsal dawned.

Now, I told myself, I must produce that note at all costs. If Tilde was not actually on her knees in the box she was, I felt sure, petitioning Heaven with piteous urgency. As the famous bars approached I tried to divert my thoughts from the danger ahead. Then I took an enormous breath and – Wham! out came that A Flat, big and vibrant, leaving me almost paralysed with astonishment.

But then I could not stop it, and had to hang on until I ran out of breath. I saw Tilde rise to her feet in the box, smiling. I was a *baritone*!

Afterwards Sampaoli came to my dressing room and said, 'What exaggeration! A beautiful top note, it's true, but far too long. You must have put together all those saved during the rehearsals.'

'Si puo' . . . si puo' . . .' (Allow me . . .) The Prologue steps before the curtain, addressing the audience directly, and proceeds to describe the nature of the entertainment which will be offered. It is almost a classic description of the *verismo* theatre.

This is a story of love and vengeance. It was a novelty which instantly conquered Milan in 1892, and presently every other opera house in the world. The feelings and emotions of the characters will not, he explains, be histrionically imitated. They will be expressed in terms of genuine truth.

'Poichè siam uomini di carne ed ossa e di quest'orfano mondo al pari di voi spiriamo l'aere.' (For we are men of flesh and blood like you and breathe the same air of this sad world.) He presses home his assertion that, for the composer, theatre and life are one and the same thing – in direct contrast to what Canio will later tell the rather cynical peasants. But then who shall say where theatre ends and truth takes over, particularly in this work?

'Poiche in iscena ancor, le antiche maschere mette l'autore,' he sings in unison with the cellos. (Since our author is reviving on our stage the masks of ancient comedy . . .) And then, 'In parte ei vuol reprendere le vecchie usanze . . . e a voi di nuovo inviami.' (He wishes to restore for you in part the old stage customs, and sends me to you once more.) There is not actually a *corona* at this point, but a pause of a value and duration required by the text and the interpreter. The thought which follows strengthens what has been announced. With a *ritenuto* the voice prepares the beautiful melody: 'Un nido di memorie . . .' (Deeply embedded memories . . .) Only one *piano* is indicated, but there is the instruction *dolce; col canto*, (*doloroso, animando col canto*).

Leoncavallo's insistence on the marking *col canto* recalls his shared interest and sympathetic co-operation with Maurel. What a joy to feel for once, if only partially, that the reins of the aria are in the hands of the interpreter!

On the score there are a great many notes and instructions, suggesting to each interpreter, with careful insistence, everything that can be conveyed in words. These reveal the culture, intelligence and sensitivity of the composer. Even when indulging in dramatic and spectacular effects he plumbs the depths of the human soul to find the true origin of the overwhelming passions which bring fatality into ordinary everyday lives. The philosophy behind it all may be almost naïve, but it is expressed in the uncontrolled violence of simple, primitive people.

There is some pretty bad language in the text, it is true, but only when the situation truly calls for it. Also, one must always consider the way in which crude words are used and the personality of the character who uses them. Such expressions must be anticipated, almost justified, by grief and despair, not just shouted boldly without restraint.

It is possible that Leoncavallo allowed himself a good deal of licence in order to make his way among the *verismo* composers, and then the brutal drama rather carried him away. But in any case it should not be forgotten that he wanted the work to be played *with truth*, and he gave freedom to the singing in order to add value to the word.

Having now over the years shot innumerable A Flats, with death in my heart and agony for any unforeseen peril, I fully agree with those purists who insist on removing all trace of questionable traditions and honouring the score. The notes originally written by Leoncavallo are more beautiful, and have a more balanced effect, than that stab in the stomach of the A Flat followed by a final G. It was Maestro Serafin who removed all my doubts and fears on this point, as he guided us through 'clean performances' which earned the interested approval of audience and critics alike.

At the opening of Act 1, in almost every score of a good edition, there are four lines which explain the exact nature and setting of the scene. It was I believe new to the world of 1892: 'Squilli di trombe stonati . . . risate, fischi di monelli e vociare che vanno appressandosi . . .' (Trumpets blaring out of tune, laughter, urchins whistling, approaching tumult . . .) and the curtain rises on the steep wooded mountains behind Montalto in Calabria, with a distant view of the Cambarie Mountains rising almost two thousand metres above sea level. It is 15 August; the festival of the Madonna.

I find amusing – but quite hopeless – the persistence with which Leoncavallo asks at almost every bar that *half* the chorus should be singing. We all know that if they are not all together they never attack in tempo; or if they do then they bawl instead of singing. Today, of course, with unions to back them, they decide these things for themselves – which means that you can have all or none.

This opening scene of great activity is fraught with unexpected perils. Once, playing *Pagliacci* in the majestic ruins of the Caracalla Baths in Rome, moving down-stage towards the light to sing my Prologue, I had my first view of that vast multitude of people and, after the first 'Si puo' . . .' had an almost irresistible impulse to gasp, '*Non* si puo' . . .' and run away. But I stuck to my post like a good trouper and, after the last triumphant note of the Prologue, I opened my arms and collected an avalanche of applause from the generous audience. Then, with a gay pirouette, I withdrew – to cling to the reins of the Sardinian donkey who was waiting for me in the wings, harnessed to his little cart.

In that little cart were Beniamino Gigli, Nedda and the big drum (*grancassa*). I pulled the donkey forward, but after a few steps he obstinately refused to go any farther on to the stage. Beniamino was nervous and certainly had no intention of singing from the wings – or jumping from the cart. What was I to do? Some forty thousand eyes were watching me, plus two which belonged to the terrified donkey.

I embraced him effusively – he was hardly bigger than a goat, poor little creature – and, lifting his two forelegs, I started dancing energetically and, with the help of Beppe, was able to take him to the centre of the stage, where he made a successful debut.

With the exception of Beppe, all the characters in this drama have strong emotions, violent thoughts and impulses and very human passions which they can hardly control. Indeed, it is because they find themselves unable to control them that crime and tragedy enter their lives. With so much excitement and drama already provided in words and music, it is wiser in my view to 'play it cool'. Self-control in the performer is vital if one is to portray the lack of it.

There is bitter irony in the fact that the first entry of the principal performers is to the watching villagers an occasion of the most light-hearted enjoyment. They crowd round demanding that the players should entertain them forthwith. But Canio – who will play Pagliaccio in the comedy later – explains that the performance will be at '23 ore'.

With admiring comments on Nedda – later to play Columbine – they begin to drift away, shepherded by Beppe, already wearing his Harlequin's costume. Tonio – later to play Taddeo, the clown – provokes few comments except of derision at his ugly face and twisted body. But, as the scene clears, the first stresses in the relationships of the principals begin to show.

Tonio, deformed in both body and face, is strong physically but weak mentally. Humble and submissive so far as his work is concerned, he goes about his menial tasks of cleaning, setting up the primitive scenery and taking care of the little donkey, his only friend and confidant. But in his muddled mind and his desolate heart he has conceived a sort of worship for Nedda, whose reaction to him is at best scornful indifference and at worst disgust and revulsion.

Nedda is beautiful, young and untamed. In her lack of womanly fulfilment she is rather innocently provocative and inviting. Her husband, Canio, adores her but, aware of the difference in their ages, he is fearful and easily roused by jealousy. He found her some years before, a little girl abandoned along the road and starving in the snow. He brought her up, taught her to read and write, and to act with him in the simple plays he presents. Then one fine day he married her, giving her his name and his status as the leader of the small company.

Owing him all this, Nedda must have undoubtedly shown him her gratitude . . . and they have been happy in their way. She has known nothing of life outside her small world of the strolling players. But the natural instincts of a lovely young girl have been rising in her, with an intense desire for some sort of real romantic love. Fatally, at this point she has met the attractive Silvio, and is ready to fall into his arms.

After the villagers have scattered Canio and Beppe go off to the tavern for a drink and Nedda, left alone, lies on a grassy bank in the August sun, singing voluptuously to the passing birds overhead, envying them their freedom and wishing that she too could be so free.

Unknown to her, Tonio is watching her, spying in a sort of ecstasy, and presently he breaks in on her happy dreams. When she sees him she is resentful, and his humble comment, 'Affascinato io mi beava' (Watching you I was in heaven) is received with contempt and a spiteful laugh.

Her laughter wounds him but he restrains himself and, with touching resignation, confesses his love for her but adds, 'So ben che difforme, contorto son io; che desto soltanto lo scherno e l'orror.' (I know I am a miserable cripple and arouse only scorn and horror.) But then, in a crescendo which excites and upsets his weak mind, he confesses that he dreams of her and longs for his love to conquer her.

Nedda laughs in his face and, his weak mind overbalanced, he tries to seize hold of her. Catching up a whip, she slashes him savagely across the face and, uttering a scream like a wounded animal, he falls on his knees and vows vengeance. Then, staggering to his feet, he runs away into the surrounding woods.

Wandering there in a daze, he presently sees Nedda in the arms of Silvio, the young village beau. He watches them and into his bewildered mind comes the speculation – was this why she rejected me? There's another man! Nedda is not after all the good wife Canio believes her to be. 'Pura e casta al par di neve alpina' (Pure and chaste as the mountain snows). She is just a whore! preparing to go off with her lover . . . and he runs to summon Canio.

The weal raised on his face by the whip burns both his cheek and his soul. He seeks consolation in thoughts of vengeance which rise irrepressibly and develop tragically during the evening's perform- ance. Tonio now holds the threads which bind all the characters in the drama, and he guides them inexorably, prompted by uncon- trolled madness.

Only at the end of the evening, when Canio cries in an agonised voice, 'La Commedia e' finita' (The comedy is ended) does Tonio realise what he has done. As though waking from a fatal trance, he stares at the two young people lying dead on the ground. Then, with a wild scream, he pushes his way through the terrified people as the curtain descends.

Canio is basically a good man with a good heart. But he is violent and primitive, even though Leoncavallo gives him words and expressions more important than his status demands. The comedies which he plays with Nedda and Beppe are simple farces to amuse simple people. He is the master and his authority is accepted and undisputed. How they all shared the cramped accommodation in the wagon is something I have never been able to fathom, but possibly Tonio slept in a sort of hammock under the wagon, and I suppose Beppe made shift in some other primitive way.

Such an arrangement could hardly have been agreeable, but until the point at which the drama opens apparently it was fairly happily accepted. One always comes back to the fact that Nedda had never known anything better, and what one does not know one does not actively long for. Then came the meeting with Silvio, just as she is ripe for love, romance and everything that can dazzle a young girl.

Silvio – young, handsome and ardent – is possibly the son of the rich man of the district. Anyway, he is well dressed and with considerable charm, and he absolutely fascinates the girl who knows nothing beyond the hard, boring everyday routine of life on the road. It is an almost inevitable conquest, despite her feeble resistance and her pleas that he should not tempt her: 'Taci, Silvio; e' follia è delirio.' (Be quiet, Silvio. It is folly – madness.)

Guided to the scene by Tonio, and goaded by the confirmation of his desperate jealousy, Canio launches himself upon the guilty pair as they take leave of each other on the revealing words, 'Tonight, love, and for ever I am thine.' He pursues the fleeing Silvio, but Silvio escapes unidentified and, in spite of a terrible scene between Canio and Nedda, she refuses to name her lover.

At this point Beppe intervenes with the practical insistence that it is time to prepare for the evening's performance. He sends Nedda away to dress for her part in the play and practically forces Canio to assume his costume and make-up. Prostrate with misery and grief, Canio sings the aria which all the world knows, and which has added a phrase to the language: 'Vesti la giubba –' (On with the motley –) 'Ridi, Pagliaccio,' (Laugh, clown, laugh).

One wretched hope remains. Prompted by Tonio, Canio believes that Nedda's lover will attend the performance, and will almost certainly reveal his identity inadvertently.

Beppe, the only one who is not a prey to wild and ungovernable emotions, is responsible for setting the evening's entertainment on its familiar routine. He is really the embodiment of the old theatrical adage that 'the play must go on', and in any case it does not occur to him that this present upset is any worse than others which have occurred on previous occasions. Possibly as a reward for his admirable stage management, Leoncavallo has presented him with the most enchanting serenade in his part as Harlequin. (A serenade, incidentally, which many a leading tenor has not disdained to appropriate for recording purposes.)

With cruel irony, the silly, stylised little comedy on the improvised stage proves to be practically a burlesque of everything that has happened in the first act. The unfaithful Columbine entertaining her lover while her husband is away, some slapstick interference from the clumsy Taddeo, the clown, and then the unexpected return of the cuckolded husband in time to see Harlequin disappearing through the window and to hear the unfaithful Columbine call after him, 'Tonight and for ever I am thine.'

'Nome di Dio,' gasps Canio in an aside, 'quelle stesse parole!' (In God's name, the same words!)

The unknowing audience are in gales of laughter over what they regard as rich comedy, though one or two are faintly disturbed by the realism of the acting. The laughter, superimposed on the agonisingly appropriate words and the ironical interjections of

Tonio, drive Canio to madness. As Pagliaccio, he tries to make Columbine disclose her lover's name, and the usual silly scene becomes a violent real-life quarrel on stage. The entranced audience, still unaware of the hidden tragedy, applaud this wonderfully realistic scene. They are still laughing and clapping when – before the appalled Beppe can intervene – Canio suddenly stabs his faithless Nedda.

Everyone rises in horror and Silvio rushes to the stage to rescue her. Dying, she gasps, 'Soccorso . . . Silvio!' (Save me, Silvio.) And Canio, at last identifying the man who has stolen his wife, stabs Silvio too. The crowd runs away in terror and, while Canio, in desolate misery, embraces the dead body of his unfaithful beloved, the curtain falls rapidly.

The speed and drama of this final scene are overwhelming, and the whole thing is a magnificent showpiece for the tenor. It begins with his very difficult outburst, 'Nome di Dio!' and then, his homicidal fury only increased by the applauding peasants, he launches himself into the bloody scene of revenge. Both singers and chorus must carefully measure out the development, which is, as I have said, rapid, taut and breathtaking for the audience.

It is a mistake for either performers or audience to regard this as no more than a shabby village crime perpetrated by rather worthless people. Swift and violent though the work is, there should be understanding and compassion for each major character:

The truly loving older husband, whose early tenderness is transformed into murderous jealousy by his desperate fear of losing his young wife.

The unknowing girl, for whom gratitude towards the older husband is not enough once she has glimpsed real love for a man she is prepared to protect with her life.

The wretched, dim-witted Tonio, whose humble love for Nedda precipitates the whole tragedy.

Even Silvio, used to relatively harmless dalliance, who suddenly finds himself out of his depth in a sea of blood, but still runs on Canio's knife in an attempt to save Nedda.

They are not cardboard figures. They are, as the Prologue says, truly characters of flesh and blood. As such they have held their place in the world of opera for nearly ninety years and will continue to do so as long as people have hearts to understand and pity.

15

La Bohème

One day, at my Opera Workshop in Italy, one of my young students was singing Mimi. The sound was beautiful, the rhythm and pronunciation good, but there was no dramatic involvement. The real heart of Mimi was not there. The shy, melancholy smile, the delicacy of her dreams, her desperate need for affection and love, all the generous human feelings and impulses were missing, or perhaps stifled inside my very shy soprano.

Again I explained the character, what is hidden in but essential to this gentle soul: her deepest thoughts, her sad, sweet memories, her brief joys, her struggle with the sickness which is sapping her life, and the loneliness, the solitude.

Before a class of over forty, composed of young singers, talent spotters, and coaches, I described, with emotion in my voice, all the humanity which Puccini has injected into this marvellous work. Then, to carry further conviction, I myself sang the role of Mimi.

I was carried away, I confess, by the beautiful, touching music and the conclusion of my performance was greeted by much blowing of noses amidst which I acclaimed the best Mimi in the business! As for my original Mimi, transported by the atmosphere, she sang the aria beautifully, then burst into tears and rushed to hide her head on my shoulder! Once again it was proved that it is important to be moved to tears oneself in order to handle one's emotions, and thus communicate them to the audience. My young Mimi now felt a new freedom and was able to convey the human feeling which, when rightly expressed, makes a singer into an actor.

And if ever a work called for singing actors it is this exquisite masterpiece, *La Bohème*. A masterpiece so melodious, so instantly accessible to an audience, that people sometimes tend to underestimate it, forgetting that only a supreme genius can convey simplicity, tenderness and true sentiment in a way which reaches all.

Here we are, then, in Paris around 1830 in the Latin Quarter. The four Bohemians – Rodolfo, Marcello, Colline and Schaunard – live in shabby quarters, sharing a life of poverty enlivened from time to time by flashes of sporadic gaiety when one or the other of them has a stroke of luck. Mimi, who has not known any of them before the opening of the opera, lodges on the top floor of the same building. Musetta, Marcello's *innamorata*, uneducated but enchanting, has little permanency in her life. She flits from one man to another, but always returns to Marcello.

These are the major characters in the work. But before we get to know them better, I think we must meet the minor characters. For any aspiring young singer is more likely to find them on the first rung of the ladder to fame. Few leap to the top in one bound. Except of course in fiction.

The first to consider is *Benoit*, the landlord, who interrupts the four Bohemians just as they are making merry over a stroke of good fortune which has come Schaunard's way. Benoit knocks on the door, reminding them that he has come to collect the promised rent.

This is the first pitfall for an insensitive player or producer, for the scene is frequently played as farce, totally opposed to the libretto and the music. Certainly Benoit is a comic character, but very human. Poor henpecked little man, he is not even aggressive about the rent – to which he is fully entitled.

The Bohemians do not start by bullying him. They are much too smart for that. Particularly Marcello. They express great cordiality, while encouraging him to drink enough to make him rather silly. Then Marcello, in this atmosphere of conviviality, leads him on to speak of a nice looking girl with whom he was seen recently.

The temptation to talk of his little conquest is too much for Benoit. He expands the story, chuckling over the details, comparing the girl favourably with his skinny wife. This is the chance the friends have been waiting for. They all express shock and revulsion at a married man carrying on in this way! They can no longer let him remain under their roof. (That it is *his* roof no one gives him a moment to point out.) They hustle him to the door and push him out before he even has a chance to pick up the receipted bill which he had brought in readiness for the expected rent.

Marcello picks up the receipt and pockets it, with the cynical remark that the next quarter's rent is now paid. Their conversation after Benoit has gone should be almost *sotto voce*, as though they think he may still be behind the door. This scene requires finesse and a light touch, nothing gross or farcical. It is pure comedy.

★

Puccini has the supreme art of putting into music the small everyday things which seem to have no importance in the life and character of the performers but which, nevertheless, accompany them and sometimes impinge on their destiny. They are all significant but must never be too strongly underlined or forced out of the frame of the scene. The next act – the street scene outside the Café Momus – is rich in these moments. It brings three minor characters on to the stage and, as they are all frequently mishandled and exaggerated, let us give them some attention.

First there is the engaging figure of *Parpignol*, the toy-seller, who appears in the busy street pushing his cart, surrounded by eager children demanding this and that. He should sing his first phrase rather far back in the wings, 'Ecco i giocattoli di Parpignol.' Then he sings it again nearer at hand, creating a sense of approach; and finally on-stage, acting the little scene without wasting time.

It is just a colourful detail in the overall picture of a square in Paris – part of a musical mosaic. He does not need to shout for attention. He is not Otello entering after the storm. Nor need he show off vocally, ostentatiously singing his rather high phrase in one breath. It is better to show good taste in creating a character than to insist on showing how accomplished your breathing may be.

I remember once at the Teatro San Carlo years ago, when Parpignol was entrusted to an old *comprimario* in need of work but with remarkably short breath. Well, he was intelligent and created a character *à la Honoré Daumier*. He uttered his two phrases with gusto, paused to give the horse to the little boy – the trumpet having already been grasped by Colline, who says, 'Falso questo re' (This

D is flat) – then laboriously pushed his cart across the stage and went on his way, having created just the amount of attention required, no more and no less.

★

In this scene within a scene we also have the *Child* who pesters everyone because he wants the trumpet and the toy horse and cart. It is customary for at least four women to grab him, immobilise him centre-stage, in front of the conductor, and beat him in time to the music. Then they smother him in caresses, stifling his one phrase, and bear him off as though he were a prisoner of war. Should the poor brat go wrong in the midst of all this there is going to be a row between conductor and *répétiteur*. As a result Parpignol is more or less ignored, the boy's real parents are in despair – and all that was really needed was to let the child alone, permitting him to think for himself and sing his phrase naturally.

Then, still in Act 2, we have the shamefully used *Alcindoro*. Shamefully used not only by Musetta, it must be said, for most producers make of him a figure of fun. This seems to me quite wrong and merely weakens a rich situation for the sake of a cheap guffaw or two.

Of course in an opera with so much pathos and veiled with sadness a comic episode is welcome. But I have often noticed that few laugh at Alcindoro as he is usually played. Their attention is already too much engaged by the movement in this lively scene, particularly by Musetta's part in it.

Why not play Alcindoro as a dignified State Councillor in his fifties, having a little diversion with an attractive girl while his wife is away on holiday? This makes him much less of a buffoon and more of a human being when he finds himself quite out of his depth, his precious dignity cruelly assailed. I visualise him very well turned out and aware of his worldly importance. Nevertheless, he could not resist that little adventure with the enchanting Musetta. Gratified, but a little confused, he has showered her with expensive presents, in expectation of some charming recompense later.

The last thing he had bargained for was a *contretemps* with a bunch of rather raffish Bohemians – one of whom seems to have so much effect on Musetta that she resorts to all kinds of outrageous tricks to attract him while embarrassing and flouting the wretched Alcindoro. His gratified pride in his lovely companion turns to anger and appalled embarrassment as she orders him about, calling him 'Lulu' as though he were a funny little dog. He now longs to escape as, in her attempts to make the jealous Marcello notice her, Musetta becomes increasingly outrageous, attracting the attention of everyone. His dignity shattered, he attempts in desperate half whispers to quiet her, and positively welcomes her ploy to get rid of him when she insists that she must have new shoes as the ones she is wearing hurt her.

Relieved, Alcindoro rushes away to do her bidding, Musetta joins her Bohemian friends and, when the bill is presented, coolly says the gentleman will pay all. Then off she goes in company with the others.

When Alcindoro returns, to be presented with the two bills, I think he should grasp at the remnants of his dignity. I should like him to take out a large bank note, toss it on the table as one who is superior to the riff-raff with whom he has been momentarily involved, clap on his hat and depart. I find that much more amusing and effective than to have him collapse among a gaggle of fanning waiters. I don't insist! I merely suggest.

La Bohème is a drama enlivened by happy episodes proper to young people living a casual life, in which a sort of fictitious gaiety casts a veil over their melancholy poverty. From time to time a sense of reality impinges upon them, and throughout the work sorrow is never far away. The approach of death, the inevitable doom of Mimi, lends a sort of fatalism to the whole, a sense of agonising resignation.

Small thoughts, events, incidents are miraculously transformed into music and become part of the life of the spectator too. It is as though one's feelings blend with those of the characters, so that one also loves, suffers, laughs and cries with them. I am not, of course, the first to make this magical discovery. But it is something to be kept in mind all the time, for part of the miracle of *La Bohème* is its basic humanity.

I have known this sense of involvement to have its comic side – which is also in the spirit of the work. I still remember with delight an occasion in Lisbon when Ramon Vinay (who was there to play Otello, with myself as Iago) could not resist the temptation to take part in *La Bohème*. We had just reached the scene at the Café Momus when we became aware of a most imposing waiter, sporting a formidable moustache and a large important looking notebook, standing with pencil poised, ready to take our orders.

Hardly able to stifle our mirth or follow our cues, we watched fascinated as Ramon made himself tremendously busy and solemn, distributing lobsters, salami and other delectable items for the meal of the Bohemians. Presently our merriment became such that it seeped down to the orchestra and finally to Maestro de Fabritiis, who also found himself hardly able to control his laughter at the sight of the great Otello taking the evening off as a waiter.

Similarly, I have seen Maestro Giuseppe Conca (a dear fellow but a tyrant of a chorus master at the Rome Opera during the reign of Serafin) don a cloak and mingle with the chorus during the performance of that scene. He would move around, supplying some difficult attack or cue, keeping the chorus most truly alive. No wonder then that to us our four Bohemians are such real people!

Schaunard is perhaps the least important dramatically, but his reactions support the actions of the others. Also he is the one who usually supplies the money! A good, sentimental sort of chap, simple, generous and (I think) short-sighted. When I was a young singer he was described to us thus by Marcello Govoni, a learned and sensitive producer in the days when the term 'producer' didn't even exist.

Govoni had been a good singer, starting as a baritone and *basso-comico* and ending up as a romantic tenor. He knew all the operas inside out. We were preparing *La Bohème* at the Rome Royal Opera under Serafin in 1939/40 – and not a bad cast it was either, now that I come to think of it. Favero, Malipiero, Perris, Gobbi, Taddei, Neri, Pacini (maybe Tajo).

The inspiration that Schaunard should be short-sighted still seems brilliant to me. He enters triumphantly, tossing his money around, followed by errand boys with quantities of food, and is greeted by his friends with delighted enthusiasm. He simply does not notice the way they throw themselves on the provisions he intended for later consumption. He is too busy cleaning his glasses and telling the story of the providential riches. No one is really listening to him, and only when he comes to the death of the parrot and they all ask in astonishment who is dead, does he put on his glasses and realise that he has no audience because they are all too busy with the food.

He runs to its defence, explaining that it is for future 'dark days'; then generously divides the money equally between them, preparatory to their all going out to celebrate at the Café Momus. Frankly, I find much linking of arms a bit overdone. There are other ways of expressing readiness to celebrate. Shining shoes with a paintbrush, anxiously combing hair, wrapping a scarf round the neck and so on gives a little more variety.

Colline, the philosopher, makes his first entrance in Act 1 like a storm: 'Gia' dell'Apocalisse appariscono i segni.' (The Apocalypse must be at hand). He is outraged because the pawnshop is closed on Christmas Eve and he has no money. He wears no coat, only a long scarf and a hat which is sprinkled with snow. Though apparently a deep-thinking and serious person, he enjoys a joke, makes amusing comments and laughs heartily.

He is more careful with his money than the others. When everyone else is spending Schaunard's largesse somewhat lavishly, Colline buys an old-fashioned overcoat – a bit worn, but dignified and suitable to his philosophical personality. He also buys a rare copy of an old German grammar, displays it a little ostentatiously, takes a good seat outside the Café Momus and expresses his contempt for the vulgar herd.

There is something almost grandiose about him, and whatever he does or says seems to emanate from profound philosophical thought. When Rodolfo presents Mimi to them all he says grandly but kindly, 'Digna est intrari' (Worthy to join us). It is all a bit of a pose, of course. But then what young man has not done something the same in his time? I remember myself as a student in Padua doing all sorts of things to be 'different'. Possibly because I came from the provinces I was determined to cut a figure in the university city. In place of a tie I would wear a sort of ribbon, usually black or dark blue, very suggestive of the Bohemians. Or I would wear spats over my shoes – but the wrong way round. I also had a friend who solemnly wore his raincoat inside out to display the tartan lining. Oh, Colline is not the only one to have his little eccentricities!

He is always an integral part of the action, well aware of all that is happening, though without showing the fact. As I see him he is tall, with long legs, walks slowly, rather majestically in his 'new' overcoat and carrying his 'rare book', and knows that he is worthy of note. Giulio Neri was superb in this role, as indeed was Italo Tajo, whose interpretation was perhaps the deeper and more subtle. But the sheer weight of Neri's voice in the 'Vecchia Zimarra' made the dark sounds seem to come heartfelt from the depths of his physical being and to express the very essence of his feeling.

The placing of this famous solo is sheer genius. In the last act Colline joins fully with his three companions as they desperately make merry over their poor meal. They dance, quarrel, fight a mock duel, but still their carefree mood conceals an inner melancholy, a sense of tragic expectancy. The shadow is at its deepest during the mock duel, when Musetta's sudden appearance changes the whole atmosphere.

I think the stage set should have more than one door – as is usually the case in an attic – and the bed could be in another room or behind a curtain. As Colline and Schaunard busy themselves carrying it to the right spot the scene is subtly transformed from comedy to drama.

We must feel Colline's presence though he has little to do. He observes Musetta and Marcello drawing together, and at this point he should find himself near where the famous overcoat hangs. Then he needs nothing more than a single resigned gesture to lift it down before singing the beautiful aria which Puccini has filled with the condensed expression of all that Colline feels and is.

Many people – performers as well as audience – see no more in 'Vecchia Zimarra' than a lovely solo for the bass who has not had much solo work so far. Nothing of the kind! It is one of Puccini's masterstrokes: the revelation of Colline as a person and a summing up of the situation by a supreme master of drama and melody. That old coat means a lot to Colline. But it is not only the coat to which he is bidding farewell. He is the one who first realises that the half sad, half gay life they have all shared together is coming to an end. Nothing will ever be the same again. That wonderful measured accompaniment, with its rhythm of a slow sad walk, depicts not only his resignation; for there is a subtle play on words when he says he will climb 'il sacro monte', which is the slang for going to the pawnshop.

Everything is so well described musically that little remains for Colline's interpreter to add; he just needs to put his soul into the musical phrases – and then go out with Schaunard.

I have decided to take *Marcello* and *Musetta* together, for they are essential to each other, and even when they quarrel and part their thoughts remain united.

Musetta is a very special figure in the Latin Quarter. A beautiful girl in her twenties, with little education but supremely attractive and a born coquette. Her station in life is perpetually changing. One moment she is richly dressed and riding in a carriage, the next she is called back by her genuine love to the attic where Marcello is always waiting for her.

She is frank about herself, declaring that a breath of luxury, a taste of wealth and some excitement are essential to her very being. Her many love affairs don't mean a thing, she insists – 'My life is a crazy song to which Marcello is the permanent refrain.'

With a natural instinct – almost a genius – for extravagance, she has excellent taste in clothes, and when a rich admirer is around she knows how to spend his money. Intelligent, clever, rebellious against any convention or restriction, she admits no rule but her own caprice. She is *not* vulgar or bawdy, as so often portrayed by poor-grade performers or producers. She has a style all her own.

The only man she really loves is Marcello – perhaps because he is the only one who can make her suffer. But luxury for her is a condition for living, almost for health. And luxury costs money, which Marcello does not have.

Marcello is certainly the most positive of the four Bohemians. He has the strength to let Musetta go and, though deeply hurt, assumes an air of nonchalance. He is the one to whom all the others appeal for advice or help, the most touching being when Mimi, after a long walk in the snow to find him at the beginning of Act 3, bursts out, 'Oh, buon Marcello, aiuto!' (Oh, good Marcello, help me!)

Later, Rodolfo greats him with, 'Marcello, finalmente!' (Marcello at last!) as though his coming may solve their problems. And, in the last sad minutes of the work, it is to Marcello that Schaunard appeals when he sees that Mimi is dead though Rodolfo has not yet realised it. 'Marcello, e' spirata' (Marcello, she is dead), as though asking what to do now.

He is a key character who must perform with very well controlled action throughout the opera. His change of mood and attitude is of the utmost importance for the four friends when they are together and must be made very evident.

In Act 2 Musetta makes her striking entrance before the Café Momus, delighting in the universal attention while her wretched escort, Alcindoro, of course wishes to heaven she would be quiet and more circumspect.

Marcello, at his corner table, is infuriated by her presence, for she is both his torment and his joy. And when Mimi asks innocently who is the lovely, well-dressed girl he replies bitterly, 'You ask me! She is like a screech-owl, feeding on human hearts, and it is my heart that she bites at the moment.'

But her fascination is something he cannot resist, as she saunters around the tables, addressing words to Alcindoro which are really intended for Marcello. Then, when Alcindoro has been dispatched to get the new shoes, Marcello opens his arms to Musetta before everyone and exclaims, 'Oh, my youth, you are not dead! If you knock at my door my heart will open it!'

In the big ensemble which follows it is Marcello's voice which soars above the others. He and Musetta embrace rapturously, and this is the only moment in the opera when we see Marcello really happy.

At the beginning of Act 3, Musetta and Marcello are together again. Both have a job of sorts – she, rather unexpectedly, teaching singing, and he painting the outside of the small tavern. They are both inside the tavern at first but, summoned by the servant to whom Mimi has appealed, he comes out. He knows that all is not well between Mimi and Rodolfo but tries to comfort her, offering her the advice to live as he and Musetta do, each having their own freedom. This philosophical mood fades, however, when Musetta is heard laughing in a provocative way from within the tavern, where she is evidently making a fresh conquest.

At the close of this act we have the incomparable quartet which Puccini has given to the two so different pairs of lovers. Marcello and Musetta part violently on a magnificent exchange of insults. Rodolfo and Mimi touchingly postpone their parting until the spring, agreeing that it is hard to be lonely in the cold of winter, 'Soli d'inverno é cosa da morire'. And then, on an exquisitely pathetic note, Mimi adds that she wishes the winter could last for ever.

Marcello and Musetta do not meet again until she makes her dramatic entry in the last act with the dying Mimi. But at the beginning of this last act there is Rodolfo and Marcello's beautiful duet in which each sings with longing of his missing love. They have neither the resolution to forget nor the courage to make some sort of new start. They admit they are cowards but kid themselves that they are acting from altruism in letting their women go to rich men.

Rodolfo is without any prospect of earning money, yet only money can buy the good food and warm clothing which the ailing Mimi needs. Poverty is killing her and Rodolfo tells himself that in letting her go to someone else who can support her better he is doing right.

As for Marcello, while truly loving Musetta, he knows that luxury, gaiety and a brilliant way of life are essential to her happiness and wellbeing. Has he the right to keep her the prisoner of a love that would inevitably wither away? By this reasoning the cowardly feeling of the two men becomes almost heroic and generous!

The dramatic entrance of the two girls – well though soberly dressed, in marked contrast to the shabby, poverty-stricken ambience – changes everything. While Mimi is tenderly helped to the bed Musetta removes her gold earrings and, giving them to Marcello, tells him to sell them and buy something for Mimi. Suddenly the two almost forget where they are, only knowing that they are together again and, in a close embrace, they go out.

And now we come to *Mimi* and her *Rodolfo*. Mimi, who is one of the most adorable heroines in all opera, is in her twenties. She is shy and retiring, pale and delicate with fine features (though admittedly not all Mimis fulfill that requirement *in toto*), and there is something unique about her.

She lives upstairs in a little white painted room (una bianca cameretta) and has probably seen the young men sometimes but without exchanging words with them. For her precarious living she makes artificial flowers with those delicate hands of hers. As she comes home on Christmas Eve up the dark staircase her candle is blown out by a draught and she knocks on the door for a light.

Rodolfo reacts to the sound of a feminine voice with gusto, and this must be emphasised. He straightens his tie, runs to open the door and does his best to prolong the visit. Mimi's entrance is very natural and again one sees how magically Puccini transforms the ordinary, everyday things into music. When she turns faint, breathless from the climb, Rodolfo is distracted. There is nothing to do but what the music suggests. The three *pizzicato* notes are little drops of water which he gently sprinkles on her face to revive her.

This being Mimi's introduction into the opera she must immediately register as the gentle, modest girl she is, with a sort of natural elegance. She must emanate such touching sincerity that Rodolfo, an expert in love and women, remains speechless before her. Indeed, during her aria, when she interrupts herself to ask, 'Lei m'intende?' (Do you understand me?) he is already so captivated by her charm and beauty that he almost hesitates before answering '. . . Sì!'

Having recovered from her faintness, Mimi stands up, preparing to leave. The candle is rekindled, there is nothing left to say but, 'Buona sera'. But Rodolfo's 'Buona sera' is not at all conclusive. The interval of seven notes has an expectant, interrogative accent. And when Mimi's candle blows out again at the door the ready Rodolfo promptly blows out his candle too, leaving them in darkness except for the moonlight.

It is by the romantic light of the moon that they exchange their simple stories. He, the poet – and indeed the verses of the librettists are pure poetry – speaks of his bohemian life, and his sensitivity to beauty and charm. With great *élan* the music soars in a beautiful phrase, '. . . talor dal mio forziere. . .' (I am a millionaire in spirit but sometimes my strong-box is robbed of all its jewels . . . by a pair of pretty eyes.) I doubt if many of the audience really concern themselves with the actual words of this famous aria, anxious as they are to hear the tenor's high C. But it is beautiful poetry clad in beautiful music. This is what attracts Mimi, who answers rather timidly, telling her own simple story.

It is something which happens every day: two young people in their first tender conversation as one heart opens to the other.

Mimi's aria seems so easy to sing, as she describes her little room under the roof. But the singer must clothe the small details with simplicity and feminine grace. She speaks of her pleasure in making her flowers, her sense of poetry peeping out when she says that alas, they have no perfume. And then comes the great outburst about the sun, guided so unerringly by the rising phrases.

When she speaks of her one great privilege – that she is the first to see the sun when spring returns – she is transported by such enthusiasm that one immediately feels that she desperately needs the sun, her best friend: that sun which enters through the window, reaches her, warms her in her bed. She feels that the sun almost belongs to her personally, giving her the wonderful feeling of warmth and health.

I never tire of explaining to my young singers this near worship which Mimi has for the life-giving sun, and how the warmth in the voice must convey to the audience the warmth which Mimi herself feels when she speaks of 'her' sun. 'E'mio, e'mio . . .' and then, with three Ms . . . 'e'mmmio!' She flies high in the sky on those phrases, and comes down to earth reluctantly to tell of her little rose tree growing on the windowsill, under her anxious care. Returning to reality, she asks pardon for being such a troublesome neighbour. It all seems so easy because it is so true. You have it on the authority of the best Mimi in the business!

At the end of her aria, 'Mi chiamano Mimi', the two dreamers are recalled to reality by the shouts of the friends waiting below, and for a moment the spell seems broken. Until this moment I think for both of them the occasion is a small one, the beginning of a little romantic adventure maybe. Nothing serious, but a lovely encounter.

Rodolfo answers his friends that he is not alone, to which they reply with ironical and teasing comments. He turns to Mimi, standing against the big window, the moonlight framing her like a vision from Paradise: a delicate silhouette, lovely profile, beautiful hair, one small hand raised in a questioning gesture, her face half in shadow. He gazes enchanted – and realises that this is his love and his destiny.

I wish I were a tenor, just to sing that wonderful phrase, 'O, soave fanciulla . . .' (O, lovely maiden . . .) 'In te ravviso il sogno che vorrei sempre sognar.' (I see in you the dream I would for ever dream.)

Carried away by his emotion, she replies with equal fervour, and they decide to join the friends.

'And later?' he asks. To which she replies with a touch of innocent coquetry, 'Inquisitive?'

By the time they arrive at the Café Momus in Act 2 their rapport is obvious. They walk together amidst the crowd, looking at shops and stalls. Rodolfo can only afford a little pink bonnet, but she loves it and is already wearing it when they meet the friends. He presents her with some ceremony to the others, anxious that she should not be mistaken for a partner in a light adventure.

'Questa à Mimi,' he says, adding in extempore verse, 'I am the poet, she is the muse. From our rejoicing souls love is born.'

They all laugh good-humouredly at this poem, accept her formally and, at dinner, everyone puts himself out to be nice to the 'lady'.

It is at this point that Musetta and the attendant Alcindoro appear on the scene. During the act which she puts on for the benefit of the jealous Marcello Rodolfo – quite capable of jealousy himself where Mimi is concerned – tells her that he himself would never, never forgive infidelity.

She answers very sweetly, 'I love you so well, why talk of forgiveness? This is love already.' And their happy pleasure in each other lasts to the end of the act.

By the opening of Act 3 things have changed. It is still winter and we can judge that it is only perhaps a couple of months since their first meeting. But living together has confronted them with the ever present problem – poverty.

Deeply in love as she is, Mimi does not mind very much. But Rodolfo has discovered that she is desperately ill, in need of good food, warm clothing and medicine, instead of hunger and draughts in the shabby attic. He has no possibility of providing her with the expensive necessities required to prolong her frail life and, though he does not know how he can do it, feels he must let her go. She is unaware of the seriousness of her condition, so that suspicions and misunderstandings have crept into their relationship and they quarrel constantly.

At the opening of Act 3, with the snow falling, Mimi appears outside the tavern at the Customs barrier. A few officials control the small crowd of market people who stand warming their hands at a street brazier. But it is quite unnecessary, let me point out, for the spokesman to bark his few phrases, as so often happens, or to hustle the little crowd in an aggressive manner. They are not criminals – just ordinary countryfolk about their lawful and familiar business.

Mimi timidly approaches the tavern and addresses a woman who is cleaning a window, asking her if she will please tell the painter Marcello that Mimi is here.

This silent performer can – and should – provide a useful reaction to Mimi's action. The latter's first request is gentle and deprecating, but then it is repeated with desperate urgency in both words and music. – Why?

Surely because the woman ignores her at first and just goes on cleaning the window. But at Mimi's piteous persistence she gives her some attention and 'Ho tanta fretta' – perhaps with a nod – goes into the tavern to deliver the message. (It is a small but good example of being 'alive' on the stage instead of simply present.)

A few seconds later Marcello appears, rubbing his hands and crying 'Mimi!' with an air of animation as he strives to hide what he suspects. For in actual fact Rodolfo has turned up at the tavern at dawn and is now inside sleeping on a bench.

To Marcello Mimi confesses her unhappiness and bewilderment. Unaware of her own dangerously declining health, which is driving Rodolfo crazy with anxiety, she thinks it is his insane jealousy which makes him watch her every hour of the day and night.

'Please help us, Marcello,' she begs. 'I love Rodolfo so dearly and cannot understand why he torments himself thus.'

Marcello offers friendly advice and then, seeing through the window that Rodolfo is waking, he encourages Mimi to go away in order to avoid any unpleasant scene. She affects to do so but, desperate to know the truth, hides behind a tree and overhears their conversation.

After complaining excitedly about Mimi's flirting – which hardly rings true – Rodolfo suddenly bursts out with the terrible reality. She is desperately ill and he can do nothing to help her. Their poverty-stricken life is killing her. The more she smiles and makes light of privation the more guilty he feels. It is better for them to part.

From her hiding place behind the tree Mimi is suddenly and brutally made aware of her condition. She begins to cry, softly and then convulsively, as she exclaims aloud in her desperation, 'My life is ending!'

At this discovery Rodolfo and Marcello run to her, trying to comfort her and reassure her. But she is calm now and determined. She says, 'Addio –' and moves to go.

All Rodolfo's heart is in his short answer, 'Che! Vai?' (What! you are going?)

'Yes,' she says, 'and with no hard feelings.'

There follows her heartbreaking, 'Addio, senza rancor.' Together they recall characteristic memories, the man remembering the sweet moments and the girl the scenes of jealousy and bad temper. She asks him to collect the few things that she left scattered around; she will send the doorman for them. She will not come herself. She tells him to look in the drawer, where he will find the little gold ring (with emphasis on that precious word) and her prayer book. The latter does not seem so important to her at that moment, though she is a religious girl. But – the ring, the little token of love, the emblem of something that was almost a marriage in her heart.

'Oh, remember,' she goes on, 'under the pillow of our bed I left the little pink bonnet you gave me that first time on Christmas Eve. If you want it – if you want it – if you want it . . .' to remind you of our love . . .' Three times that 'Se vuoi' is repeated, each with a different, heartbreaking expression.

The first time it is quite loud, almost aggressive, as though to say, 'You silly man!' The second time almost pleading. The third time she means: '*Please* keep it as a token of love,' the voice rising, almost breaking. 'Goodbye – without hard feelings.' It is a masterpeice of musical psychology.

There follows that most touching duet in which they decide to postpone the actual parting until the spring, because it is so hard to part in winter. That is the moment when Mimi adds with indescribable wistfulness that she wishes the winter would last for ever. Mimi! – to whom the sun is life itself.

Meanwhile, at the other side of the stage, Musetta and Marcello are quarrelling violently and abusively over her friendliness with the stranger in the tavern. They part on the spot, but Mimi and Rodolfo stand there almost afraid to make the first step. Finally, in a close embrace, they move slowly towards home.

Remember – very little action, but intense in its quality. Give the right dimension and weight to each word. Don't rush, don't worry about that final note. If you understand the true meaning of what you are doing there will be no problem. Just be a good interpreter.

In Act 4 Mimi, who has fainted on the stairs, is helped into the room only seconds after Musetta's dramatic entry with the announcement of her collapse. At first she appears to see no one. She does not even look around. Again – don't worry. Just wait. The time for recognition will come, but at the moment she has only enough strength to ask Rodolfo sweetly in a whisper if he 'really wants her to stay'. This entrance must be so well performed that everyone must appear to realise the gravity of the situation while rejecting the very thought of what is inevitable.

She sits down on the bed and then leans back, her movements slow and no longer co-ordinated. Every gesture must betoken an enormous effort. Don't strive for a beautiful vocal sound at this point, but for a beautiful *colour*. Quality is more important than quantity throughout this last, infinitely touching scene. The sound of a dying girl – very sweet, very lovely and fragile – can easily be broken by faulty breathing. Take care.

Presently she realises that her friends are around her, and greets them, for each one a different colour of inflection: 'Buon giorno, Marcello –' the favourite friend. 'Dear, good Schaunard – Colline –' the tower of strength – 'Good morning.'

Her voice, the very turn of her head, suggest a little bird returning to the nest even before Rodolfo says, 'Torno al nido la rondine e cinguetta.' (The swallow is back home and chirps.)

Like a flame flickering to extinction, she now and then seems to find enough strength to say a loving phrase or two to Rodolfo. But when, in fuller voice, she says, 'Si rinasce, ancor sento la vita in me,' (I am reviving, I feel new life in me,) the hearts of her friends are not deceived. When she says her hands are growing so cold Rodolfo takes them in his, recalling that her cold little hand in his was the first revelation of their love.

The friends exchange a few desperate words, knowing there is nothing in the house to help her. Then Musetta removes her gold earrings and tells Marcello to sell them and buy food and medicine. He is deeply touched and presently they go out together. Colline goes to sell his famous overcoat; Schaunard, on Colline's advice, also slips away, leaving the two lovers in precious solitude.

Mimi rouses herself a little and confesses with a faint mischievous smile that she had feigned sleep in the hope that they would be left alone. He cannot do enough for her, with his little gestures and words of tenderness. From time to time she says anxiously, 'You're not leaving me? Time is so short.' And he replies that he will never leave her.

Then he produces the pink bonnet which he has cherished and she gives soft little exclamations of pleasure. In tender phrases and with touching musical reminders of that first meeting they go over that happy time together, and on a note of wistful fatality she declares that he was both love – and life – to her.

Presently the others return, Musetta bringing a little fur muff, which Mimi receives with almost childlike joy. It is so soft, so warm, and she puts her cold hands into it. Those delicate, express-ive, easily chilled hands which have a special significance with Mimi even in the last minutes of her life.

'Is this a present from you?' she asks Rodolfo. But before he can reply Musetta quickly says, 'Yes,' on his behalf, at which Mimi gently chides him for his extravagance, and he cannot control his tears.

'Don't weep, love,' she says to him. 'Why should you weep, my love? I am well, . . . here . . . with you . . . ever with you. . . .'

Otello: Placido Domingo.

La Traviata. Maria Callas *(opposite and left)*; Joan Sutherland and Amelita Galli-Curci.

La Bohème: As Mimi and Rodolfo: Katia Ricciarelli with Jose Carreras (*top left*); Ileana Cotrubas with Neil Shicoff (*top right*); Kiri Te Kanawa with Luciano Pavarotti. *Opposite:* Thomas Allen as Count Almaviva in *The Marriage of Figaro*.

Mario Persico.

Riccardo Zandonai.

Bernardino Molinari, with his wife Mary.

Ildebrando Pizzetti. In the background, my father-in-law Raffaello de Rensis.

Maestro Tullio Serafin.

Ermanno Wolf-Ferrari. He dedicated his *Canzoniere Italiano* to me at the time of my marriage.

From left to right: Umberto Giordano, composer of *Andrea Chénier* and *Fedora;* Lorenzo Perosi, eccentric musician and priest; Pietro Mascagni, creator of *Cavalleria Rusticana.* They are seen in the uniform of the Accademia Italia.

Then drowsily she adds, 'My hands are warmer now . . . and I . . . will . . . sleep . . .'

The others converse in whispers, and Rodolfo, eager to do anything for Mimi's comfort, goes to pull the curtain across the window. I like to think he goes there in a sort of trance, his eyes filled with the image of his little love as he first saw her, standing against that window in the moonlight.

Behind him the others realise what has happened and when, without turning, he says, 'You see – she is quiet now,' they can find no reply.

Only when the silence lengthens unnaturally does he turn and rush to the bed, to find that Mimi has died – as gently and unassumingly as she lived.

Don't spoil this marvellous moment by yelling, 'Mimi, Mimi –' hysterically. The fragile tenderness of the scene requires no tenor trumpeting.

The directions for playing this wonderful last act are precise and very clear, and I always suggest that they should be followed as closely as possible. At the same time, I like a certain freedom of interpretation, some little variation in expression which, while in no way changing the original, keeps alive that flame which is the soul of the interpreter.

16

Tosca

It may surprise you to know I am an amateur cook. My engagements and social life, not to mention the various hobbies which fill
my days, ended up recently with a partial occupation of the kitchen.
My delicious inventions – which I pretend are innocent of butter, oil
or any other fat – have by now conquered the dinner table with the
inexhaustible fantasy which cooking can suggest.

I have finally obtained the official approval of the family and, just
as I open windows on opera, so I also manoeuvre and open pots and
jars in the kitchen like a modern alchemist – a Cagliostro pretending
to create gold. I find it very relaxing to spend a few hours among
innumberable jars of every size, with herbs, flavourings, essence –
which I don't always use but I like to have handy in the background,
just in case.

Like painting and other means of self-expression, cooking sets an
example for a performer. You have to 'dress' your characters
(whether historical or imaginary) with exciting bits of information

or hearsay which may appear to have little to do with the story but, if used in the right place and at the right time, can add new 'flavour' and revive the vitality of the presentation.

From a culinary point of view you can, of course, haunt Fortnum & Mason or some of those exclusive delicatessens for the delicacies which work havoc upon the waistline . . . thus encouraging the fashion of the unbuttoned jacket. From an artistic – or, more specifically, from an operatic – point of view, you must gradually build up your own stock of factual or imaginative 'flavourings' which add fresh paint and interest to a familiar story.

So – without pressing the analogy too far, I am going to apply this idea to the tragic history of the love and death of Floria Tosca.

Some say that Tosca was Roman. But I prefer to think of the beautiful Floria as born somewhere between Verona and Vicenza, among those lovely verdant hills which have produced so many heroines of history and legend. In my opinion she *cannot but* be Venetian, one of those radiant women painted by Paolo Veronese or the lovely Madonnas of Jacopo da Ponte, 'Il Bassano', or of Francesco Guardi.

The action of the opera covers no more than a matter of hours, from the morning of 17 June 1800 to the dawn of the 18th, and takes place in Rome. On the morning of the 14 June the Battle of Marengo was won by the Austrians. But a swift and sudden counter attack by the French revolutionary forces under Napoleon that same afternoon reversed the position, making Napoleon the victor.

News travelled more slowly then, and the report of the initial Austrian victory reached Rome on the morning of the 17th. Hence the jubiliation of Sacristan and choir in the first act. By evening came news of the dramatic reversal of fortune – in time to provoke Cavaradossi's outburst of triumphant joy in front of Scarpia in the second act; a defiant indiscretion which sealed his own fate.

His Excellency Baron Vitellio Scarpia, Chief of Police appointed by Caroline, Queen of Naples, had been sent by her to Rome to suppress the Republican riots, the Pope being then in exile.

Scarpia is rapid in his decisions and sends any suspects directly to Castel Sant'Angelo with no question of defence. Executions are daily events. Postponement would create a backlog and make for disorder. The whole process is a routine one, and this should be plain on the faces of the execution squad – and more particularly on the face of the jailer.

But there are other windows to be opened on to the background of this opera; windows which give a longer perspective on the events leading up to those few dramatic hours which encompass the fate of Floria Tosca, Mario Cavaradossi and Scarpia himself.

In June 1796 Napoleon was in Bologna and imposed on Pope Pius VI (born Giannangelo Braschi in Cesena in 1717 a very severe armistice, followed by the harsh Treaty of Tolentino in February 1797. Meanwhile, Joseph Bonaparte was in Rome, where the Directory proclaimed the First Roman Republic (15 February 1798) of which Angelotti was a Consul. At this point the 81-year-old Pope was taken prisoner and brought to Siena five days after the proclamation of the First Roman Republic, thence to Florence in June, to Parma in March 1799, and finally to Turin. From Turin, gravely ill and in a state of collapse, the old man was taken to France, across the Alps in acute discomfort. On 13 June 1799, he was locked up in the fortress of Valence, where he died of consumption.

His body would not be brought back to Rome until 1801, when this was ordered by the new Pope, Pius VII (Gregorio Luigi Chairamonti, who, like his relative and predecessor, was also born in Cesena). The new Pope postponed his arrival in Rome, entering there only on 4 July 1800, when Napoleon, after his victory of Marengo, proposed a treaty which was signed after 15 July.

In Puccini's opera Tosca kills Scarpia on the night of 17/18 June 1800. Legend has it that when the new Pope Pius VII entered Rome in July he was pleased and moved by the scenes of general rejoicing as he passed through the streets. On enquiry, however, he discovered that the joy was not on his account, but for the death of the hated tyrant Scarpia.

Well, well! Having represented Scarpia on-stage nearly a thousand times, I would not be the one to question his importance. But I confess that I find fifteen days of celebration for his abrupt removal a bit excessive. Did someone slip up over the date? Or perhaps the news was not 'leaked' for some days?

Be that as it may, I add it to my store of flavoursome details. Why not? There was a cook once, somewhere around 1500, who used to throw half-plucked chickens into a big pot of boiling water, claiming 'Tutto fa brodo!' (Everything makes a broth.) And so I throw everything into my broth to increase and improve the flavour. I mix legend with history, truth with fiction, reflections and interpretations – my own and other people's. But I choose with good reason, of course, keeping in mind the atmosphere of the country, the state of civilisation at the time, the historical period.

Relationships are important too – both probable ones and those that are only suspected. Even a touch of gossip may have its importance – and so on. Then I mix everything and taste it, perhaps adding a necessary pinch of salt or, even better, some pepper. When

my soup is ready I drink it all! I do not offer it to my audience in its
original state. *I* drink it. And then – if I make myself clear – what my
audience is subtly aware of is the aroma which exudes from my
pores.

That is why everything to do with the characters and scene comes
usefully to my hand. For instance, I appreciate knowing that Mario
Cavaradossi (the painter who, strangely, left no trace of his art) was
working in the studio of the famous David. (Should not then his
painting of the Maddalena show a suggestion of the David school,
now that I come to think of it?)

Mario was the son of a French mother and a Roman father, a
follower of Voltaire and a friend of Diderot. Had he come to Rome
for political reasons, or were his artistic pretensions genuine and did
he come for the Prix de Rome? Anyway, one day his destiny took
him to the Teatro Argentina (looking for a job as designer perhaps?)
He did not get one, but he saw the dazzling Floria Tosca, the star par
excellence, and promptly fell in love.

Meanwhile, in both Naples and Rome rioters were clamouring to
establish a Republic. But in both cities the first attempts were of
short duration. For more than forty years the Bourbons – Ferdinand
and Caroline (daughter of Maria Theresa of Austria and sister of the
ill-fated Marie Antoinette of France) had been on the throne. The
revolution forced them to flee to Sicily, accompanied by the whole
Court.

Then a mixed army of Bourbon soldiers, brigands, peasants,
Russians, Turks and English, led by Cardinal Fabrizio Ruffo,
liberated the city of Naples, and the Bourbons, escorted by Nelson
and the English Fleet, were put back on the throne. A proclamation
issued by Queen Caroline and signed by King Ferdinand com-
manded fierce reprisals, which brought Scarpia to Rome. It is said
that during this period of terror about 40,000 Roman people
suffered confiscation, imprisonment or summary execution.

On 17 and 18 June, according to Sardou's drama – from which
Illica and Giacosa constructed the libretto of Puccini's opera – there
was certainly real slaughter on the banks of the Tiber. Angelotti
committed suicide, Scarpia was stabbed to death, Cavaradossi was
executed, and Tosca threw herself from the heights of Castel
Sant'Angelo. Perhaps Spoletta and Sciarrone survived by hiding
themselves in some abandoned catacomb of the Agro Romano?

And so to the point of the story when Puccini's opera begins. It is
the morning of 17 June 1800 in the Church of Sant'Andrea della
Valle in Rome, and the imprisoned Angelotti has just escaped.

★

Before coming to the principal dramatic roles, however, I should like again to start with the minor figures, each one of them a human being, though some are sadly lacking in what we really mean by humanity.

Among those who act but do not sing I should like to insert a little invention of my own: a Majordomo who attends Scarpia, giving more importance to the 'povera cena interrota' (my poor interrupted supper). He pours the wine from a crystal decanter, moves silently around, opens the window, saving Sciarrone work, and discreetly withdraws. His is not a vital role, but the way he watches every gesture and glance of his master emphasises the authority of Scarpia and the refined and luxurious way in which he lives.

I should also like the Sergeant of the execution squad to have a certain personality of his own. The soldiers are Austrian and, therefore, used to strict discipline, which shows in every movement. They should be like tools of a so-called justice, impersonal, cold, with no feelings about the rights or wrongs of their job. But the Sergeant should salute Cavaradossi I think, when he refuses the bandage to cover his eyes, in a sort of approval of one brave man for another. These figures all come from a past period and if not faithfully reproduced will presently pass from our memories, which would be sad.

The voice of the little *Shepherd*, heard offstage at the beginning of Act 3, must give a sense of distance by diminishing the volume of the song as he walks away. This indicates the countrified Rome of the period, when the roads had no pavements and the Agro Romano reached into the environs of great palaces, houses and historic ruins alike.

The opening of Act 3 is very beautiful and should be left as the composer conceived it, reducing scenic movement to the minimum in order to enjoy the inspired music. The chiming of bells all over the city gives a unique effect and is still the way in which Rome greets the rising of the sun.

Sciarrone, a gendarme, is one of those vital characters referred to in the chapter on so-called small parts. He is a hard-headed man whose obedience to his master is unquestioning, all human feelings deliberately suppressed. This makes all the more effective the occasional outbursts which do erupt at some unexpected catastrophe. When, for instance, he announces the disastrous defeat of Marengo, he stands there panting and stammering, all his military self-control lost. Discretion and policy should have made him whisper the news confidentially to Scarpia. As it is, Cavaradossi also hears every word and, when he staggers to his feet with the cry of, 'Vittoria, vittoria!' Sciarrone sees the mounting rage on his master's face. At Scarpia's violent, 'Take him away!' Sciarrone is only too glad to comply – administering savage blows on the prisoner as he goes.

With much clicking of heels, standing rigidly to attention and thrusting out his chest, he is pretty busy scenically but has little to sing. His utterances are brief: short, dry phrases but with a variety of expression. In the torture scene, off-stage, he reports to Scarpia like a man not used to thinking for himself:

'Nega,' (he denies it,) he says, and his anger shows in the one word – his determination to make the victim speak.

'Tutto?' (Everything?) he exclaims incredulously as Scarpia, with inexplicable clemency, bids him cease the questioning.

The third comment, 'He's fainted,' merely expresses contempt for a weakling who can't stand up to a little pain.

In this particular scene it is important that those backstage should be able to follow closely what is happening onstage. Otherwise some remarkable misunderstandings can arise. Once, I remember (fortunately at a rehearsal), in answer to Scarpia's 'Che dice il cavaliere?' (What does the cavalier say?) Sciarrone popped in briskly with 'Tutto!' (Everything.) At which Maestro de Fabritiis remarked from the podium, 'Ah well, then we can all go home.'

Sciarrone's most important part in the third act is to rush in with the news of Scarpia's murder, and his words *must* be completely clear. 'E'lei!' (It is she,) he cries, identifying Tosca as the murderess. A confused trumpeting behind the scene will not do. He watches her mount the parapet and throw herself into the void. It is not necessary for him to go to the parapet and look down. That is the business of the squad – and well must they be coached in their actions.

There is a delightful story of a performance in which the producer, with insufficient time to give full instructions to the squad, had to rely on a few (foreign) words and some gestures from the wings to indicate that they should rush to the wall and look down. Confused but willing, the squad thought they had got the message. They rushed to the wall and, one after another, leapt over in the wake of Tosca. I hope the story is true. Mass suicide by the firing squad makes an enchanting finale to *Tosca*.

The Jailer can be performed in one of several ways. After the bell tolls four o'clock he has two Es in which to announce that the time has come: 'L'ora.' These two notes are so expressive of sad and human sympathy that I like to think the poor man is obliged by need to perform a task he abhors. He should be shabbily dressed, and answer the salute of the sentries with a tired, dispirited nod. He drags his feet a little as he walks and looks sadly at the latest victim of oppression, impotent rebellion lapsing into resignation.

On receiving the portfolio from the Sergeant he slowly reads the name – 'Mario Cavaradossi' – signs his acceptance with a cross and returns it – 'A Voi.' The Sergeant withdraws with his soldiers. Then, without movement and speaking slowly in a stifled voice, he says 'Vi resta un'ora . . . Un sacerdote i vostri cenni attende.' (You have an hour . . . A priest is ready if you wish.)

At Cavaradossi's tentative request for a favour he waits to make sure all are gone before he says softly, 'If I can,' and listens with sympathy to what undoubtedly is to him the story of every dawn. Quietly but firmly, he refuses the offer of the ring and, turning abruptly, sets paper and charcoal for the unfortunate prisoner. Then, with a nod, he says briefly, 'Scrivete . . .'

He meets the grateful, surprised eyes of Cavaradossi, moved at finding a human heart in the midst of such misery and injustice. Then he withdraws.

Later, I should like him to look furtively for the secret letter Cavaradossi had been writing – and which could compromise him! The writing of it was interrupted by the unexpected and unhoped for arrival of Tosca. It is a nice detail – if he succeeds in taking the letter away, then pockets it and goes away with the others. He does not want to see the execution.

Spoletta, faithful to his master in all things, is a sullen man, malevolent and vicious. He is arrogant with his inferiors, much involved in actions of subtle cruelty, and well aware that only absolute obedience and precise execution of orders can keep his head on his shoulders and avert the sudden rages of Scarpia.

On his side, Scarpia can abuse him foully: 'Ah, cane, ah, tradi-tore, ceffo di basilisco –' (Dog, traitor, reptile) and then mock him ironically as 'galantuomo' (honest man) and 'quel bravo Spoletta' (the excellent Spoletta). He never shows him the least confidence, keeping him always at a distance, the master giving peremptory orders.

In Act I Spoletta enters the church, moving aside to admit Scarpia, his eyes fixed on the Baron's face, awaiting his orders. To his superfluous question: 'Sta bene. Il convegno?' (Right. The meeting?) Scarpia gives him an angry glance and answers with annoyance: 'Palazzo Farnese.' As though to say, 'Where else?'

Spoletta must then disappear without being noticed, hiding in the shadows among the crowd assembling for the Te Deum. He must never make himself conspicuous when giving orders, so that everyone can see him and run away. All Rome trembles before Scarpia, and it is the duty of his 'sbirris' to keep alive this reputation.

A Chief of Police so refined and elegant, sinister but impeccable in his clothes and gestures, a man who delights in precious crystal and gold and silver dishes for his 'poor interrupted supper', who embellishes his study with *objets d'art* of great beauty and value – this man would certainly not tolerate a deformed Spoletta of shabby appearance. All the ugly features of Spoletta, both body and soul, are superficially concealed under a correct appearance – but only on the surface. It is not necessary to opt for the first idea which comes to you after studying the libretto – or Sardou – or Puccini. As with any character, there are endless possibilities in the realisation of Spoletta. A touch of bigotry would not come amiss – and would please his master.

Angelotti is a nobleman and a man of courage; his family has a private chapel in this church and I do not like to see him drag about the church floor like a worm, even if he is at the end of his tether. Better that he should be seen to make enormous efforts to fight his extreme exhaustion, and not fall about in the church for all to see. Let him, instead, lean against pillars, railings and a kneeling stool. If he knows his role well – and is not trembling for fear of missing his cues – he can easily search for the key in time to the music, instead of grovelling about on the dusty floor.

When producing this scene, I heighten the tension by the simple device of making him lack sufficient strength to turn the key. (Cavaradossi later does this for him.) Then, at the sound of the Sacristan's approach, I send him into the confessional box, to conceal himself with perilous insecurity. As the Sacristan walks around dusting and talking to himself he actually flicks his duster over the confessional in a casual manner, creating a moment of acute suspense.

Later, Floria and Cavaradossi also go near, and Angelotti is an unwilling witness of their love passages. Once she has gone he emerges, and is in a good scenic position for his duet with Cavaradossi, after which both flee through the private chapel, the existence of the secret passage being thus underlined: 'Un canneto che va lungi pei campi alla mia villa' (A reedy fen going along the fields to my villa).

I have always been puzzled by the fact that Cavaradossi knew the secret passage from the Attavantis' chapel, which took him to the 'orto mal chiuso' (scarcely locked orchard) by way of the reedy fen and so on to *his villa*. Bah! I suspect our painter is hiding something that Sardou whispers in our ear. We already know that he is less than truthful when he says to Tosca, 'La vidi ieri ma fu puro caso.' (I saw her yesterday by pure chance). For the chatty Sacristan has already referred to 'the unknown woman who during the past *days* came here to pray.'

The Sacristan is a beautifully drawn figure, as he goes about his daily work of keeping the church clean and tidy. He grumbles all the time – to the pillars, the open door, the extinguished candles, to himself, to the Madonna, to the Saints. Apropos the painter he grumbles about the followers of Voltaire, and then about the gowns of some of the women who presume to compete with the Madonna – although they smell anything but sweet.

He is a sterile, sour tree and finds comfort only in keeping his church clean and exercising paternal discipline over the choirboys. Always slip-slopping around, he wears a black shawl around his shoulders and a little cap to protect his head against the morning dew. He pretends not to like Cavaradossi, but really enjoys serving him, pestering him with news and gossip and, above all, profiting from the often rejected lunch basket.

The entrance of Scarpia terrifies him and he tries to stammer out harmless explanations in answer to the Baron's questions. Then he recovers a little and feels important as he drops an indiscreet word here and there. 'Nella cappella? Non ne avea la chiave.' (In the chapel? He had no key.)

Repenting, however, he becomes uninformative once more with regard to Tosca, ending with, 'Il pittore Cavaradossi? Chissa'dove sia svani sgattaiolo' per sua stregoneria . . .' (The painter Cavaradossi? Who knows where he is? He vanished, slipped away with his magic.)

Somehow he defends his church from any complicity and is beaming triumphantly once more when leading the choir in the great procession for the Te Deum.

He has a slight nervous tic – a small, gentle musical tic, almost elegant, like the music which repeatedly describes it. Don't exaggerate this!

His Excellency *Baron Vitellio Scarpia,* Chief of Police, is a character I can fairly claim to know pretty well, but every time I approach him I find new facets in him. This many-sided man is something of an exhibitionist, always on show, covering the centre of the picture.

He was not born a nobleman, and his title could not have come from the church, as when he was appointed in Rome the Pope was already the prisoner of Napoleon. The honour must, therefore, have come from Queen Caroline, either for services rendered, as the saying goes, or for more personal reasons. In any event, his fame as a ruthless executioner was what probably commended him to Queen Caroline, who sent him to Rome to suppress all signs of rebellion.

An ambitious *arriviste*, he is well described by Cavaradossi as 'Bigotto, satiro che affina con le devote pratiche la foia libertina,' (Bigot, satyr, concealing his libertine's lust under a semblance of religious devotion). Enough to make all Rome tremble, indeed! – and doubtless Ostia and Civitavecchia too. The nearest comparison in more modern times would be, I suppose, some of those who appeared at the Nuremberg Trials.

Overweaningly proud in his absolute authority, in his old-fashioned style of dressing, he is an elegant sadist, indulging himself in both physical and psychological excitement. In the famous Te Deum we have the complete picture of the bigot, who passes naturally from heroic exultation to the 'Mea culpa', as he beats his breast in a theatrical display of public repentance.

He uses the letter of the law to justify any wickedness in which he wishes to indulge. And – his position unchallenged – he loves all the luxuries, all the beautiful things long coveted and now *his*.

From whence did he originally come?

I remember once I was driving through Paternò, a town near Catania, in Sicily, when I noticed an old palace, heavy and dismal in its severe architectural design. Workmen were busy restoring it and I stopped and went in. The rooms were large and dark, the high windows protected by iron gratings. And I thought to myself, 'Here young Vitellio once played as a boy. Here he was born around 1750. Wonderful!'

Is anyone going to deny it? – Surely no more than they will question the dramatic touches with which Sardou overloads the evidence against Lady Hamilton, the Marquis Attavanti, Cimarosa and Paisiello in his original play. In such an orgy of history and fantasy I claim the right to fix Scarpia's birthplace. As I said before – I *know* him well.

Scarpia is so sure of himself and his success that he almost believes in his own sincerity and honesty. He does not fear the authority and responsibilities he has taken upon himself. He does not follow the law – he makes it. He does not accept the brutality of his own actions since he regards them as totally justified. He is confident of his own irresistible charm, malevolent and dominating, supported by the terror he exudes. His success is easy because he does not care about his victims, nor the misery he inflicts in order to reach his goal.

His erect figure, the stiff neck, the fixed inquisitive eyes under the heavy lids, the hard mouth smiling coldly, the slow, controlled gestures – all make him an enigmatic and frightening figure. Within there are violent, terrible instincts, generating outbursts of anger, but it is seldom that these crack the veneer of his haughty self-restraint. Occasionally, however, his suave manner is shattered by an outburst of hysterical laughter which comes like a whiplash to disconcert his unhappy opponent.

To suit his own ends he can be gallant, almost mellow, and he is patient in his determination to pursue his ruthless purpose. He is a great actor and as such can overact. It is that over-confidence which eventually proves his undoing.

Tosca requests the safe conduct for herself and her Mario to leave Rome, and Puccini marks Scarpia's reply of, 'Partir dunque volete?' (You wish to go away?) *dolce*. For a moment he has been wounded in his vanity, his *amour propre* flicked by her obvious indifference to – indeed loathing of – him. Then he recovers his sense of irony and answers *con galanteria* 'Si' adempia il voler vostro.' (Your wish shall be granted.) After all, he is not looking for love, only to satisfy a whim, and his confidence is fully restored.

So, with the safe conduct in his hand, he rushes – for once defenceless – into the embrace which ends his wicked life.

Traditional in his views on life and fashion, and loathing the French influence (which will in any case be offensive to the Queen), he wears a wig – white or silvery grey – a lace jabot above his high pointed collar and a dress-coat similar to the Venetian 'velada'. His costume is completed by knee breeches, high boots and a light cloak, with a baldric-like sash in the Roman colours.

When I played Scarpia I never changed my costume for Act 2. Everything happens in the same day, and Scarpia dines alone in his study, nervously awaiting news. He does not feel like attending the reception, even though it is taking place in the same Palazzo Farnese. Knowing full well that if he does not produce the escaped Angelotti he may pay for the omission with his own life, he is not in the dressing-up mood! It will be sufficient for him to excuse his attire with a small gesture as he welcomes Tosca, who is in full gala dress.

I admit that not all producers accepted my views without objection. But the fact is that this costume gives Scarpia a more authoritative and dramatic appearance in Act 2, and the death becomes more spectacular. It is a giant who collapses under Tosca's knife. Not just an elegant gentleman in silk stockings and pumps.

His first entrance into Sant' Andrea della Valle in Act 1 is always (or should be!) immensely impressive. I recall an occasion in the

Arena in Verona, where the stage was large enough to present the whole panorama of Rome, the church occupying only the centre front. This meant that Scarpia's arrival at the outer door of the church was part of the scene – and it was decreed that I should gallop in on horseback. It was very, very effective, of course. But there was the little problem of the horse, who was the restive type. So every night I held firmly to the reins and tried to look as though all Rome trembled before me, while feeling a little shaky myself. But it was worth it.

Scarpia is of course one of the great theatrical characters of opera and, while still in the shadow of his personality, I feel this is as good a place as any in which to give one or two basic rules for dramatic self-expression.

To achieve harmonious acting a performer must find the necessary dimension in which to express his own character without being extinguished by those who want to excel at all costs. This does not mean continually seeking the limelight. On the contrary, to fade into the shadows at the right moment makes it possible to take the light again more effectively. (This is the idea behind the flashing light in an advertisement. A static luminous sign is much less effective than one which goes on and off at irregular intervals.)

Never indulge in excessive and pointless movements, which only block and embarrass your colleagues. Above all, refrain from filling your performance with countless illogical contrivances. This is confusing, untidy and extremely boring. Every movement must have a logical relation to the words, must be expressive and must coincide with the length of music and singing.

Be sure that you enter the scene with the expression and attitude required by your character at that specific moment.

Remember that every period of history requires not only a costume but a *manner* which belongs to it. Each period has a special way of walking or sitting, acting and thinking. To cross your legs when seated is a bad habit only recently accepted, and to precede your elders or your social superior is not to be entertained in almost any period if you are impersonating a well-behaved young character.

The audience is ready to be moved to tears or laughter when the story calls for it, but to make the audience laugh in the wrong place just to be noticed means that you undervalue them. It is playing of the worst kind.

To be ignorant of all these things is not sufficient excuse if one is expecting to be listened to, admired and highly paid. Each singer has an individual way of performing according to his or her personality and experience, but if the performer is a good one the audience should be convinced at that moment that this is the *only* way of doing it.

However different they may be, all good performers strive to recreate the composer's idea. But the gradations of tone, the breathing between phrases, the pauses, are expressed individually, for there are no rules for interpretation, and each individual acts with his or her own personal feelings. Thus, although I play Scarpia in the way which seems right to me, there is no definitive interpretation of any role – only a deep conviction within oneself.

And so we come to *Mario Cavaradossi*, painter, lover, revolutionary perforce and, above all, tenor.

The character is a rewarding one to play, for he changes and develops in each act, gallantly facing up to the tragic situation into which he is so unexpectedly plunged. In Act 1 he is a young man with scarcely a care in the world, enjoying to the full the love between him and Floria Tosca. It is an intensely romantic love, strongly sustained by a reciprocal physical attraction. It is a beautiful relationship, but they seem to have no common interest outside it.

He is so little interested in her singing that, when she tells him she is singing that evening – 'Stassera canto' – she finds it necessary to add that the performance will not be long. 'Ma è spettacolo breve . . .'

On her side, although she has an almost poetic way of painting a scene in words, she shows no interest in his art, walking up and down in front of his picture without so much as a glance at it until the moment when she is leaving. Then it is jealous curiosity rather than artistic pleasure which makes her enquire about the original.

To both of them their happy love is all that matters. Work is just a tyrant which keeps them apart. Even her much discussed jealousy melts like snow before the warmth of his ardent words. Her anger is a passing cloud without thunder or storm. Indeed, for a man in love as Cavaradossi is, her whims and jealousy are charmingly flattering rather than irritating.

The discovery of Angelotti hidden in the church upsets Mario's plans and changes everything. At first he is not deeply troubled; but when he realises the tragedy of his friend's predicament, the playboy of 1800 begins to change into a responsible even a heroic man, to whom the life of a friend is sacred – like freedom and the rights of man. 'La vita mi costasse vi salverò,' he says. (I will save you though it cost me my life.)

But, in the second act, to conceal his strong emotion in front of Scarpia or his anxiety at the sudden appearance of Tosca, must test him to the limit. It is a mistake for the interpreter of Cavaradossi to act without fear. To be most effective and command all our sympathies he should show, to some degree, that it is his courage which dominates his very real fear as he answers the pressing questions of the terrible Chief of Police with apparent indifference and coolness.

To treat Scarpia with scorn, trying to make him look like some small provincial policeman, does not increase Cavaradossi's stature. On the contrary, he is a human being who finds himself in a tragic position almost before he realises what has happened. I have sung with several tenors in my time who are mainly concerned with looking important every second they are on the stage. Such a stupid attitude could only infuriate Scarpia, and I had to react with violence – in turn cynical, icy and cutting, reducing the unfortunate young man to utter dejection.

This is all right for Scarpia, from whom all sorts of wickedness can be expected, but it is not helpful to Cavaradossi's image. Also it weakens the dramatic impact of his 'Vittoria, vittoria!' when it does come. This must be sudden and unrestrained to make the right effect – let alone to bring out that top note. With agony in his face and in his heart, uncertain of the future, appalled by the realisation of Scarpia's machinations (not to mention the entry of the Executioner and his assistants, who make no mystery of their job) Cavaradossi feels his mind and his senses assailed on all sides.

All this must be clear behind his outward calm, for only thus shall we see him growing into the man of courage who is prepared to face martyrdom rather than betray a friend. In short, this role requires fine and intelligent acting. It is not just a matter of waiting for arias or striking top notes.

In Act 3, dragged forcibly away and brought to the Castel Sant' Angelo, leaving his Floria defenceless at Scarpia's mercy, Cavaradossi is racked with anguish. Desperately aware of the few hours slipping away, he goes to the castle rampart, stretches his arms wide and bids his last farewell to Tosca and this city of Rome where, until yesterday, he had been so happy.

His beautiful aria is filled with memories, the music evoking each remembrance with poignant pain. Almost in tears, he utters the heart-breaking words, 'Io muoio disperato e non ho amato mai tanto la vita.' (I die desperate – and never did I love life more.)

He goes to write his last words on the paper provided by the kindly jailer – Tosca interrupting him when she rushes in with the safe conduct, the music soaring in exultation as they embrace over a sonorous chord.

In the first moment joy and hope rise in him. But when she tells him her story everything collapses for him. 'Scarpia che cede?' (Scarpia yielding?) he exclaims incredulously. Though he immediately understands the deception of the safe conduct, he pretends to accept it in order to postpone to the last minute the realisation that all her efforts to save him are in vain.

He wants to fill his soul with the dear sound of her voice. 'Parlami ancor, come dianzi parlavi, è cosi dolce il suon della tua vocé.' (Speak to me once more as you were speaking just now, the sound of your voice is so sweet!) – what marvellous words – and he goes along with her in her dream of their escaping over the sea together into the sunset, light breezes wafting them to freedom.

Determined there shall be no tears in her loving eyes when he has his final glimpse of her, he lies to the end, even joking with her over her professional instructions on how to fall realistically. Then, rejecting the offered bandage for his eyes, he is able to gaze upon her to the last moment of his life.

Floria Tosca, as described in the Sardou play, was born a poor shepherdess and brought up by the Benedictine friars near Verona. So well did she respond to her lessons that by the time she was sixteen she was already a young celebrity. The Pope himself released her from her religious vows, saying, 'This is also a way of praying to God. Go free, my child. You will melt many a heart and make people shed sweet tears.'

Her beauty is arresting, dominating and proud, but she is also blessed with the irresistible charm of grace and elegance. Spontaneous and natural in her every gesture, she shows how well she has profited from the Roman society in which she lives, both loved and admired.

She dresses with taste, eschewing any excessive display of jewels, and retaining an almost childlike innocence in her movements and in the fleeting fancies which she pursues impulsively lest they should escape her. It is obvious that she loves long and poetic descriptions, full of happy memories and sensations – and fortunate is she that Puccini was there to give her the right music for these!

As a true woman, she is inspired by the admiring glances of her audience, glowing as though in a warm light in which she can give of her best. For this reason I prefer my Tosca not to enter the church excited and ruffled, anguished and inelegant, as though drawn there by the reins of jealousy. Her entrance music has written over it, *Andantino sostenuto dolcissimo e con tutta l'espressione,* in complete contrast to the later '*con una specie di violenza*' (with a sort of violence) when she pushes Mario from her.

There is a choice to be made in that entrance and, as always, I prefer the one suggested by the music, like the rhythm of a light carriage or the cantering of a little horse on parade. (The great Claudia Muzio almost floated in on the magical triplets Puccini has supplied. I saw her only once, when I was quite young, but I have never forgotten that incredible harmony of movement and music.)

Tosca's first questions – cool and without preliminary greetings – are nervous: 'Where is that woman? I heard quick steps and the rustle of a gown.' But as soon as Mario replies, 'I deny that and I love you!' a smile irradiates her face and the light cloud passes.

A darker one looms up, however, when she takes more time to examine the painting and recognises the Marchesa Attavanti. (Personally, I think she had some reason for her jealousy, too, for Mario's casual explanations don't quite hang together!) However, he manages to reassure her.

Later in the scene, Scarpia's advances are obviously distasteful to her. But she makes an effort to control herself and courteously accepts his offer of the holy water – and his implied reprimand for entering the church without crossing herself. As he plays on her suspicions of her lover, however, she falls inevitably into the trap he is setting for her.

It is more interesting if she is seen to make an inward struggle against her suspicions, rather than falling headlong at the first hint. She goes out, clutching the fan, determined to have Mario's explanation, and unaware that Spoletta and his minions are at her heels.

Obviously at Cavaradossi's villa she learns many things of which she has been blissfully ignorant. This makes her wary and more careful when she is dealing with Scarpia in the second act. But her secret fear is tormenting her, and she betrays her weakness when, entering the study, she runs impulsively into Mario's arms. This is in itself enough to alert Scarpia to the situation and she becomes an easy victim to his subtle manoeuvres.

The contest is totally unequal and, in the end, she loses all control. When he finally forces from her the secret of Angelotti's hiding place she touches the lowest rung of her defeat. In face of Scarpia's sadistic, almost frenzied amusement, she is sick with fear and loathing. Still, however, she does not actually plan to kill him, though the idea passes through her mind as she stares in fascination at the knife on the table.

She is trembling and half fainting when Scarpia, triumphantly sure of himself, rushes towards her with the safe conduct in his hand, and as he seizes hold of her, her reaction is instinctive and instantaneous. She grasps the knife and stabs him. In the violence of her reaction she screams words of hate at the dying man. But when she sees him dead at her feet she seems to wake from a nightmare.

'E' morto . . .' she says and crosses herself 'or gli perdono.'

Then, in a moment of half superstitious forgiveness, she sets lighted candles on either side of the corpse and puts a crucifix on his breast. Then she feverishly collects her stole and furtively goes out on the last notes of the scene.

If the character is deeply felt I think there are no more explanations or details to be added. Living vicariously through the terrible tragedy which has befallen this defenceless woman is in itself a terrific experience. The attitudes, expressions and inflections for the right interpretation are endless. It is simply a question of choosing those which most naturally result from one's own feelings and possibilities.

Tosca hurries home, orders a carriage and, taking her jewels, flies on the wings of love to the Castel Sant'Angelo. The safe conduct seems to work, and she finds herself escorted by Sciarrone, Spoletta and the officer – all still completely unaware of Scarpia's death.

She throws herself into her lover's arms and, with mingled pride and disgust, recounts the story of her encounter with Scarpia. Then, as he pretends for her sake to share her happy confidence, they dream of escape together from all their recent misery. Right up to the end she believes that the execution is a pretence, and is full of a blissful, triumphant excitement. When she finally makes the fearful discovery that Mario is in truth dead, soldiers and guards are already returning, mounting the stairs to arrest her.

Without a moment to reflect, she knows exactly what she must do. She runs to the highest point of the castle wall and, in a last outburst of theatrical fervour, she calls on Scarpia to appear before the judgment seat of God. Then she plunges to her death.

*

Melodrama? Of course it is. In the truest sense of that much misused word. It is great theatre, resistible only to those with no red blood in their veins. That is why *Tosca* is an opera universally loved.

I remember once, in the second act, at the moment when Cavaradossi is dragged away with Tosca clinging to him, one of the men (as the action demands) pushed her away and, as she staggered back, she either forgot or did not notice that there was a small step behind her and she fell heavily. Maria Callas as Tosca was partnering my familiar Scarpia. From the other side of the stage I asked her with my eyes 'Are you hurt?' and with an answering glance she was able to reassure me. But, realising what a fine piece of stage business we could make of this, I went over to her and disdainfully extended my left hand to her. Immediately, also realising what could be done, she almost clawed her way up my arm on the pleading word 'Salvatelo!' (Save him!') To which I replied ironically, 'Io? – Voi!' ('I? – No, you!') and let go of her, whereupon she dropped back despairingly on the ground with such apparent helplessness and pathos that a slight gasp of indignant sympathy ran through the house. She needed no instructions, no hint of what was in my mind theatrically speaking. She *knew* and made the perfect completion of what I had started.

With Maria it was not performing but living.

In January 1964 Callas made her great comeback in *Tosca* at Covent Garden (after two or three years of semi-retirement.) It was an event of worldwide interest. It is impossible to describe the sensation it caused and, to a creature of Maria's sensibility, it must have been sheer torture. I suppose there are few more appalling ordeals than to make a stage comeback when you are headline news; far worse than any début. Mercilessly caught in the crossfire of public searchlights, you hang there suspended for all to observe and criticise. Triumph or crucifixion? You are battling for the one, but fate may deal you the other.

Everyone at the Royal Opera House was frantically afraid that she would cancel at the last moment. Sander Gorlinsky, her manager, had no time for anything else. The strictest orders were given that no one should be admitted at any rehearsal and the only reports issued were brief ones to the effect that everything was going well.

One charming incident in connection with this secrecy is worth recording. Maria stayed away from a rehearsal of Act 2 one day because of a slight cold, and John Copley stood in for her. On this occasion it so happened that a distinguished titled lady came to the box-office to pick up her tickets and, realising that a rehearsal was in progress, she implored Sergeant Martin to allow her just one glimpse of the diva: if he would just open the door a single crack . . . The poor man, with all the solemn authority for which he was famed, explained that he simply could not do so, not even for such a distinguished lady. Well, would he just for one moment open the little window connected with the house so that she might at least hear a note or two from that famous voice?

With this request Sergeant Martin complied and at that moment John Copley, lying in my arms with beard and glasses, let out an excruciating shriek: 'Ah piu' non posso, ah che orrore.'

'Ah, the unmistakable voice! whispered the delighted lady to Sergeant Martin. 'Thank you, thank you.' And she went away quite satisfied.

But there were not many of these lighter moments for any of us as the first night drew near. To some extent David Webster had put Maria in my care – to coax, to reassure, to support her insofar as one colleague can support another; and never, I think, did I prize a trust more highly. We worked very hard, since Maria was always a tremendously disciplined artist, but after the long rehearsals she would phone me at great length to discuss our parts and go over them all again. At the dress rehearsal, looking a mere girl in the beautiful pale pink dress which Zeffirelli had decreed for her, she was scared to death but sang resolutely and acted superbly. The clicking of cameras backstage made the place sound like an office with twenty typists and, in the atmosphere of nervous tension, even David Webster must, I feel sure, have had some difficulty in maintaining his slight customary smile.

21 January, 1964. Here is my wife Tilde's description of that never-to-be-forgotten night, written in her diary next morning.

'What a night! A beautiful performance, though for the first time in my life I heard the "Vissi d'arte" go without applause.' (My own view is that the audience was too spellbound by the drama to interrupt with ill-timed applause.) 'The second act was unbelievable: two giants, and they bowed to one another before the curtain like two gallant opponents. The stage was invaded after the endless ovation. I have seen for myself the self-controlled English people go mad, take off their coats, scarves or whatever and wave them in enthusiasm. Tito was great and it was wonderful to see the perfect reactions of the two of them. Maria certainly gave a big shake-up to the character of Tosca, making her much more human and extrovert. But this can be done *only by her*. Others who would try to imitate – beware!'

In spite of her tremendous, unparalleled triumph she remained desperately nervous. On each day of performance she would phone me to say she could not sing – she had no voice left, or else she must change everything in the second act. I would be half-an-hour on the telephone consoling the poor girl and encouraging her. 'All right,' I would say, 'you don't sing. It is enough for you to appear. You just act and I'll do the singing. – All right, you change whatever you want. You know we understand each other –,' and so on.

In the evening she would come by my dressing-room before going on stage and I would take her to the wings, holding her icy hand and whispering encouragement while rivulets of perspiration would be running down her neck and the edge of her dress. Yet when she came off-stage after her exquisitely sung duet with Cioni she would clasp my hand and wish me luck and stand there waiting until my first phrase had been sung. Indeed, there was something utterly touching in the way she would show endearing flashes of concern for others however deeply absorbed she might be in her own ordeal.

We gave six performances in London and we repeated the same team-up in Paris and New York. I doubt if anyone who was present at those performances will ever forget them. I know I never shall – not only for the artistic peak which they reached but for the extraordinary rapport and understanding between us.

Probably millions of words have been written about La Callas, and quite a few about the vulnerable, lonely, elusive creature who was Maria. There is little I can add. She shone for all too brief a while in the world of opera, like a vivid flame attracting the attention of the whole world, and she had a strange magic which was all her own.

I always thought she was immortal – and *she is*.

17

Il Tabarro

Over the first line of music in the score of *Il Tabarro* Puccini has written, 'The curtain rises before the music begins.'

This is something which can be enormously effective, and I myself like to use the idea whenever it is appropriate. In *Il Tabarro* it is particularly so. With the orchestra silent, and with no action to distract the spectator's eye or attention, the audience immediately becomes at one with the ambience and atmosphere of the drama.

For the music Puccini has used a varied and dramatic palette of colours with which he instantly captures the spectator as he enters this world which holds no smile. From the first notes the music flows like the river on which the dark action takes place, and the contrasting twilight atmosphere reflected by the little out-of-tune barrel organ, set against the violent happenings of love and blood on the barge, impart to the work an air almost of nobility.

It is a hard world in which the grim struggle for existence has extinguished the light of hope, a world where passions creep along the walls like shadows in the night. And when dawn comes another kind of darkness falls on bent shoulders – the darkness of the weary effort to cope with what the day may bring.

The reactions of the characters are slow and heavy, the dialogue difficult, just as life is difficult. 'Com' è difficile esser felici' as Giorgetta says. (How hard it is to be happy.) Each character follows his or her own thoughts without paying much attention to the others, the dreams and fantasies mostly poor or tragic.

Tinca, one of the stevedores, has found his solution. 'Wine is the spice of life,' he declares. 'When I drink I stop thinking. It's thinking which makes me miserable.'

Talpa, another stevedore, lets his wife Frugola do most of the talking. For him life is just the ordinary round of hard work, perhaps a fairly good supper and then sleep.

Luigi, the youngest and liveliest of the stevedores, has other, more passionate dreams. He loves Giorgetta, the wife of Michele the barge master, the boss. She and he come from the same district on the outskirts of Paris and share memories of a brighter, happier existence; recollections innocent enough in themselves, but dangerous now in their inescapable contrast with the gloomy life on the barge.

Throughout the action one should be keenly aware of life being lived literally on two levels. Above the wharves and the river bank is Paris, with its midinettes, its happy lovers, its ballad vendor, its organ grinder, the passing figures with their carefree relationships. They may be poor, but they have their simple pleasures and their moments of joy.

Below, on the barge moored on the bank of the Seine, is a world in which the troubled souls of the utterly defeated move sluggishly, like the water in the river. That world sinks into oblivion at sunset, just as Paris is coming to life for the gay, simple pleasures of evening. Only the light of secret passion will briefly illumine the dark night hours on the barge.

From far away comes the sound of sirens from barges sliding up and down under the bridges of the Seine. The embankment is the horizon, and from up there come the sounds of motor horns, laughing voices, silly love songs, to remind those below that life on that other level is somehow better, even the air is clearer. Down on the moored barge the air is thick, like fog, with the same dreary thoughts repeating themselves each day.

The usual activities are going on around the barge when the scene opens. Men are loading and unloading, Giorgetta, weary and impatient, is hanging out a few articles of washing, Michele sits silent in the prow of the barge, smoking his pipe, lost in thought as he absently watches the sinking sun. He rouses himself when she addresses a few words to him, but when he gently tries to put his arm around her, she turns her head away from his kiss and, defeated by the rebuff, he goes silently below.

Above, the organ grinder – probably at the end of a tiring day – stops at Luigi's invitation, puts down the leg of his instrument and mechnically turns the handle. His thoughts are already moving to someone who is waiting for his return. The shabbiness of his old instrument is at one with the patient face and the kindly eyes. There is a long story behind his slightly bowed shoulders, but he has a certain dignity, pleasant and gracious, like the out-of-tune waltz which comes from the old musical box. It is difficult to express artistically the 'nothing' which the old man has to do, but the music describes his resigned attitude, in subtle contrast to the rebellious reactions smouldering in Giorgetta and Luigi.

Luigi calls to the old man to play, and Giorgetta, in a rare moment of gaiety, dances with one of the men, chides him for his clumsy footwork and yields immediately when Luigi takes her in his arms and dances with her voluptuously. The scene is interrupted by the return of Michele; the old man accepts a coin from Luigi and then goes slowly on his way.

Almost immediately, on that 'other level' comes an exquisite little sketch in complete and innocent contrast to the tension on the deck of the barge. A ballad vendor slowly approaches from up-stage, followed by a group of laughing midinettes. He stops once or twice, singing nostalgically, echoing the music of Mimi in *La Bohème*. The girls laugh and comment, while below on the deck of the barge Giorgetta and Michele exchange no more than the monosyllabic dialogue of two people who are worlds away from the lighthearted scene above.

As the group drift away in the wake of the ballad vendor Talpa's wife Frugola enters, and Michele, annoyed at the interruption of his conversation with Giorgetta, abruptly leaves.

Frugola's name describe's her exactly – the one who goes around the streets and alleys picking up bits and pieces here and there, rummaging in odd corners for odd things. She dreams of a country cottage somewhere. She is never going to have it, of course, but she dreams all the same. Meanwhile, she finds pathetically cheerful comfort in the company of her beloved Tabby cat, Caporale, which she describes with endearing partiality immediately understandable to anyone with a cat, a puppy, even a plush teddy bear in their lives.

I see Frugola gentle in her poverty, moving with a not quite forgotten grace, an ex-cabaret actress perhaps. She has lots of coloured ribbons about her and dresses rather theatrically for her performance of . . . the next moment. She believes firmly in what she says and does, and she is essentially generous, willingly giving away the best items among the poor odds and ends she has collected.

Rummaging in her sack, she imagines the story connected with every object she produces, describing with gentle movements and quick, lively glances what she thinks is suitable to each article. Her laugh is sharp, a little hoarse perhaps from her tendency to a drop of rum – but I protest strongly against any idea of her as a witchlike creature with a coarse guffaw. She is the cleanest character of them all – not literally perhaps, but in her disposition – and when speaking of her Caporale she must be moving and inspire tenderness. Her 'ron, ron, ron' must be a sweet imitation of the philosopher cat purring, not a horrible grunt. Nothing in the score suggest the over-accented, steam engine rhythm which has become almost a tradition – and a most unacceptable one.

As she sits on the deck, waiting for her husband, she talks to Giorgetta about the cottage she would love to have one day, and in excited contrast Giorgetta speaks of her own longing for life as it once was in Belleville, from which both she and Luigi come. Luigi joins her in describing the happy life which they shared with the other young people in Belleville, and it becomes painfully clear how much Giorgetta loathes, and longs to escape from, life on the eternal barge. She is deathly sick of going up and down the river with no real joy to sweeten existence.

The exchange of memories between Giorgetta and Luigi amounts almost to a love duet, in spite of the presence of Frugola and the other stevedores. For a brief moment Frugola also understands their longing for the life they describe; but then, full of her own dreams, she prepares to drift towards home, accompanied by her husband.

She and Talpa sing a little song as they go: 'Ho sognato una casetta' (I have dreamed of a little house), and this must be sung with a sad smile in the voice, while keeping the musical rhythm. It is the sad smile with which they contemplate their beautiful, unattainable dream. Not a tarantella or a dancing folk song, but the expression of a nostalgic, hopeless thought which grows heavier as the song slows down and dies away in the distance. That smile in the voice covers tears. Many people can teach how to suffer and weep, but very few how to smile over sad dreams never to be realised. It is a wonderful human glimpse in this opera of violence and passion.

As Frugola and Talpa leave the stage the two lovers are left alone in dangerous isolation. Passion breaks out afresh between them, though expressed for the most part in breathless undertones, for they fear the return of Michele at any moment as Luigi makes passionate love to Giorgetta.

The duet is no longer one of dreams and regrets. Now they are alone there is a dark strain of irresistible passion running through it, as violent as their need to break loose. Dreams and poetry are not sufficient now – and then suddenly they are interrupted by the return of Michele.

He is not suspicious, but there is a great weight on his heart and spirits. His few answers are cold and brief, and when Luigi bids him good night there is a *rallentando* in his answering 'Buona notte,' before he goes below.

The love duet takes fire ever more feverishly and desperately. Impatient with sexual desire, mad with jealousy, Luigi swears he will grab a knife and kill. Giorgetta agrees to meet Luigi again during the night on deck; the signal to let him know the coast is clear will be her striking a match. When Luigi runs off she complains 'Com' è difficile esser felici.' (How difficult it is to be happy.) Then Michele returns to hang up the lighted lamps.

He speaks to her movingly of other days when they were happy together. She still loves her husband and cannot forget that they once shared the joy of their child. But, torn between pity for him and her love for Luigi, she begs him not to torment her – and himself – by talking of happiness which is past. Her reluctant compassion becomes nearly unbearable when he refers almost humbly to the gap in their ages: 'I miei capelli grigi mi sembrano un insulto alla tua gioventu.' (My gray hairs are an insult to your youth.)

He is beginning to suspect her infidelity but, in a last desperate attempt to win back her love and understanding, he takes her into the shelter of his great cloak, reminding her of the time when they loved each other and he used to gather her and the child into his protecting arms beneath the cloak.

With an anguished cry he implores her, 'Resta vicino a me, la notte è bella.' (Stay with me, the night is beautiful.)

Tormented though she is by his appeal, she feels she is a prisoner of some sort of inescapable destiny and, hardly knowing what to do or say, she struggles free from his embrace with the feeble excuse, 'Casco dal sonno.' (I'm so sleepy.)

He waits hopelessly for a kinder answer, even the smallest gesture of comfort. Motionless, he follows her with his eyes, no expression on his face, until she disappears. Then, like some great tree struck by lightning, he collapses and, in a burst of anguished fury, he utters the one word, 'Sgualdrina!' (Strumpet!)

Again from above drift back the voices and sounds of the city. Words of love are carried on the wind from a self-absorbed world which knows and cares nothing for the misery of others. Michele is sunk in his own dark thoughts – death and a wish to kill. Throwing his great cloak around him, he leans on the tiller of the barge. The aria 'Fiume eterno' (Eternal river), which expresses his misery and rage, was changed by Puccini into the more dramatic monologue 'Nulla, più nulla' (Nothing, nothing more) as Michele reflects on what may have caused this unhappiness between them.

He drops his head on his arms, then feels mechanically for his pipe and strikes a match to light it. All unknowing, he has given the sign for which Luigi, waiting on the bank, is watching. As the flame flares up in the darkness, Michele suddenly becomes aware that someone has stealthily moved towards the gangplank which connects the barge with the shore. Startled, he withdraws into the shadows – and then sees it is Luigi who has stolen back on board.

Michele throws himself upon the intruder and seizes him by the throat. There is a fearful struggle, Luigi trying desperately to get hold of his knife. But the enraged Michele is the stronger of the two and, tightening his grip on Luigi's throat, finally forces from him the confession that he has come to meet Giorgetta and that he loves her.

In his final contortions as Michele strangles him, Luigi continues to clutch his assailant with dead, stiffening hands. And at that moment Giorgetta appears on deck, gazing frightened around her.

Michele, the cloak now wrapped closely around him and the dead Luigi, is sitting quite still, apparently calmly smoking. Giorgetta approaches him timidly with an appeal for forgiveness. She is sorry she was so unkind – she cannot sleep for thinking of it, and she wants to be near him after all.

'Where? – under my cloak?' he asks her heavily.

'Yes,' she agrees. 'Quite close to you.' And she reminds him how he used to tell her that every man needs a great cloak in which to hide his secrets – sometimes of joy, sometimes of deep sorrow.

'Sometimes a murder,' he rejoins savagely. 'Come under my cloak. Come here – come!'

And he rises to his feet. Then, opening his cloak and tearing the dead man's grip from him, he throws Luigi's corpse at her feet.

The role of Michele is a very powerful one, which I always enjoyed playing. But I should like to add a few paragraphs on my relationship with the work as producer.

Towards the end of 1982, at the invitation of Dr Otto Herbst, I went to produce both *Tabarro* and *Gianni Schicchi* for the Bayerische Staatsoper in Munich. Some years before I had staged the same two operas for him in Zurich on the beautiful sets by Pier Luigi Pizzi. I myself sang Schicchi, and I was delighted to renew the contact.

In Munich the sets were ten years old but, with the changes allowed to me, they were tremendously effective, proving my contention that expensive new sets are seldom essential to a fine performance.

The casts were very good indeed. In *Tabarro* Carlo Cossuta was Luigi, Marilyn Zschau was Giorgetta, and the Michele was Garbis Boyagian, with a clever group of supers.

For *Gianni Schicchi* – with which I shall deal in the next chapter – I had the authentically Tuscan Rolando Panerai for Schicchi himself, the enchanting Lucia Popp for his daughter, while Zita was none other than the superb Astrid Varnay. The Rinuccio was Peter Kelen, who, having arrived late, provided me with quite a problem. I found he spoke nothing but Hungarian while I was almost totally ignorant of that language. During my long, detailed and mimed explanations he remained like a statue, without a hint of acknowledgment. But, to the surprise of everyone, including myself, at the rehearsal this young tenor performed exactly as I wanted!

I have to say it was all rather hard work, but tremendously rewarding. For the performance was greeted with great enthusiasm from the company as well as all the musical and stage assistants. My collaboration with Maestro Sawallisch was complete, loyal and with a most gratifying identity of viewpoint, resulting in a sincere friendship which I venture to say was not confined to professional contact only.

The stage rehearsals took place at the Prinzregenten Theater, which brought back moving memories to me of the time just after the War when I sang Simone Boccanegra there. I still remember the storms of cheers and tears and applause which continued endlessly after Simone's 'E vo' gridando pace e vo' gridando amor' (I plead for peace and love).

Every producer naturally hopes to show something new in a fresh production of an opera, and I am no exception. On the other hand, it is with me an article of artistic faith that the producer must always remember he is not an originator; he is merely the interpreter of someone else's invention. To distort a masterpiece in a cheap bid for notice does nothing for the composer and, in the long run, precious little for the producer.

When I took over this particular production of *Il Tabarro* my biggest problem concerned the lighting. The scenery had originally been conceived with the idea of starting in the dark of night and proceeding towards dawn, whereas in fact Puccini planned the action to begin at sunset and continue into the night.

The stage directions are quite explicit about this. When the curtain goes up Michele is sitting facing the setting sun and the whole barge, though sunk between the banks, should be lit by the red evening light. 'Questo sole che muore nella Senna,' (This sun sinking to its death in the Seine), as Giorgetta says. But in spite of all my efforts with projectors and spotlights, not to mention the most earnest help of the co-operative lighting designer, night would fall too swiftly on the black sets.

I needed that light badly! So I conceived the idea of installing a lighthouse at the not too distant harbour. This projected a beam of light every seventeen seconds which travelled slowly across the stage from right to left also in seventeen seconds. Like an eye slowly searching out the dark corners of the barge, it then slid along the pier with its piled up sacks, creating a suggestive atmosphere which added real strength to the drama. At the end the light plumbed right on the dead body of Luigi, then moved relentlessly on its way until the curtain descended.

I am not claiming this as a stroke of genius. I merely give it as an instance of reasonably intelligent direction solving a practical problem without either great expense or trendy insults to the composer.

As drama pure and simple (if such a term can be used of such a story!) *Il Tabarro* would be little but a tremendously effective piece of *Grand Guignol*. With the addition of Puccini's magnificently penetrating and expressive music, however, it becomes something much finer. Shock and horror give way to irresistible compassion for the poor human flotsam and jetsam drifting on the waters of the Seine. If this impression is not achieved then I am afraid either producer or performers must take the blame.

18

Gianni Schicchi

He was called Fulmine – a solitary cavalier of the streets in my native city of Bassano. Several times, as a boy, I saw him on the Ponte Vecchio or on the road that leads to the heights, declaiming ancient poetry to the glory of the river and the mountains. In summer he used to sleep on park benches, his hat over his eyes, his feet – in shoes of two colours – thrust out in front of him, the thin ankles showing beneath the too short trousers. His coat was tight and always buttoned up, a safety pin securing the silk scarf '*à la belle époque*' in place of a shirt. His bamboo cane twirled at intervals between fingers covered with exotic rings, which he made himself from candy papers. His hat, large-brimmed and feathered, was turned up at the sides and the face beneath it, of uncertain age but distinguished, was faintly reminiscent of Don Quixote.

With short birdlike steps he made the rounds from bar to tavern, where he was always given a biscuit or an 'ombra' (a small glass of wine which, if repeated too often, blurs the sight). This disturbed his balance at times but not his humour, though he never laughed out loud, not even when he dextrously filched a cigarette from the fingers of a passer-by.

Everyone knew him and let him live in peace. If offered money he absent-mindedly turned his glance the other way, and then took off his feathered hat and bowed. To the inevitable jokes of the youths he responded by leaning on the wall and looking them over from top to toe with half closed eyes, smiling complacently. When winter's cold came Fulmine, with great ingenuity, would let loose a horse or cow from the market and run shouting, 'Stop, thief! Stop, thief!' Then he would let himself be captured and end up in prison for a few days, provided with warmth and a bed – though with the door always left open because he suffered from claustrophobia.

His aristocratic voice was husky with the smoke of cigars and cigarettes, the butts of which he picked up everywhere and stuffed into his pockets. I am afraid he was not particularly clean but he smelled quite pleasantly of grass and tobacco.

Once the priest from the mission, Don Giovanni Bragagnolo, managed to get him to church, with the intention of having him make confession. But Fulmine promptly took himself off again, protesting that he resented such curiosity about his private affairs.

When I was a child I used to see him every day on my way to school, and he used to greet me as 'Parosin' (little master), lifting his cane to his hat. Once I offered him the snack which my Nanny, Maria, had prepared for me (under the affectionate delusion that I was half starved at school). Fulmine bent over the package and opened it.

'Oh, what beautiful cherries!' he said and took one. But when I pressed him to take more he replied courteously, 'Thank you, Parosin, but no. I am tall, you see, and can pick them whenever I want from somebody's garden.'

Then one day Fulmine disappeared. He had been taken to the hospital in urgent need of attention. And there, in the cool, clean hospital linen, he died, lamented by all as a lovable rogue who was unforgettable.

I am moved to recall Fulmine because the moment I first read the libretto of *Gianni Schicchi* I thought of him: his lively glance, his one-sided captivating smile, the short thick eyebrows, the long ruffled hair falling over his shoulders, the expressive 'bejewelled' fingers. He returned to my memory fully alive and somehow helped me to penetrate the mediaeval character of that other engaging rogue, Gianni Schicchi, with surprising ease. I could say that we *both* examined Franz Hals portraits for the idea of 'our' make-up, knowing that what was needed was the face of a Tuscan man of the people, acquisitive and sly, apparently humble but very astute.

> L'altro che la' sen va, sostenne
> Per guadagnar la donna della torma
> Falsificar in se Buoso Donati
> Testando e dando al testamento norma.

> As that man who goes yonder [Gianni Schichi] once devised,
> To gain the lady of the stud, how he
> Buoso Donati's self might simulate
> And make a will and frame it validly.
>   Translation: Jefferson Butler Fletcher

So Dante Alighieri describes the sly Florentine who impersonated a dead man and remade his will to his own advantage. And on this glimpse of a character in *The Inferno* Gioacchino Forzano wrote one of the most brilliant libretti in all opera and the incomparable Puccini supplied the music which turned it into a masterpiece.

My first close contact with *Gianni Schicchi* came in 1939, when the Rome Opera gave a series of performances in the Opera House in Adria (near Venezia). The Schicchi was Benvenuto Franci and I revelled in the tremendous power of his characterisation, the sonority of the middle and lower notes, the marvellous colouring of the voice, the inborn shrewdness of the Tuscan accent, the heavy step with which he made his bold entrance. I was particularly well placed to note all this for I (almost a young beginner then) was Betto di Signa, the poorest of Buoso Donati's relations, the least important, the one who is always snubbed and pushed around by the others.

At a later date, when I was myself studying Schicchi, I had the unparalleled good fortune to become a friend of its librettist, and many are the precious recollections which I have of that association. Once, Forzano and I were so deeply immersed in our study that we even forgot to laugh at the many jokes and witticisms scattered so lavishly through the work. But when I remarked on this the sharp retort I received from the witty Tuscan was: '*Our* work must be serious. It is for the other people to laugh and enjoy it.' How true! Nothing is more destructive of a good joke than to laugh when telling it.

On another occasion, when I returned from an engagement abroad, I told him how I had been persuaded to give the last words of the opera in English: 'Ditemi, voi Signori . . .' (Tell me, gentlemen, etc.) to make it more easily understandable to the audience. He gave me a black look and replied, 'And didn't you have to bite your tongue to please those barbarians?'

He was very jealous of his works and woe betide anyone who dared tamper with them. It required all my patience and diplomacy to persuade him to accept the slightest licence. At the end he said nothing, but he gave me a lovely Schicchi-like smile. When I first came to produce the work I had no chance to discuss it with him, and I cannot say if he would have accepted all my ideas with resigned friendship. But I think of that smile – and hope.

Forzano wanted the performers to play as much as possible to the proscenium, so that the audience could enjoy the comedy and costumes to the full, so I used the idea of a sort of promenade. The curtain rose in absolute silence, disclosing a backdrop, practically a wall, looking like an old Florentine street of 1299, the whole scene bathed in mellow September sunlight. In the middle sits:

Betto di Signa. He is a clumsy figure, with muddy old boots and a shabby peasant cap. He is timid, but with the lively eyes of a ferret. His movements are slow and awkward and although he does not look any special age he has a bent back. Later, when he talks, it will be seen that he spreads his fingers as though seeking the right word. He is sitting near a hen coop containing two live chickens, and on his arm is a basket of fresh apples and pears, which he is in the habit of taking to his cousin, Buoso Donati. It is 8 am and he is waiting for a decent hour to make his appearance, ignorant of the fact that his rich relation is seriously ill.

Marco and *Ciesca* powerfully excited, enter from the left. They are the son and daughter-in-law of the sick man's important cousin, Simone. Very conscious of their social superiority to Betto, they hurry past without even acknowledging his greeting. Behind them comes Rinuccio, also excited, and gesticulating to Betto to come quickly.

Rinuccio is the nephew of Zita, another influential cousin of Buoso Donati, usually referred to as 'The Old Woman'. He is in love with Lauretta, the daughter of the graceless Gianni Schicchi, and very much aware that a match with her would be totally unacceptable to his grand relations.

Next arrives from the right the majestic notary, *Ser Amantio di Nicolao*, followed by the professional witnesses, *Pinellino* and *Guccio*. He passes by, his long notary's robe flying out behind him. Then, with some commotion, yet another group of relations hurry in. These are *Gherardo*, Buoso's nephew, who drags behind him his wife *Nella*, who drags behind her the small boy *Gherardino* who, in his turn, drags a little wooden cart with a missing wheel which creates an unwelcomed clatter.

The notary disappears left and the others hasten to the right, with a passing greeting to *Doctor Spinelloccio*, who advances pompously at that moment, merely inclining his head slightly *en passant*.

Betto collects all his things and, last of all, makes his exit right. The stage darkens, the street backdrop flies up and, as the orchestra begins, the light at the same time comes on to disclose the big room of Buoso Donati, who lies dead in the bed.

This short preliminary action has the sole purpose of introducing the characters, the historical period and the scene of action, at the same time clarifying what can sometimes seem a confusing opening with no useful pointers. The make-up, costumes and acting for the scene that follows should not be exaggerated. The balance of performances should be respected so that a minor role does not overwhelm another without good reason.

Buoso's two cousins Zita and Simone are already at Buoso's bedside, holding a wake for the dear departed, and at this point, they are the only ones who actually know that he is dead. The others have been drawn there by the report that he is dangerously ill. Co-ordinating with the music, the relatives enter from upstage, displaying signs of inconsolable grief.

Zita, like a sullen old vulture, is perched on the best chair in the place. Bent with age, her round eyes wide open and watchful, she receives the respectful homage of the lesser members of the family. Rinuccio arrives first and kisses her hand. The others follow close behind, Marco and Ciesca making loud sounds of lamentation. Gherardo, Nella and Gherardino, still with his cart, come next and are immediately ordered to keep away. Betto, perhaps the only one who truly cared for the old man, gives vent to a sincere outburst of grief, at which the others hush him so violently that he drops the basket of fruits and does not dare pay Zita his respects.

Simone, sitting almost in the shadow of the bed, has received a respectful salute from each member of the family as they compete for a place near the bed and the opportunity to make the most conspicuous display of grief.

Feeling excluded from the general mourning, Betto is bored, he slowly approaches Nella and whispers in her ear that in Signa it is rumoured that if Buoso dies it is the monks who will be the richer. The others, kneeling as they are, keep vigilant eyes and ears open for any hint of the real situation and watch the conversation between Nella and Betto closely. Then, still on their knees, they shuffle nearer and ask plaintively, 'What is it that they say in Signa?'

This is Betto's moment. Important at last, he repeats that in Signa everyone is saying that the monastery will inherit everything from Buoso. Incredulity then desolation overwhelm all.

Buoso Donati's relations cannot, of course, bear each other. The grades of relationship (not to mention expectations), the different social stations, the sheer jealousy, combine to divide them into groups. Probably Marco, for instance, son of the influential Simone, lives with his wife in the centre of the city, while Gherardo and Nella and their tiresome offspring are on the outskirts. Rinuccio has a certain status as Zita's favourite nephew, and the one who has no status at all is Betto, a poor countryman who lives outside the city in Signa. These degrees of relationship and social standing, if properly differentiated, add enormously to the comedy of the situation.

By the time Betto makes his disastrous announcement all the characters in this masterly comedy have been clearly drawn and, small though some of the roles may seem, they all require intelligent singers, a fine sense of interpretation and moderation in acting. *Gianni Schicchi* is *not* a farce, though ignorant directors have often fallen into the trap of trying to make it one. It is a superb comedy in which both words and music give the clearest indication of what is required – which is *recitar cantando* (acting in singing). If supported by absolute musical and vocal security, the real singing actor can only delight in the privilege of taking part.

As the full implication of Betto's news sinks in they all turn to Simone, as the eldest, for guidance. He is rather gaga, but his slow reactions are stimulated by the compliment of their attitude and for once he guesses right. If, he declares, the will is in the hands of a notary all is lost. 'But should it still be in this room, misfortune to the monks and hope for all of us!'

Forgetful of the deceased and any necessity of registering seemly grief, everyone starts on a mad and shameless search through everything in the place. It is Rinuccio who finds the will and, without hesitation, tries a bit of blackmail. Holding the document well out of their reach, he asks – On such a day of rejoicing will Aunt Zita agree to his marrying Lauretta, Gianni Schicchi's daughter?

All say, 'Yes, yes –' and he hands over the will. But he has the forethought to send young Gherardino to fetch Schicchi and his daughter.

Carefully Zita unfastens the ribbon binding the parchment and, with a generous gesture, hands the cover to Simone, after reading aloud: 'To my cousins Zita and Simone –'

General commotion, during which Simone, despite his ingrained parsimony, walks to the bed and reverently lights three candles amidst a chorus of approval. Then, finding that the one sheet of parchment handed to him by Zita is no more than the outer covering, he throws it on the floor. Meanwhile Zita goes on removing the seals and declares the will open.

They group themselves behind her in a sort of pyramid, anxiously hopeful, smilingly expectant, then obviously follow line by line, silently mouthing some of the words, as gradually black consternation replaces hopeful expectancy. The first one to move is Simone, who goes back to the bed and savagely blows out the candles so prematurely lighted in honour of the deceased.

As dismay turns to rage the air is filled with cries of fury and disappointment. All eight are for once united in the single emotion of frustrated greed. Then Rinuccio, usually a rather submissive fellow, dares to put forward the suggestion that the resourceful Gianni Schicchi might perhaps be able to help them. At first everyone rejects the idea. But then he breaks into his glorious aria in praise of Florence and her great men, 'Firenze è come un albero fiorito', claiming that Gianni Schicchi, the smart guy, is not unworthy to be included.

Fascinated by the young man's enthusiasm – and the discovery that behind that submissive exterior there is after all a real man – they finally applaud with fervour. They are still doing so when a knock on the door announces that Schicchi has arrived, and all immediately assume a suitable attitude of mourning.

What a moment for one's entry! My heart used to beat fortissimo as, tightening my hand round that of Lauretta, I stood in the wings counting the bars. Then with four steps I went forward with extended hand straight to Zita, who peevishly rejected my greeting. Then I went to the bed – and discovered the corpse. Finally, putting my arm around the shoulders of Betto – a poor man like me – I tried to console him and at the same time learn something of the situation.

The Donatis make no attempt to conceal their spiteful scorn for Schicchi, a quarrel blazes up and he prepares to depart again, dragging his reluctant daughter with him. But she, knowing that her happiness and Rinuccio's also is at stake, falls on her knees and begins her appealing aria, 'O mio babbino caro.'

This aria – too often presented with unmixed pathos – is really a marvellous amalgam of sincere and pretended despair. There is nothing Lauretta does not know about twisting her old Dad around her little finger – though of course this situation is more serious than any she has ever had to tackle before. So there she is in tears – a few of them genuine – and she even threatens to settle the matter by throwing herself from the Ponte Vecchio if he remains adamant.

With a sniff, Schicchi wipes away a tear or two of his own, relents and asks to see the will.

I maintain that it is artistically wrong for Schicchi to stand there unmoved, just waiting for her to finish her aria, collect her applause and give him a chance to continue. Where is action and reaction then? I know not everyone agrees with me. Indeed, one London critic – who shall be nameless because I think he may have learned better by now – stigmatised my acting as 'villainous' (a very unkind word) because I allowed Elizabeth Vaughan's adorable performance to draw a sentimental tear or two from me at Covent Garden.

Well then, Schicchi examines the will and finally sees his way clear to deal with the problem, but dispatches Lauretta to the terrace 'to feed the bird' so that she shall not be involved in what promises to be a very dishonest masquerade.

After agonising cogitation, during which the relatives follow him about the stage, he informs them that the will cannot be changed, *but* if Donati could be brought back to life for a vital half hour or so a new will could be made. He himself will impersonate Buoso Donati.

Enchanted, the relations haul the corpse out of the bed with scant reverence and hustle it into a closet. Zita instructs Rinuccio to fetch the notary and he rushes away. But then, to the horror of all, the doctor knocks at the door on his daily visit, and Schicchi has just time to leap into the bed and draw the curtains.

Enter *Doctor Spinelloccio* while the frightened relatives flutter round him, keeping him as far as possible from the bed. The note on the score says 'a nasal voice and Bolognese accent' for the doctor but, while agreeing with the accent, I would question the nasal voice and suggest instead a round, pompous voice, calculated to impress his patients. Schicchi, when imitating the voice of Buoso (a Tuscan), is bound to use characteristic 'yellow' nasal voice, particularly as he is impersonating a quavery old man. To have two similar voices in this vital conversation of deception is confusing, whereas a contrast can be very funny.

Schicchi triumphs brilliantly in the first round. His imitation of Buoso begging the doctor to leave him in peace and return later succeeds perfectly. On the doctor's departure the relations almost dance for joy as they discuss the possible partition of the goods, their affectionate euphoria prompting Schicchi to comment ironically on the beauty of family love. This sweet scene, however, is already showing signs of turning sour when everything is brought to a standstill by the tolling of a bell in the piazza outside, signifying a death.

As they gaze at each other in horrified alarm, fearing that somehow the news of Buoso's death has leaked out, Lauretta appears from the balcony to say innocently, 'Papa, what do you think? The bird won't eat any more.'

'Then give him a drink,' replies her distracted father, and she disappears again as Gherardo, who has rushed out to make enquiries, comes panting back with the news that the tolling bell was for somebody else. Nothing to do with their dear departed. They all sing an ironical 'Requiescat in pace' and return to business.

There follows the dressing of Schicchi for his vital role, a delightful musical page in which, while the women play around him coquettishly and the men watch sardonically, all in turn make an opportunity to ask Schicchi to see that some coveted item shall be theirs. To each he promises that it shall be so.

But then, feeling that the time has come to put the fear of God into them, he brutally recalls them to reality by warning of the penalty for all should their dishonesty be discovered – the loss of a hand and exile from Florence. And here he sings the wonderful little phrase 'Addio Firenze', so exquisitely full of nostalgia and yet so menacing that all stand motionless, listening. Then they repeat the phrase with terror in their tone, a terror which must be clearly manifested, since it is sufficient to restrain them later in front of the notary, even though Schicchi is dictating a will which disinherits them and enriches himself.

At this point Rinuccio returns anxiously announcing that the notary is approaching, and once more Schicchi just has time to leap into the bed and rearrange the curtains before the entry, to solemn music, of *Ser Amantio di Nicolao*, accompanied by the two professional witnesses, Pinellino the shoemaker and Guccio, the dyer. I call them professional witnesses because they obviously live and work nearby, their work allowing them to leave at any time and follow the notary to earn a little extra money. It is a familiar experience for them and I personally would prefer Pinellino not to burst into tears from time to time, even though he does say, 'Mi vien da piangere' (I'm going to cry.) It covers the triplets which underline the ideas flashing through Schicchi's ingenious brain. Better perhaps that he should just smile foolishly. Both are curious people and only listen for a while to the dictation of the will. Then their attention wanders and the notary has to recall them.

Ser Amantio di Nicolao enters Donati's home like a king,

pausing for a moment as though looking for the red carpet. He then sits down at the desk which the relatives have prepared for him in the farthest corner, divests himself of his headdress, opens his portfolio, arranges his papers – and gives the chatty Pinellino a sharp tap on the belly with his stick to indicate that proceedings are about to begin.

How I always enjoyed the dictation of that will, with its thousand colours, inflections and accents! I could, as the saying goes, have died with laughter instead of just impersonating that corpse.

A very special voice is needed for Schicchi. The voice of a mature man of course, but with here and there a touch of sharpness, some subtle inflection reminiscent of youthful cheek. It is an essential part of Schicchi's personality which sometimes escapes the audience, involved as they are in the brilliance and vivacity of the acting. He is a man very much alive to the situation, but still keeping the character of the roguish Florentine boy he once was, ready to make fun of everything and everyone and turn all to his own advantage.

This is what I always look for and try to express, just as intensely as I study make-up and movement. Note, for instance, how he appears to approve all the aspirations of Buoso's heirs, while having really worked out his plan in his own acute brain. Also how, in a moment of danger, he reminds them skilfully that they are all accomplices, all equally at risk in this piece of roguery. Puccini's Schicchi is a countryman, shrewd and full of commonsense, determined to fight for his daughter's happiness, scornful of authority and always ready with an answer.

There are no rules for the interpretation of the wonderful will-making scene, which offers infinite possibilities. I used to enjoy making mock of my so-called relatives, sometimes taking them by surprise so that their reactions were spontaneous and genuine – though always respecting the music and text, of course. For that in my view is a *must*.

In the character of Buoso, Schicchi begins by complimenting the notary, describing him as 'solemne et leale' (solemn and loyal), knowing his vanity will be gratified and that he will then be in a co-operative mood, ready to accept the explanation that paralysis has affected the sick man's power to sign. The relatives dutifully chant, 'Poor Buoso' in melancholy unison, at which Amantio glances at them briefly over his glasses. (Spectacles, incidentally, were invented in Pisa in 1295, four years before these events, so our notary is very up-to-date.)

Accepting the sad explanation, reinforced by a feeble wave of the hand between the curtains, the notary states firmly, 'Testes viderunt,' (The witnesses see this), and uses his stick once more to recall them from their wool-gathering. Then he begins to intone the preamble to the will.

This reading, strictly in tempo, must sound monotonous but very clear, with emphasis on the underlined words. Gianni knows the significant bits pretty well and takes the notary by surprise when he asks, in a tremulous voice, to have added, 'Annullans, revocans et irritans omne alliud testamentum' (annulling and revoking all other wills).

Ser Amantio hastily writes in the words he had forgotten and, although irritated by the family's chorus of approval and nervous at the many interruptions, he queries nothing until Schicchi comes to the very meagre legacy of five lire for charity.

'Don't you think that is too little?' he protests. But Schicchi, always imitating Buoso's voice, replies that when you leave to charity, people say: 'It is stolen money.' Then the united chorus from the family of, 'What wisdom, what clear thinking!' wins the day.

The sly Schicchi generously disposes of the minor items of the estate, allowing himself an amusing *rallentando* when he gets to Ciesca and Marco: 'The property of. . . Quintole,' as though there are so many names and properties to remember that he might forget some vital matter. When he leaves the 'beautiful mule to *his* devoted friend . . . Gianni Schicchi' the comments and interruptions become so loud that the confused notary finally strikes a blow with his stick on the desk and, in the pregnant hush, states in a resonant voice: 'Mulam relinquit eius amico devoto . . . Gianni Schicchi.'

The protesting cries of the family are drowned by the descending notes of the orchestra, except for Simone's honeyed protest that a mule will be of no use to Gianni Schicchi.

The terrifying reply from the supposedly dying man is: 'Lo so io quel che vuole Gainni Schicchi.' (I know what Gianni Schicchi likes.)

The notary sits down again to write, but is up once more in almost no time, shouting over the clamour of the relations who now realise that every item of value may well go to Gianni Schicchi. At first the relations had in turn approached the bed to express thanks for small mercies. Now their choked and furious protests delight the amused Schicchi as one item after another is consigned to 'my good friend, Gianni Schicchi'.

He declares plaintively to the notary, as though apologising for the conduct of his excited relations, that he will leave his goods to whom he pleases. 'This is my will, and such it must remain,' he says, adding menacingly, 'and if they yell about it I shall keep calm and hum the old refrain.'

The helpless, infuriated relatives realise that he means, 'Addio,

Firenze –' the warning of the punishment for the fraud in which they are all involved.

Over the final and most valuable bequest, the sawmills of Signa, he lingers with exquisite pleasure as he prolongs the anguish of the family in a passage that resembles a vocal acrobatic display, imitating Buoso's voice for the notary and using the Schicchi voice to hold the relatives in helpless fear. To achieve a good result it is absolutely imperative to follow Puccini's directions exactly, not quickening the tempo too soon but keeping it rather *sostenuto* and without precipitating, 'Ecco fatto.' (It is done.) This should be very clearly pronounced, as though it were the simplest matter in the world.

The witnesses put their cross on the document, and the notary quickly stows away the papers in his portfolio. Then, still trembling with indignation over the disgraceful scene, he prepares to depart, but is arrested by the feeble voice from behind the bed curtains directing that he shall receive a hundred florins for his services and that the witnesses shall have twenty florins each, the whole to be paid by Zita from her own purse.

Enchanted by their rewards, all three of them would have liked to approach the bed and express their overwhelming gratitude. But the weak hand of the 'dying' man waves them away, and the terrified relations block their path.

With bitter reluctance Zita doles out the promised sums, and the notary and the two witnesses withdraw, expressing their appreciation in chorus: 'What a man! What a loss!'

It is to be noted that Rinuccio is cleverly kept out of all the most disgraceful plotting and quarrelling. After Schicchi's success in deceiving the doctor, Zita takes over the management of the plot and orders Rinuccio to run and fetch the notary. The young man obliges and therefore is not present during the shameful scene of offered bribes and the attempts to 'seduce' Schicchi. He is present again during the first part of the will and is amongst those to express thanks for the small bequests. Then he rejoins his Lauretta.

Possibly they listened at the keyhole, in order to follow events on which their happiness depends. After all, she is the daughter of a rogue, and he is the offspring of a bunch of greedy, ruthless vultures, so we must not expect the highest morals from them!

'Anyway, they are children,' Forzano told me. 'Come on, would you have rejected such a fortune?'

'I hope I would,' I replied, reflecting on the occasion in my own family when something curiously similar happened. We were the five children of my father and the favourites among my grandfather's six grandchildren. But when he died my father was abroad and his brothers (a sort of modern Donati group) took everything, with the complicity of a blind notary, assuring the witnesses that the dying (or was he already dead?) man had confirmed the bequests with a nod.

But, to return to the realm of comedy. Paralysed by their catastrophic loss, the Donati relatives remain silent and motionless at first. Then, as the door closes behind the notary and witnesses, they turn as one against Schicchi. He is, however, waiting for them, standing on the bed, armed with a big knotty stick which he always carried, and which he had with him when he entered. (I always took the precaution to hide it immediately on my first entry, after Zita had refused my outstretched hand and I had gone to the bed to inspect the corpse. As I said, 'Oh, he is dead,' I leaned forward – and deposited the stick. It is as well to remember that! There is so much action in this work that everything must be perfectly timed and organised.

The word, 'Ladro!' (Thief!) which Zita utters first, is pronounced with a long 'A', without changing the stifled, voiceless note . . . Then all together rush towards Schicchi, who deals out heavy blows right and left, halting their attack but not their screaming.

Then a state of wild pillaging breaks out, everyone taking whatever is to hand; even the sheets are dragged from the bed. Betto grabs his hen coop, and Schicchi does not interfere. But when Simone tries to drag away the large silver candlesticks Schicchi makes him drop them and run away. The little boy, forgotten in a corner (or in the room on the right, according to the score) falls in the middle of the great confusion, adding to it by running off with his still noisy toy.

Both men and women steal indiscriminately and rush for the staircase. But let me warn the cast to get out singly. Otherwise you will pile up at the door and, unable to squeeze out, be soundly beaten by Schicchi.

The stage clears, the screams of the women grow more distant, the final shouts of Schicchi, 'Via, via!' (Go, go!) are heard as the glass doors on the balcony swing back to disclose the happy Rinuccio and Lauretta silhouetted against the panorama of Florence. They hold hands and sing their wonderful final music without coming down-stage. Meanwhile Schicchi, a comic figure in his long nightgown and loaded down with the loot he has managed to retrieve from the fleeing Donatis, re-enters.

I always give the lovers time to finish their beautiful music before uttering the phrase 'La masnada fuggi' (The gang ran away) on the third beat, and only after that do I noisily throw the stolen goods on the floor and burst into a hearty laugh. I cut it short on suddenly seeing the children and, with the sweetest and most human expression allowed by the make-up, I turn to the audience and say: 'Ditemi, voi, Signori . . .' (Tell me, gentlemen . . .) Then, going towards the happy couple with open arms, I laugh and applaud.

These final phrases cost me many hours of patient rehearsal with Forzano, who was never satisfied. Neither was I! It is easy to write, *licenziando senza cantare* (playing it freely) – but to address the audience with complete conviction and spontaneity, without emphasis or theatrical exaggeration, is another matter. This phrase must be part of the frame of the work, provided by the colour of the voice and the intensity of the sound. It belongs to the opera and must be uttered in the same tempo.

One day I thought: 'Supposing I write the notes to suit myself?' I tried, but unsuccessfully, and I began to think that the comedy was going to end in tragedy so far as I was concerned. Finally I sat down at the piano and started to work it all out on a single note – the G flat major. Finally, as an extension of this idea, I spoke the famous words, avoiding all discordant sonority . . . and I think I succeeded.

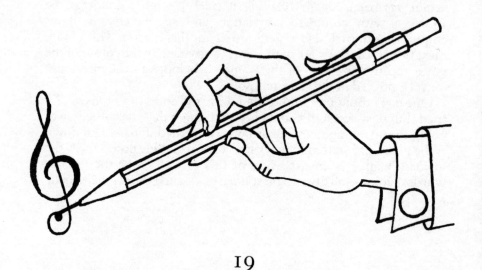

19

Some Composers of My Time

While opening this somewhat random selection of operatic windows for my readers I have inevitably cast some nostalgic glances through them myself. And now I have come to my last chapter I realise that for some time there have been insistent signals to me from figures I would not wish to ignore. These are the composers whom I have been privileged to know personally and in whose works I have appeared.

They do not include the giants of operatic composition – I was born a little too late for that! – but they do number among them some extremely distinguished composers, with a legitimate claim to be part of the wider operatic scene. In some cases I knew them well enough to discuss their works with them at some length. In others I knew them only passingly, but can perhaps give the personal glimpse which sometimes serves to transform a name on a printed page into a real figure.

My first acquaintance with many of them was in the studio of my father-in-law, Raffaello de Rensis, where the walls were covered with photographs of musicians and composers of all countries. I always looked at them with respectful curiosity, and one in particular attracted my attention – that of a priest.

The inscription read: 'Al karissimo amiko Raffaello de Rensis affettuoso rikordo del suo Pietro Piolti', and the date was as strange as the spelling, with its 'k' instead of 'c's. Then I discovered that Don Pietro Piolti was a fake signature, the real name being *Don Lorenzo Perosi*, and on further enquiry I was told the whole sad story.

It seemed that, as a young priest, Perosi had composed an opera *Romeo and Juliet*. But then he began to worry lest this 'profane' composition were against true religious principles, unfitting work for a priest. Haunted by thoughts that it might be a mortal sin for him to have put into music a drama of human passion, on a sudden mad impulse he threw the manuscript into the fire, destroying the work of many years.

Apparently after this his mind became sometimes vague. He would suffer from strange harmless manias such as reforming the alphabet and the calendar; and, denying his real identity, he insisted that his name was Pietro Piolti. Otherwise he was a delightful person with a phenomenal memory for certain things. He used to call me 'Mezzo Tedesco' (Half German), having heard that my mother came from an Austrian family!

He always dressed as a priest, was usually kind and spoke in a soft voice . . . but to rehearse in his presence was far from easy. He wrote a great number of oratorios, restoring to Italian sacred music a new vigour and light. I sang in several of these works, my special favourite being his *Resurrection of Christ*. But my first experience in connection with this was hair-raising.

I had already worked for five weeks at it with Maestro Bernardino Molinari, resident conductor at Santa Cecilia in Rome. Incidentally, he himself was not an easy man to work with and, although I was a close friend of the family, during rehearsals he became a tiger. In the *Resurrection* there is a most beautiful phrase written high up in the stratosphere which Jesus (my role) sings to Mary Magdalene: 'Noli me tangere . . . Nondum ascendi ad Patrem meum.' (Do not touch me. I have not yet ascended to my Father.)

It starts with a high F on the 'Noli', and Maestro Molinari, in spite of my clear, young voice, demanded a *mezza voce* up there – a *pianissimo* which the difficult *tessitura* made well nigh impossible.

If I managed it the first time that was not enough! I had to repeat it again and again just to make sure, so that in the end I was hoarse –

and stopped. A terrific scene ensued, in which he banged on the piano and shouted picturesque words of abuse. I was tempted to run away, but could see the sweet face of his wife, Mary Molinari, peering at me through the crack of the half-open door, her hands clasped imploringly as she silently begged me to stay and not irritate him further.

After having blown his top Molinari would become the nicest man imaginable . . . and I knew he was well aware that the composer could be very difficult and that all this was in preparation for a Scala performance. So I stayed, of course, and everything calmed down, and off we went to Milan next day, to be greeted enthusiastically by Don Lorenzo.

But, alas, at the first rehearsal he shouted at his 'Half German' that he did not understand what I was singing and that he had not written this music at all. I was petrified, and watched in horror as he tore two pages from the score and begged me for the love of God not to sing them in the performance. I promised (what else could I do?) and the rehearsal ended.

Terrified and dismayed, I had to be comforted by Maestro Molinari, who told me it was just one of those strange mental crises which came upon him sometimes. 'Don't worry,' he insisted. 'He will forget all about it.'

All very well for him, of course! I, poor trembling wretch, had to sing with Molinari on the podium and Don Lorenzo Perosi sitting in the front row. With my heart in my mouth I attacked the two rejected pages.

Nothing happened – and with general relief we completed the work. The shadow had passed and poor Don Lorenzo had forgotten all about it.

*

While speaking of priestly musicians, I immediately recall an entirely different one:

Don Licinio Refice was an extremely outgoing person. He seldom wore his cassock and spoke without inhibitions. (No qualms of conscience troubled *his* operatic leanings.) I met him at the Rome Opera, where I sang in two of his operas. He was what we call 'simpatico', a delightful man and a greater raconteur with a fund of stories which, I am bound to say, sometimes left me dumbfounded!

I sang Arsenio in his *Margherita da Cortona* replacing a colleague who had had a fall from his horse. And I also sang Tiburzio in his opera *Cecilia* in 1942. I have no very clear recollection of either work, and neither of them had a long run. The real claim to fame in the case of *Cecilia*, however, was that the first interpreter of the name part was none other than the great Claudia Muzio. Two very beautiful records of her singing in the role still exist.

Both operas were realised on a grand scale and the music was at least pleasant, but I think neither had enough strength to hold a place in the general repertoire.

★

About that time I also met *Franco Alfano*, and recall very well that great mane of white hair which imparted to him such a romantic air. Besides the ungrateful and demanding task of completing Puccini's *Turandot*, he wrote a number of good operas in his own right. To me far the best of these was *Resurrezione*, based on the novel by Tolstoi. I sang the role of Simonson in it and received from the Maestro nothing but encouragement and appreciation. It is not always easy to please the composer, mind you, and I remember this with grateful appreciation.

I loved the part. But, above all, it gave me the thrilling experience of being at the side of Giuseppina Cobelli, the great interpreter of Katiusha; a role which she invested with almost unbearing poignancy.

★

Now I come to a very good and special friend of mine, *Annibale Bizzelli*. Bibi to his friends, he was a Bohemian in the true sense of the term. Under cover of a careless, light-hearted manner, he was in fact a very fine musician and a most cultured man. In his youth he composed an opera, *Dr Oss*, which Maestro Serafin himself conducted at the San Carlo in Naples. It was a success with public and critics alike, and should have been the beginning of great things for him. But somehow – incorruptible and delightful though he was to his friends – his unstable ways hampered his musical career.

We remained friends to the end of his life, and I studied a lot of music with him, doing the 'refining' job, guided by his extraordinary musical taste. Most of the time we would seclude ourselves at Santa Severa, my summer home, and work there peacefully, preparing programmes and scores.

After composing operas, ballets and songs without much sign of success, he made his living mostly from composing music for films and from coaching, for which he was much sought after. He could have made a fortune coaching Mario Lanza in Rome, but could not put up with the singer's eccentric habit of going around in the nude all the time! He loved to work with Pia Tassinari, Ferrucio Tagliavini – and, he told me, myself. But his crowning glory was the tour with Toti dal Monte in the Orient; he would tell endless anecdotes about 'La Totina'.

He was a man of modest tastes, and his enchanting American wife, Alva, had to make do on next to nothing. Finally, she persuaded him to go to the States, where in no time a man of his experience and musicianship was kept busy from dawn to dusk – so much in demand that he was soon making a great deal of money. We thought with relief that now he must finally be happy. But not at all! Amid the glory of the skyscrapers he missed the familiar little square with its friendly 'local', where he would sit for hours on end with a small cup of coffee, a glass of water and a newspaper. He fell seriously ill, and his poor wife had to bring him back to his familiar surroundings and take care of him for a long time while he recuperated and eventually became once more his delightful useless self.

*

Enter *Ermanno Wolf-Ferrari*! A powerful open white Austro-Daimler containing two people dressed all in white, with a huge Great Dane sitting upright in the back, came to a halt in front of the de Rensis residence. The Wolf-Ferraris had arrived for their customary spring visit – and quite a spectacular appearance they made too. Both were tall and slender and with their huge dog made a sensational group.

It was a great joy for the whole family, including me (though in the beginning I was just half-family, being no more than a fiancé). The Maestro and Papa Raffaello were very fond of each other and would sit talking in the studio, Papa Raffaello seated at the desk and the Maestro 'stravaca', stretched out full length in an armchair which is now in my home.

Mimi Wolf-Ferrari was much attached to Mama Giuseppina, and so their visit was always the pleasantest of events. To Tilde and Franca the Maestro was 'Barbazio' (Uncle) and he immediately christened me 'Novizzo' (the promised bridegroom). He would always speak his Venetian dialect unless some official occasion required otherwise.

When Tilde and I were married he was her chief witness or 'testimonio'. But he promptly called us back from our brief honeymoon because he wanted me to sing his new *Canzoniere Italiano*. It is a lovely collection of songs on Tuscan popular rhymes. Some of them, for baritone, he dedicated to me (the Novizzo!) in lovely words surrounded by little flowers:

'Questi sono i fiori che dovrebbero nascere dalla gioia al caro Tito' and, on another page, 'Altri fiori per lui.' (These are the flowers which should blossom from joy – to dear Tito . . . More flowers for him.)

Sometimes we would meet in Venice, and there again the fine tall couple made everyone turn and comment. But the one who really drew most attention was the Great Dane, looking even bigger among the small 'calles' and bridges of Venice. Nothing could restrain a Venetian at such a sight. They would cry, 'Varda, varda sto can, el pare un védelo!' (Oh, look! look at this dog. He's as big as a calf!)

Ermanno Wolf-Ferrari died in Venice – the Venice he had so often extolled in song. A long procession of gondolas followed the one which contained his bier, with the choir from the Fenice singing, 'Bondi, Venezia cara, Bondi Venezia mia . . . Veneziani sioria . . .' (Hello, dear Venice! Hello, my Venice! . . . Venetians, your servant!) It was a last salute to his beloved Venice, taken from his opera *Il Campiello* (The Little Square). The people lined the canals and bridges and sang and cheered him as the gondola passed on its way. An unforgettable occasion which one would like to think he himself enjoyed.

He was a fine musician, with characteristically elegant instrumentation, and a delicate touch with which he turned many of the Goldoni comedies into successful musical works. I myself sang in *I Quattro Rusteghi* (*The Four Curmudgeons*) and *Il Segreto di Susanna* (*Susanna's Secret*), both comedies, and also in *I Gioielli della Madonna* (*The Jewels of the Madonna*), a strongly dramatic opera set in the middle of the last century in Naples among the 'camorristi' (the gangsters) who to this day go happily on their way!

My role was that of the Boss, a 'guappe' (impudent criminal), arrogant and with a sort of outrageous charm. This role, like those of the soprano and tenor, is very strong; and to work with the Maestro (delightful though he was) was hell. To him perfection was merely the starting point, and I would leave the rehearsal room exhausted, voiceless and empty-headed. Yet when he lifted his hands from the piano and looked at me with his good, heart-warming smile, I was ready to start all over again if he wanted it.

As a matter of fact, my actual debut at the Royal Opera in Rome was (all unexpectedly!) in his *Le Donne Curiose* (*The Curious Women*). It was hastily thrust upon me owing to the sudden indisposition of another singer; but with the unstinted help of my colleagues I carried the ordeal to a triumphant conclusion – the memory of which warms my heart to this day.

Years later I succeeded in bringing *The Four Curmudgeons* to the Teatro Nacional de San Carlos in Lisbon. There was a sparkling cast including Italo Tajo and Tagliavini, and an intelligent producer who left us free to express ourselves. As a result, in spite of the Venetian dialect, the audience thoroughly enjoyed the brilliant comedy. The performance was good and we also enjoyed ourselves enormously, presenting opera as theatre. I was pleased that the San Carlo repeated the work the next season.

★

I have vivid and precious memories of all the many composers I met during my long career, even when my involvement with them was not extensive. Among the most celebrated of these was *Italo Montemezzi*, whom I remember with great pleasure. When the Rome Opera opened the season with his *La Nave* (*The Ship*), I sang the very smallest part, that of the helmsman, and had to remain perched on the prow during the whole of the first act. It seemed a very long act to me, and I could hardly wait to come down and run away, so I saw the impressive figure of Montemezzi only from afar. But a few years later when – so they said – I had shown some gift for the stage, I was assigned a delicate task.

My good friend and mentor Pino Donati, then Director of the Bologna Communale, asked me to sing in *L'Amore dei Tre Re* (*The Love of Three Kings*). Maestro Montemezzi – looking to me rather more like a successful business or professional man than an artist – wanted to have someone who would give more character to the role of Manfred, who tended to appear somewhat sheepish in a less than heroic part.

On the strength of such authority – and rather flattered, to tell the truth – I studied my new part very hard. But I disliked Manfred, and I did not very much like his music either. None of it seemed to fit me. So I went to Bologna and frankly explained my feelings and my my fear that I could not do justice to the opera.

Donati was very understanding, and Maestro Montemezzi – formal but kind – admitted that I should be running a real risk of damaging my young voice with such a strenuous role . . . So I was released – and I never sang Manfred.

★

Then there was *Ludovico Rocca*, an excellent composer. He had his moment of glory during the reign of Serafin, who presented both his important operas. A terrific cast, made up of all the young singers of the company, performed the works very well indeed, *Dibuk* in 1938 and *Monte Ivnor* in 1939 – in which Gino Bechi shone particularly.

Maestro Rocca was shy and retiring and never approached any of us except through the conductor. *Dibuk* had a real triumph, and we

were all very happy after so much rehearsal. The second performance, as everyone knows, is always much more relaxed – and
anything can happen. Well, there we were, a group of high-spirited
young people on the stage, singing and dancing: 'Ballo tondo,
buoni Ebrei, ballo tondo, ballo tondo . . .' (Dance around, good
Jews, dance around, dance around.)

Suddenly, because of some silly slip in the wording, one of us
started to laugh, and in his desperate efforts to suppress his amusement began puffing in such a funny way that we all found ourselves
copying him until we laughed unrestrainedly. Maestro Serafin,
without even glancing at the stage, went on conducting until the act
ended. Then, when he came up from the podium, we were all
drawn up a little anxiously to make way for him. His face was like
thunder and as he passed he looked fixedly at each one in turn and
said between his teeth, 'Vergogna!' (Shame on you!)

Somehow the joke had lost all its flavour. But at least Maestro
Rocca had already left and so was spared this incident. When war
broke out, being a Jew, he was retired from the directorship of the
Turin Conservatoire where he had studied and which he had always
loved and he went into obscurity. But his work will always remain,
and I have heard with the utmost satisfaction that his operas are now
being revived.

★

Another composer whose works Maestro Serafin put on with casts
of younger singers was *Ezio Carabella*, who had a great success with
a lovely ballet *Volti la Lanterna* (Turn Your Lantern) and was then
encouraged to try his hand at an opera. This was *Il Candeliere* (*The
Candlestick*) from de Musset's work of that name. We had a whale
of a time, bursting with pride that Maestro Serafin entrusted us
with such important roles.

In *The Candlestick* I was a swashbuckling Captain Clavaroche,
with engaging moustaches and a brilliant costume. Carabella
laughed so much at my portrayal of his character and was so happy
about it that we became good friends. He loved to discuss his
characters with us, especially with the leading lady – understand-
ably so since she was the starry-eyed Margherita Carosio.

★

Ildebrando Pizzetti was something very special. He had an intensely
personal musical language – beautiful *recitar cantando* with long
extended phrases that always fascinated me. At the Rome Opera I
sang a small role in his *Lo Straniero* (*The Foreigner*), in which the
great bass aria – sung at that time by Giacomo Vaghi – is inexpress-

ibly beautiful. I also sang the Bishop in *Fra Gherardo*, and felt myself
invested with tremendous authority while the divided chrous
stormed with amazing contrast.

Maestro Pizzetti was a small man, shy and fragile, with a soft
voice and a faulty R which gave to his speech a particular sound.
One could not imagine how such a frail man came to choose great
biblical tragedies and impart to his music such enormous strength.
When he was really old he yet produced *L'Assassinio nella Cattedrale*,
a work of immense power.

As a very young man I went to the opening performance of
Pizzetti's opera *Orseolo*. By now I rather fancied myself as part of La
Scala. I had still never appeared on that illustrious stage, it is true,
but in my own estimation at any rate I could at least cut a
distinguished figure amongst the audience. So, on this particular
night, I was sitting in a box, very elegant in white tie and tails,
surveying the Milanese smart set assembled in the opera house and
occasionally waving a gracious hand to one acquaintance or
another. Then into this scene of glory stepped a disquieting figure,
who informed me that I was required backstage. Surprised and a
trifle disturbed, I followed him as he led me to a maestro standing in
the wings, who informed me with brutal brevity: 'Signor So-and-
so is ill, so you will have to take his place.'

At this terrible announcement the stars fell out of my brilliant
night sky and darkness enveloped me. I protested faintly that I
knew nothing but was immediately cut short. There was nothing to
it, I was told: only one easy phrase, all on one note, as I had to
announce to Orseolo: 'La Signoria del Doge e del Sena-a-a-ato.'

I was sent upstairs to be costumed and made up, and all the way I
sang under my breath on my one note: 'La Signoria del Doge e del
Sena-a-a-ato.' In a corridor I met what seemed to me to be a
wonderful creature, regally dressed and of imposing physique,
trying his voice up and down. He looked at me with a patronising
air and asked: 'Are you the young man who is going to sing the
Herald? You are? Then come here, my boy, and I will make you up.
I will do your face because you have no experience in these matters.'

Then he sat me down before a mirror and began scratching my
face with the most frightful old sticks of make-up. They were worn
right down to the metal foil in which they were wrapped, so that in
no time my wretched face did have colour on it, but mostly my own
blood. Looking perfectly horrible, I was then tried out for the
enormous costume. At that time I was thin like that famous page to
the Duke of Norfolk, so they had to wrap the dreadful thing round
me, securing it with safety-pins in such haste that they pinned in bits
of me too. All this, however, was nothing compared to the glory of

singing at La Scala so, setting my teeth, I accepted all the anguish and made my way to the stage, still repeating my single phrase to myself.

'Who are *you*?' asked the maestro in the wings.

'Gobbi,' I whispered back, divided between pride and terror. 'I'm the replacement for the Herald.'

'Well, keep quiet and wait until I tell you to go,' he replied. At that moment I saw my great man from upstairs who had so condescendingly scratched make-up on my face. But now he was incredibly transformed. Trembling and crossing himself and kissing holy medals before his entrance on stage, he was no longer a demi-god: just a terrified human being.

This metamorphosis in one who had seemed so sure of himself increased my own fears, and I kept on asking anxiously: 'When is my turn, Maestro?'

'Wait,' the good man told me reassuringly. 'I'll tell you when to go.'

But he had no idea that I was totally ignorant of anything concerning a performance and had never set foot on a stage before. Consequently I knew nothing about the timing of an entrance. When he told me, 'Go!' I leapt forward like a runner at the sound of the starting pistol, flung open the door and, ignoring the great Tancredi Pasero singing his aria, shouted as loud as I could 'La Signoria del Doge e del Sena-a-a-ato' at least half a minute too soon.

Pasero stopped dead, his mouth open, while the other great man turned a look of fury upon me. Maestro Pizzetti, who was conducting his own work on his important occasion, nearly had a stroke, while the prompter, leaning from his box, hissed: 'You idiot! Who sent you here? Go to hell!'

I was utterly bewildered by the insults and furious looks and had no idea what to do next. But somehow I got myself off the stage, forcing my way through the Signoria who at long last were processing solemnly on to the scene.

My humiliation and sense of injustice were total as I made my way back to the dressing-rooms, divested myself of my elephantine costume and removed at least some of the make-up which disfigured my face. I dragged on my own clothes again just anyhow – not at all as the handsome young cavalier in the box had worn them – jammed on my hat at a desperate angle and left the famous Scala, telling myself that if this were a sample of an operatic appearance I had had enough of it.

My own happiest memories of Maestro Pizzetti are in Siena, where I sang the world premiere of his beautiful *Epithalamium*

(*Wedding Hymn*) in the gardens of the Palazzo Chigi Saracini. We talked together between rehearsals, and my father-in-law interviewed him. Meanwhile his young son Ippolito strolled around carrying a hawk!

I always wanted to sing his beautiful song *I Pastori* ('*The Shepherds*') with the words by D'Annunzio, but there was no way of transposing it. Every time we met he promised he would make the small change necessary; a small change indeed, but it had to be made by himself. Only somehow it never came about. Later I would not have wanted anyone else to arrange it – and so in the end I never sang it. But the Siena period lingers in my mind as an idyllic interlude.

★

Umberto Giordano was not only the celebrated composer everyone knows. He was also a very imposing and handsome man, who had only to appear for everyone else to be overlooked. He knew it very well, and had created the right voice to go with such a person. His conversation had a rather professorial tone, but was not haughty. A great charmer, he was a long-time friend of Pietro Mascagni, and they were kept pretty busy covering up for each other's gallant adventures in order to escape the wrath of their respective wives.

Maestro Giordano was very nice to me and I must say very patient too. I had already sung in his *Fedora* at La Scala, Venice and Rome, and now I very much wanted to sing in *Andrea Chenier*.

'You must sing in *Fedora*,' he used to say, 'which could have been written just for you.'

But I still pestered him because I wanted to sing Gérard in *Chenier*.

'You are too young,' he would say.

'Maestro, I've already sung a number of roles more difficult than Gérard,' I protested, 'and I've sung in *Fedora* so many times –'

'So you're no longer interested in it,' he cut in.

'But, Maestro, I . . .'

'All right, all right. Get to work and you will sing in the next *Chenier*.'

And so I did – but a few years later.

★

Pietro Mascagni I hardly knew. I used to see him during rehearsals, of course, when I sang Franz in *Lodoletta* and the Rabbi in *L'Amico Fritz*. He looked tired, but still had the fire of his music in his eyes. His voice was high pitched, with its Tuscan accent, his fund of stories unfailing and extremely witty. It was a true Tuscan wit for which he was very well known.

I never sang in *Cavalleria Rusticana*, not feeling right for Alfio, a character which my colleagues tended to make a heavy and loud sort of chap. But I did record it. Keeping in mind the innate Sicilian dignity, and wanting to pay my tribute to the memory of the great Maestro, I represented Alfio as a decent man, full of humanity but jealous of his honour – just singing the beautiful music with the right meaning, without noise or shouting.

★

Mascagni, Giordano and of course above all Puccini, together created a sort of post-Verdian opera which continued the great heritage. And not at all unworthy to stand in their company was *Franceso Cilea*, with whom I had a very warm and somewhat touching friendship, although it started with what might well have been a stage disaster.

During the 1941 season I was singing the role of the shepherd Baldassarre in Cilea's *L'Arlesiana* when something went wrong with the electrical system which raised and lowered the curtain. Instead of remaining down throughout the orchestral prelude, as is usual, up went the curtain on the first bars, disclosing not only the scene but me too! There I was on my knees with my back to the audience, smoothing down the floor covering under the ricketty bench on which I would have to sit when the action began.

Hissing sounds of warning from the wings informed me that something was wrong, and I realised that I was in full view of the audience and something had to be done immediately.

With slow, weary movements suitable to the old shepherd I got to my feet and sat down on the bench. Then, with my big, multi-coloured handkerchief, I signalled to the Innocente (the retarded boy), who was also not ready to perform, that he should come and crouch at my feet. I had him pick up my pipe – which I had purposely dropped – and made him sit near me on the grass. Then I moved around, collecting the other children now sent to me from the wings by the producer.

In short, I tried to fill the time in harmony with the music without overdoing things, and sailed smoothly along to the end of the prelude. Meanwhile, Maestro de Fabritiis, reversing the usual procedure, took his cue from me. Dispensing with the pause for applause which usually greeted the end of the prelude, he went straight into the first scene while I continued my new role of mime.

The audience had no idea that anything had gone wrong. But Maestro Cilea, bless him, was the happiest man alive! Trembling with emotion, the dear old man, with touching insistence, kept on telling everyone, 'What a splendid idea, indeed a splendid idea!'

I had the privilege of travelling with him almost every day on the street car on our way to the Opera, and he made this 'surprise happening' the subject of long and pleasant discussions on how much one should plan in detail what one offers to an audience.

I sang a number of times in this opera in Italy – both the baritone roles Metifio and Baldassarre – and often included in concert programmes the sad but lovely fairy tale of the goat and the wolf which Baldassare tells to the Innocente. It needs long breath and sustained notes, but the *tessitura* is comfortable for a baritone.

My great colleague and rival, Gino Bechi, and I had a sort of competition between us as to who could sing this aria better, and even to this day I have the stupendous voice of Bechi in my ears.

The old shepherd tells the story, imitating the voice of the wolf, to amuse the poor simple boy who is trembling for the sad fate of the goat. Cilea is a gentle and delicate composer, his melodies extending smoothly as he describes the sunset, nightfall and finally the sunrise as it touches the poor Innocente, who seems to react and understand a little. His music is full of compassion, and among the great interpreters who were happy to sing it were, besides Bechi, Tito Schipa, Beniamino Gigli and Gianna Pederzini.

L'Arlesiana (the Girl from Arles) is a woman of bad reputation. Everybody talks about her – but she herself never appears. Which reminds me of a charmingly ironical story in connection with this non-existent character.

One day when I was in the office of Maestro de Fabritiis at the Rome Opera the telephone rang, and I could see from his expression in the first few minutes that a delicate situation had arisen. In actual fact the caller was a politician or government official of some importance and was asking, pressingly and with some authority, that a small role be found for Miss So-and-so, his protégée.

'Yes, Your Excellency,' I heard de Fabritiis say. 'Certainly, Your Excellency . . . I see . . . Yes . . . Well, please ask her to come and see me. I shall do my best . . . but you know the Season is already in progress.'

The baby doll appeared next day and gave an excruciating audition. Then de Fabritiis, after making sure that she did not know the opera *L'Arlesiana* asked her to be ready in the title role of that opera by Cilea.

Drastic perhaps. But effective.

L'Arlesiana is almost forgotten now, but Cilea's *Adriana Lecouvreur* survives partly because it was beloved by several famous prima donnas – and still provides a most attractive vehicle for a really talented singing actress.

The baritone role of Michonnet, the shy, retiring sort of stage manager and general factotum who is hopelessly in love with the famous Adriana, is beautifully conceived. His monologue as he watches her, worshipping her and following every phrase, prompting her under his breath from the wings, is deeply moving. It is really a lovely recitative over an equally lovely melody, which ends in a short, half stifled aria.

I loved the role, and was already pretty well known when I came to sing it at the Rome Opera with Maria Caniglia. The Maestro was immensely gratified, saying that he appreciated what he was kind enough to describe as 'a great artist' consenting to take 'a small part'. But Michonnet is not at all a small part. It is subtle, moving and requires a very rich palette of vocal colouring.

Nevertheless, dear, modest Cilea paid me many affectionate compliments, marvelling with a sort of generous naïveté at my make-up and bearing, by which I contrived to change a big man into a slightly bent, retiring person.

Since Michonnet knew so well how Adriana should sing her great aria, perhaps I can press my role a little farther and give a few hints to aspiring Adrianas!

When Adriana is addressing the Prince and the Abbot, who are extravagantly applauding her while she rehearses a dramatic phrase, do not stifle or 'pinch' your tone in an effort to produce a *pianissimo* which was never required by the composer. She is gracefully and modestly parrying their praise, claiming she is only 'umile ancella deo genil creator' (the humble handmaid of the creator's genius). It is simply sung *andante con calma*. The double *pp* required for really soft singing comes in the finale, where Maestro Cilea asks for 'un fil di voce' (a thread of sound).

There are many other indications which are quite explicit and give the singer every opportunity to express herself. These should be followed carefully, for Cilea was the last person to want unauthorised excesses. These so easily harden into 'tradition' in the wrong sense of the word, and are merely bad habits perpetuated.

★

If I had to name someone who was the complete antithesis of the modest, appreciative Maestro Cilea I think my candidate would undoubtedly be *Georgio Federico Ghedini* who made an opera with the same title from Max Beerbohm's story of 'The Happy Hypocrite' *L'Ipocrita Felice*. He had a great reputation as a serious and cultured composer, but I doubt if he ever enjoyed any real popularity. Anyway, the opera was performed at the Piccola Scala with myself in the lead as Lord Inferno, the excellent mezzo being Anna Maria Canali and the accomplished director Margherita Wallman.

I must say that it was we who created the show visually speaking, for that side of it had hardly been indicated. In one scene, I was sitting in a theatre box as Lord Inferno with the Lady (Canali) and, at a certain moment, took a hand mirror and held it before my face as though looking at my reflection . . . But when I put it down again my make-up was totally changed. The audience gasped aloud in one long, 'O-o-oh!' It was really enormously effective.

Well, the performance was certainly very chic, rather snobbish, and absolutely suited to the kind of audience! As for Maestro Ghedini, he never showed up to utter half a word of appreciation for the many weeks of hard work which had *made* his opera for him. He must have wished to remain faithful to his reputation as the coolest man on earth.

*

Someone very different was *Riccardo Zandonai*, who came from much the same part of Italy as I do, though I met him first when he came down from Pesaro to visit my in-laws, who knew him well. In no time he and I were talking in Venetian dialect and enjoying each other's company. There was, I found, a simplicity about him – almost an innocence – which was extremely engaging, and in marked contrast to his strongly personal, powerful music.

With the possible exception of his *Francesca da Rimini*, a really splendid work, his beautiful operas, even now, do not rank as popular favourites, for which I am sorry. Even more do I regret that the baritone role in *Francesca*, that of Gianciotto, was much too strenuous for my voice. So, apart from a strange character in *I Cavalieri di Ekebu* – in which I merely crossed the stage in company with Giuseppe Taddei – I never sang anything by Zandonai.

*

Ottorino Respighi I also met in the de Rensis home – and then in his beautiful villa in Rome, where his wife Elsa entertained most hospitably. The whole musical world gathered there, and Elsa – charming and intelligent hostess that she was – even provided dancing room for the young people.

Maestro Respighi wanted me to sing his *Belfugor* (The Devil), which I believe would have been a role to suit me. But at that time the reigning Devil was Mariano Stabile, and for some reason or other I never did get round to singing in this opera.

I had to content myself with the powerful song *Nebbie* (Mists), the words by the Sardinian poetess Ada Negri. It is a wonderful drama in miniature which I sang in concerts all over the world and also recorded.

*

Having rather early acquired a reputation for 'creating characters' I was over the years often given new operas, and very glad indeed I was to perform them. They gave me the opportunity to refine my work and to meet the composers, and in so doing I entered a new world and could understand the works better. In this connection two Neapolitan composers come to mind, although they were strongly contrasted. The first was *Mario Persico*, an extremely gentlemanly person with whom I struck up a warm friendship which enriched the rapport I felt with his work. I used to visit him in both Naples and Rome and found this cultured man an ideal companion with whom to discuss dreams and hopes for the future.

It was in Rome that his opera *La Locandiera* (The Innkeeper), based on the play by Goldoni, was presented for the first time. The cast was splendid: Mafalda Favero, Ferrucio Tagliavini, Mariano Stabile – and there was a nice brilliant role for me. Nevertheless, throughout the rehearsals and the first performance poor Maestro Persico was to be descried in the wings in agonies of anxiety, looking very much like an expectant father, but I am glad to say that in the end the performance was worthy of the lovely opera.

★

The other Neapolitan composer whom I knew very well was *Jacopo Napoli*, for whom a brilliant future was predicted when his opera *Il Tesoro* (*The Treasure*) was given in Rome. I was summoned about five days before the first performance, the original singer having fallen ill, I suppose. On the principle of always helping a theatre in need, I swallowed the role in a few hours – and my overwhelming reward was to have the composer say afterwards, 'Tito, you just made the opera by creating such a splendid character study.'

To tell the truth, I had great fun with that role! I was to be a little old man, a story-singer, and I made myself up to be small and lovable, with a few teeth missing and round glasses low down on my nose. It really is one of the joys of our profession when we can change our whole personality. For myself, I always found it absolutely intoxicating.

★

On various previous occasions I have spoken of *Agostino Zanchetta* as my valued mentor. Hearing me – as a boy at a tennis party – bawling some popular song he looked out of his window and called: 'Who is that singing?' I said it was I, and he immediately summoned me and made me sing for him. Then he informed me positively that I was a baritone (and fortunate is the singer who is accurately told by a knowledgeable person what type of voice he or she possesses), and he gave it as his opinion that perhaps I should consider the possibility of singing as a profession.

Barone Zanchetta was a most distinguished musician and composer. Spending as I did many of my vacations in his hospitable villa, I often heard him at work and was constantly amazed by his extraordinary keyboard technique. It was a technique which stayed with him to the age of ninety, and was such an integral part of him that even in his operas his music displayed pianistic features.

He was essentially a romantic composer, with many good works to his credit. But, as a nobleman living in his secluded paradise, he had few occasions to enter the world of professional music. His output included songs, piano pieces, oratorios and operas, in one of which I had the real pleasure of singing – in the critical city of Reggio Emilia. The opera was *David* and my role was that of King Saul.

Many years later the city of Bassano organised for him a beautiful celebration. I gave a short talk, and some of my students presented a concert of his works. Mani Mekler and Louis Manikas (both now well known singers in their own right) sang items from *David*, and the conductor Baldo Poldic played the Barone's piano concerto most beautifully. It was a very happy occasion for us all – and for me especially it was a most moving drawing together of threads from the past, the present – and the future.

★

To take one step from the Barone Zanchetta to my next composer would seem to require the seven-league boots of the fairy story, so widely do they differ in person and work.

Bruno Barilli was feared by every performer as the most ferocious and unpredictable of critics. Endowed with great culture, an immensely talented pen, and very questionable taste – he was always dirty and shabbily dressed at a time when these habits had not become fashionable and were greatly despised – he led a disorderly life, sitting by the hour in coffee houses, eating a lot of pastries, and scratching his great mane of hair with his dirty hands.

But he certainly could write, and people in the musical world had to put up with him as he was. He had been a marvellous travel correspondent in his time, sending absorbing, colourful reports from abroad, but music was a touchy subject with him and he would slash the most famous conductors, singers and instrumentalists without mercy. In short, he was – and he is not the only one! – a disappointed composer turned music critic.

Nevertheless, the Rome Opera put on his *Emiral*, and I sang in it.

He hardly spared a glance for us poor things, struggling with his music, but I do recollect that the story was an Oriental one and that I wore a splendid costume with bejewelled turban, scimitar and all. I looked terrific. It is unnecessary to add that his review was very good.

★

To turn to *Gian Francesco Malipiero* is to go from the almost ridiculous to the occasionally sublime. It took the general public a long time to give him even a grudging acceptance, especially as an opera composer. But he is a great musician and I have learned to love much of his work. His reputation abroad was very considerable; certainly greater than in his own country.

In 1934, when I was a young student and more or less engaged to Tilde, I was invited to the world premiere of *La Favola del Figlio Cambiato* (*The Fable of the Changing Son*) by Pirandello, with music by Malipiero. It was a marvellous occasion, the scene in the house as dazzling as that on the stage. The ladies were richly gowned with splendid jewels, the gentleman sporting white ties and all which that implies: not at all democratic, of course, but decidedly more attractive than an audience where each one dresses according to his or her own queer whim.

As I have said, Malipiero was not popular with the audience, and some of them had come prepared to disturb the performance. The curtain had scarcely risen before groans and signs of disapproval started. Whistles pierced the air, noses were vociferously blown and so on. Anything, in fact, to drown what was passing on the stage and demonstrate the superior intelligence of the audience.

When the end of the performance had with difficulty been reached pandemonium broke out afresh, and people seated in the stalls rose to express their loud disapproval of – not the public but the composer. He, however, having sat calm and erect in a box throughout, ignoring the turmoil, now also stood up, applauding vociferously and shouting, 'Bravo, Malipiero!' at the top of his voice.

I thought, 'What courage, by golly!' and I liked him from that instant.

He certainly was an eccentric, living in his beautiful villa at Asolo, surrounded by animals of all kinds. He insisted on – and obtained from the priest – permission to take his dog to Mass. 'He is one of God's creatures,' he declared, 'and he understands all right.'

An extraordinary man, he had found his own way of life and insisted on living it: and although people came from all over the world to try to meet him, he would receive only those he liked or his personal friends. I regard it as a compliment that I earned his sympathy, at least as a performer.

I sang in his opera *Ecuba*, which did not cause so much scandal, and several times the lovely *Sette Canzoni*. Also I was privileged to sing in the very first performance of his beautiful mystical *San Francesco*, an oratorio based on the lovable Saint of Assisi. The last thing I sang of his was *Il Finto Arlecchino* (*The False Harlequin*) a light affair with little real substance to it.

At one point he took me aside and asked, 'What do you think of it?'

'Well,' I began, somewhat embarrassed, 'hm . . .'

'You are perfectly right,' he said promptly. 'It's nothing. But it amuses me.'

Naturally all the composers mentioned in this chapter were Italian, for they belong to the first years of my career. To know them in any degree was an immensely valuable experience, enabling me to learn how to tackle so many different kinds of music. The traditional barriers were down. I was treading fresh paths and, although I did not know it then – I was heading for *Wozzeck* in the not too distant future.

★

I wish I could end by asserting that one of the most gifted composers of that period was a young chap called Tito Gobbi. But truth forces me to say that the most I ever achieved in that direction was to act in a sort of advisory capacity when in 1949 I took part in a British film, *The Glass Mountain*. Fortunately this proved to be extremely popular, and even today you can sometimes catch it on American television around some ungodly hour like three o'clock in the morning.

The cast included Dulcie Gray and Michael Denison, two excellent British performers, and the young Valentina Cortese, who was later to become a most impressive actress. I myself had a splendid time impersonating an opera singer turned partisan.

The music was to be supplied by Nino Rota, a successful composer and a delightful man; indeed, when he was writing the music for my part he displayed the patience of a saint. I did not really like his first attempt and ventured to direct him to the songs of our mountains, which were completely in character for the story of the film. Especially did I introduce him to the one called '*La Montanara*' (Mountain Song). I sat beside him at the piano, suggesting, requesting, demanding this or that phrase – and in the end he composed the lovely music which is still popular today.

From Cortina in the mountains, where the film was shot, we

went to Venice to record at the Fenice, with Franco Ferrara conducting. While he was having a look at the score we were joined by several good friends of ours with whom we talked until the rehearsal started. Then suddenly, in the middle of a *fortissimo* passage from the orchestra, Franco Ferrara, who had a phenomenally fine ear, declared that the flautist had something wrong with the mouthpiece of his instrument.

Rota said, 'You must be crazy! How could you hear it?'

Giudo Cantelli – the young musical prodigy whose life was to end so soon and so tragically – was equally incredulous.

Then Massimo Amphiteatroff, the celebrated cellist, joined us and supported our view that there could be nothing wrong.

Finally we had a bet on it. Franco Ferrara called over the flautist – and in no time discovered a little split in the mouthpiece of the instrument!

We were all astounded, and Rota decided this called for a celebration. So presently off we went to dinner – Rota, Ferrara, Cantelli, Amphiteatroff and myself – a most congenial group, and all of us in a suitably romantic mood as later we strolled through the narrow streets and across the bridges of moonlit Venice.

Finally we fetched up at the Piazza San Marco, the Mecca of all strollers in Venice, and paused to admire the front of the Basilica, where the moon now picked out every detail. Then I suggested we should go to the other side of the Square, from which I promised them a magical sight.

We all walked over and sat down on the low steps. And there before us, indeed like a magical, almost diaphanous vision, the Basilica seemed to be floating in the moonlight on a bank of low-lying mist.

Presently, who should come along but the great Italian actor Memo Benassi, who promptly joined us. And there we sat, talking idly for hours. Such hours! Never to be repeated, but also never to be forgotten. Like jewels set in the crown of one's youth.

By the time we realised that the divine mist was chilling us to the bone the first light of dawn was breaking.

And by that light I see now, through the last of my windows, that the many figures who appeared in this chapter are no longer there.

Have they vanished into oblivion?

Some of those about whom I have written – yes. And perhaps deservedly so since their claim to lasting fame is not a powerful one. Others retain a certain place because of one or two works, or the odd aria made famous by celebrated exponents. But there remains much of very real value which is totally ignored today by the many busy opera houses and companies scattered over the world.

Instead, we are treated to second-rate mutilations of acknowledged masterpieces, presented with questionable taste and little musical knowledge. On these strange abortions much money seems to be lavished by companies who constantly plead poverty.

Would it not, I venture to ask, be more sensible, more exciting and indeed more profitable to revive from time to time some of these neglected works of genuine merit, even if they are not in the top flight?

In this sense too there are many windows to be opened. And, with my hand on my heart – and on this book – I can truly claim that window-opening has a fascination beyond all expectations. Try it! Throw back a few of those shutters and follow the one word of advice offered by that guide in San Gimignano –

'LOOK!'

Index

Adorno (in *Simone Boccanegra*) 110, 111, 113–15, 123
Adriana Lecouvreur 248–9
Adriana (the character) 249
Alcindoro (in *La Bohème*) 180–1, 185
Alfano, Franco 239
Alfio (in *Cavalleria Rusticana*) 246–7
Alfredo (in *La Traviata*) 102, 105, 106, 107
Almaviva (Lindoro in *The Barber*); in *The Barber* 41, 43–9; in *Figaro* 50–2, 54–6; character of 53, 55, 56
Almaviva, Countess (in *Figaro*) 51, 53–6
Amelia (in *Boccanegra*) 110, 111–12, 114, 117–20; shields her father 110, 114, 118–19; duet with Simone 118; duet with Adorno 119
Amelia's personal attendant (in *Boccanegra*) 111–12
Amico Fritz, L' 246
Amore dei Tre Re, L' 242
Amphiteatroff, Massimo 255
Andrea *see* Fiesco
Andrea Chenier 246
Andreolli (*comprimario*) 20
Angelotti, Roman Consul 196, 197
Angelotti (in *Tosca*) 201–2, 206
Anna (in *Don Giovanni*) 33–4, 35, 36
Annina (in *La Traviata*) 105, 107
Antonio (in *Figaro*) 54
Aremberg, Countess (in *Don Carlo*) 129, 136
Arlecchino (in *Pagliacci*) 21, 173, 175
Arlesiana, L' 247
Arnoldo (in *William Tell*) 59–61, 64, 65
Arsenio (in *Margherita de Cortona*) 238–9
Assassinio nella Cattedrale, L' 244

Attavanti, Marchesa, portrait of 209
Attavanti, Marquis 203
Autori, sings in *Rigoletto* 80
'Ave Maria' 18

Baldassarre (in *L' Arlesiana*) 247–8
Balfe, Michael 157
Barbarina (in *Figaro*) 52, 55
Barber of Seville, The 38–50, 53, 84; 'La Calunnia' 22, 42, 44, 45; Sergeant in 22; vocal technique for 38; films of 38–9, 40; liberties taken with 40; recitatives in 41, 44; played during the War 41; and Figaro's cavatina 39–40, 41, 42, 45; Gobbi first hears 42; vocal challenge of 'cunning little fox' 46; shaving scene in 48; storm 48; comic masterpiece 49–50
Barbier de Seville (Beaumarchais' play) 40, 50
Barbiere di Siviglia, Il (Paisiello's opera) 50
Barbieri, Fedora 130, 161
Bardolph (in *Falstaff*) 159, 160–1, 164, 166
Barilli, Bruno 252–3
Bartolo: in *The Barber* 22, 40–9; 'La calunnia' 22, 42, 44; in *Figaro* 52, 54, 55
Baseggio, Cesco 40
Basilio (in *The Barber*) 22, 44–9; played by Neri 84
Basiola, sings in *Rigoletto* 80
Bassi, Calisto 57
Bayerische National Staatsoper, Munich 219–21
beards 26
Beaumarchais, Pierre-Augustine Caron de 40, 50, 51
Bechi, Gino 26, 242, 248

Beerbohm, Max 249
Belfugor 250
Benassi, Memo 255
Benoit (in *La Bohème*) 178–9
Beppe (in *Pagliacci*) 172, 173; his
    Harlequin serenade 175
Berganza, Teresa, 56
Berta (in *The Barber*) 43, 46, 48–9; 'Il
    vechiotto' 43, 48
Betto (in *Gianni Schicchi*) 224, 225,
    226–7, 228
Bis, Hippolyte Louis-Florent 57
Bishop (in *Fra Gherardo*) 243–4
Bizzelli, Alva 240
Bizzelli, Annibale 239–40
Boccanegra, Simone, first Doge of
    Genoa 109, 121–2
Boccanegra, Simone (the character)
    109–10, 113–14, 116–19, 120–4;
    acclaimed Doge 110; Verdi's view of
    120; Radius on 120; appearance
    121–2; at end of study scene 123;
    sung by Gobbi at Munich 220
Bohème, La 177–93, 216; Rodolfo's
    aria 16–17; the theme analysed 181;
    Ramon Vanay as waiter in 181–2
Boito, Arrigo 109, 123, 144, 158; on
    Paolo in *Boccanegra* 112
Bologna Communale 139, 242
Bonaparte, Joseph 196
Boncompagni, Elio 67
Borgioli, Dino 42
Borsa (in *Rigoletto*) 81, 88
Bragagnolo, Don Giovanni 223
breathing 16, 17
Browenstijn, Gre 130
Burlador de Sevilla, El 30

Cajus, Dr (in *Falstaff*) 159–60, 164
Callas, Maria 25, 95, 96–9; plays
    Tosca 210–13
Campiello, Il 241
Canali, Anna Maria 249–50
Candeliere, Il 243
Caniglia, Maria 25, 95, 123, 161, 249
Canio (in *Pagliacci*) 172, 173–6
Cantelli, Guido 255
Canzoniere Italiano 240–1
Caporale (in *Il Tabarro*) 216, 217
Capsir, Mercedes 95
Captain of Arms (in *Boccanegra*) 111,
    119, 121

Carabella, Ezio 243
Caracalla Baths, Rome 172
Carlo I, King of Spain *see* Charles V,
    Emperor
Carlo, Don *see* Don Carlo
Caroline, Queen of Naples 197,
    203
Carosio, Margherita 95, 243
Caruso, Enrico 21
Caruso, Mariano 20
Cassio (in *Otello*) 21, 145, 149–52
Castello Sforzesco, Milan 169
Cavalieri di Ekebu, I 250
Cavalleria Rusticana 246–7
Cavaradossi (in *Tosca*) 195, 197,
    198–9, 200, 201–2, 206–8;
    relationship with Scarpia 207, 208;
    aria 207
Cecilia 238–9
Ceprano (in *Rigoletto*) 81, 88
Ceprano, Countess (in *Rigoletto*) 80
Charlemagne, Emperor 72
Charles V, Emperor 68–9, 125–6, 127,
    140, 141
Child (in *La Bohème*) 180
Cherubino (in *Figaro*) 52–3, 56
Chitty, Stella 130
chorus: in *Ernani* 67–8; in *Rigoletto*,
    member hit by folly 90; in *Pagliacci*
    172
Christoff, Boris 129–31, 132
Ciesca (in *Gianni Schicchi*) 225, 226,
    227, 232
Cilea, Francesco 247–9
Cimarosa 203
Cioni, sings with Callas 212
Clavaroche (in *Il Candeliere*) 243
Cobelli, Giuseppina 239
Colline (in *La Bohème*) 178, 179,
    182–4, 192; played by Neri and Tajo
    183; his 'Vecchia Zimarra' 183–4
Commendatore, Il (in *Don Giovanni*)
    36–7
comprimario, role of 20–1, 136, 150,
    179–80
Conca, Guiseppe 182
Copley, John 211
Corelli, sings in *Don Carlo* 132
Corneille, Pierre 30
Corradi, Nelly 40
Cortese, Valentina 254
Così fan Tutte 31

Cossuta, Carlo 115
Costa, Mario 40
Court Usher (in *Rigoletto*) 79–80, 82
Covent Garden 56, 58, 130, 167, 211–13, 229
Crimi, Giulio 122
Crimp, Bryan 65

da Ponte, Jacopo 195
da Ponte, Lorenzo: his *Don Giovanni* 30–1; his *Marriage of Figaro* 50, 56
da Vinci, Leonardo 121
dal Monte, Toti 42, 80, 240
Dante Alighieri 224
David (opera) 252
David (painter) 197
Davis, Colin 167
de Fabritiis, Maestro 182, 199, 247, 248
de Jouy, Etienne 57
de Paolis (*comprimario*) 20
de Rensis, Franca 240
de Rensis, Giuseppina 240, 250
de Rensis, Raffaello 77, 237, 240, 246, 250
de Rensis, Tilde *see* Gobbi, Tilde
de Sabata, Maestro 167
de Zamora (playwright) 30
del Monaco, Mario 22, 26
Denison, Michael 254
Desdemona (in *Otello*) 145–6, 155–6
Devil (in *Belfugor*) 250
di Nicolao, Ser Amantio (in *Gianni Schicchi*) 225, 230–3
Dibuk 242–3
Dobrowen, Issay Alexandrovich 48
Don Carlo 84, 125–41, 167; Auto da Fé 22, 132; historical background to 125–6; original version 126–7; Song of the Saracen 128; trouble with dogs in 130–1; prison scene 139–40; last scene 140–1
Don Carlo (the character) 126–7, 131–3, 134, 138, 139–41
Don Carlo (in *Ernani*) 68–73, 74–5; his 'Vo' salvarti' 70
Don Giovanni 29–37, 56; libretto 30–1
Don Giovanni (the character) 30, 33, 35–6, 37; his virility 35
Donati, Buoso (in *Gianni Schicchi*) 224, 226, 229
Donati, Pino 139, 242

Donne Curiose, Le 241
Dr Oss 239
Duphol (in *La Traviata*) 105, 106

Eboli (in *Don Carlo*) 128, 131, 134–5, 136–7; her Saracen song 128; her 'don fatale' 135
Ecuba 254
Edwige (in *William Tell*) 59, 64
Elizabeth of Valois (in *Don Carlo*) 125, 126, 127, 128–9, 131, 134, 137; in final scene 140
Elvira (in *Don Giovanni*) 34, 35
Elvira (in *Ernani*) 68, 69–73, 74–5
Emilia (in *Otello*) 21, 152–3; her part in the quartette 153
Emiral 252–3
Epithalamium, by Pizzetti 245–6
Ercolani (*comprimario*) 20
Ernani 67–75; difficulties of 67–8, 73; Gobbi's production in Naples 67–8, 74–5; historical background to 68–9
Ernani (the character) 68, 69–74
Evans, Sir Geraint 56
expression, importance of 23–4
eyebrows 25

Falstaff 144, 157–67; Verdi on 158–9; Gobbi produces in Paris 161; BBC TV production 163
Falstaff (the character) 26, 27, 157–8, 159–60, 161, 162, 163, 165–7; his Honour Monologue 158, 160; Gobbi in TV production of 163; his monologue in Act 3 164–5; his character and appearance 166; played by Stabile 166
Favero, Mafalda 182, 251
Favola del Figlio Cambiato, La 253
Fedora 246
Fenton (in *Falstaff*) 161, 163–4; Verdi on 164
Ferdinand, King of Naples 197
Ferrara, Franco 255
Fiesco (in *Boccanegra*) 109–10, 111, 114, 115–17, 121, 123–4; played by Neri 84
Fiesco family, in history 116
Figaro: in *The Barber* 39–41, 43–9; cavatina of 39–40, 41, 42, 45; in *Figaro* 50–3, 54–6; cavatina of 51
Filippeschi, as the Duke in *Rigoletto* 84

Filistrucchi, wigmaker 26
Finto Arlecchino, Il 254
Fletcher , Jefferson Butler 224
Flora (in *La Traviata*) 21, 100–1, 106
Florence Communale 139
Ford (in *Falstaff*) 159, 160, 162–3, 167; his aria 162–3; Verdi on 164
Ford, Mistress (in *Falstaff*) 159, 160, 165
forme chiuse 144–5, 162
Forza del Destino, La 16
Forzano, Gioacchino 224–5, 233, 235
Fox, Carol 58
Foy, Patricia 163
Fra Gherardo 243–4
Francesca da Rimini 122, 250
Franci, Benvenuto 224
Frank de Bellis Collection 111
Franz (in *Lodoletta*) 246
Freni, Mirella 56
Friar (in *Don Carlo*) 126, 127, 137, 141
Frugola (in *Il Tabarro*) 216–17; her 'ron, ron, ron' 217
Fulmine, a citizen of Bassano 222–4

Galeffi, Carlo 42
Gavazzeni, Gianandrea 167
Gedini, Georgio Federico 249–50
Genna, Irene 40
Gerard (in *Andrea Chenier*) 246
Germont, Père (in *La Traviata*) 99–100, 104–5, 107
Gessler (in *William Tell*) 59, 62–5
Gherardino (in *Gianni Schicchi*) 226, 227, 234
Gherardo (in *Gianni Schicchi*) 226, 227, 230
Giacosa, G. 197
Gianciotto (in *Francesca da Rimini*) 122, 250
Gianni Schicchi 223–35; produced by Gobbi 219; period of 225; make-up for 226; relationship of characters 227; will scene 231–3; timing in 234; *see also* Schicchi, Gianni
Gigli, Beniamino 80, 172, 248
Gilda (in *Rigoletto*) 79, 80, 83–4, 85–8; sung by Pagliughi 84; hazards of the role 85, 87
gimmicks, beware of 16
Gioielli della Madonna, I 241

Giordano Umberto 246, 247
Giorgetta (in *Il Tabarro*) 215–18, 219, 221; played by Zachari 220
Giorgetti (*comprimario*) 20
Giovanna (in *Rigoletto*) 82, 85, 152
Giovanni, Don *see* Don Giovanni
Giraldi, Cinzio 146
Giulini, Maestro 130, 167
Glass Mountain, The 254–5
Gobbi, Cecilia 122
Gobbi, Tilde 65–6, 77–8, 169–70, 240, 253; on Callas' Tosca 212
Gobbi, Tito: experience at San Gimignano 11–13, 256; on interpretation 12, 121, 191, 193, 206; on the gift of a voice 15–18; on gimmicks 16; on preparation 16, 17, 99–100; on high notes 16–17, 169–70; on quiet passages 17; on stance and breathing 17; on stage movement 17–18; on emotional involvement 18, 92–3, 122–3; on playing small parts 19–22, 148, 198; at the Teatro Reale 20–1 *et passim*; on cheap buffoonery 21–2; on make-up 23–8; on wigs and eyebrows 25; on beards 26–7; on hands and neck 28; on recitatives 30–1, 41, 44, 56, 86, 145; on the Italian language 30–1; on the 'fisic du role' 39–40, 122; on the manners of each period 41, 205; performances during the war 41–2; plays Figaro with Simionata in Chicago 46; on singing Mozart 52–3; on the fight for freedom 61–2; on choruses 67–8, 74, 90, 172; on the 'marriage' of word and action 76–7, 96; his over-enthusiasm for the role of Rigoletto 77–8, 90; on overloaded stage effects 80–1; his brush with Callas 97–9; at 'Il Riposo' 102–3; 'discovers' Boccanegra's Captain of Arms 111; foils recording thieves 115–16; on the singer as actor 140, 170, 205–6, 227; on the 'crisis' in opera 142–4; on opera 'stars' 150; his last Falstaff at Covent Garden 167; discovers he is a baritone 170, 251–2; on self-control 172; at his Opera Workshop 177–8; as a student in Padua 183; on opera as

cooking 194–5, 196–7; on producing opera 220; his boyhood in Bassano 223; on telling jokes 224; on his grandfather's will 233–4; his debut at La Scala 244–5; on the audience's dress 253; and *The Glass Mountain* 254–5; on forgotten works 255–6; and modern productions 256; *see also* individual operas, characters and composers

Goldoni, Carlo 30, 241, 251

Gorlinsky, Sander 211

Govoni, Marcella 84

Govoni, Marcello 182

Grand Inquisitor (in *Don Carlos*) 131, 133–4, 137–8, 140; played by Neri 84, 137–8

Gray, Dulcie 254

Gualtiero (in *William Tell*) 61, 65; played by Neri 84

Guardi, Francesco 195

Guarnieri, Antonio 91

Guccio (in *Gianni Schicchi*) 225, 230

Gutierrez, Antonio Garcia 109

Hals, Franz 223–4

Hamilton, Lady 203

hands, use of 28

Harlequin (in *I Pagliacci*) *see* Arlecchino

head-dresses, effect of 25

helmsman (in *La Nava*) 242

Henry II, King of France 126–7

Henry IV (plays) 157, 158, 166

Herald (in *Orseolo*) 244–5

Herbst, Dr Otto 219

Hernani 68

Hugo, Victor 68

Iago (in *Otello*) 144, 145–6, 181; his character and appearance 146, 156

Illica, L. 197

Inferno (in *L'Ipocrita Felice*) 249–50

Inquisitor (in *Don Carlo*) *see* Grand Inquisitor

Ipocrita Felice, L' 249–50

Italian language, its importance to opera 31

Jailer (in *Tosca*) 199–200

Jemmy (in *William Tell*) 59–60, 63, 64

Juan of Aragon 72, 73

Karajan, Herbert von 167

Katiusha (in *Resurrezione*) 239

Kelen, Peter 220

Langdon, Michael 56

Lanigan *(comprimario)* 20

Lanza, Mario 239

Lauretta (in *Gianni Schicchi*) 227, 228–9, 233, 234; played by Popp 220

Leoncavallo, Ruggero 168, 171, 172

Leporello (in *Don Giovanni*) 34–5, 36, 37

Lerna (in *Don Carlo*) 127, 133, 136

Leutoldo (in *William Tell*) 60, 64

Levine, James 138

Ligabue, Ilva 56

Lindoro *see* Almaviva

Locandiera, La 251

Lodoletta 246

Lodovico (in *Otello*) 147–8

Lucia di Lammermoor 21, 98

Luigi (in *Il Tabarro*) 215, 216, 217–18, 219, 221; played by Cossuta 220

Luisa Miller 145

Lustigen Weiber von Windsor, Die 157

Lyric Opera, Chicago 21, 58, 112, 139

Macbeth 144–5

Macbeth (the character) 19

Maddalena (in *Rigoletto*) 82–3, 84

Maggi, wigmaker 26

Majordomo (in *Tosca*) 198

make-up 23–8; in *Tosca* 24–5; for ladies 25; in *Pagliacci* 27; in *Gianni Schicchi* 223–4; for Michonnet 249; in *L'Ipocrita Felice* 250; in *Il Tesoro* 251

Malipiero, Gian Francesco 182, 253–4

Manfred (in *L'Amore dei Tre Re*) 242

Manikas, Louis 252

Mantua, Duke of (in *Rigoletto*) 80, 83, 88–9; played by Filippeschi 84

Marcellina (in *Figaro*) 52, 54, 55

Marcello (in *La Bohème*) 178–9, 181, 184–6, 191, 192

Marco (in *Gianni Schicchi*) 225, 226, 227, 232

Marco Polo 150

Marengo, Battle of 195, 196

Margherita da Cortona 238–9

Maria (Boccanegra) *see* Amelia

Maria (Fiesco) 109–10, 116, 124

Marie of Portugal 126
Marriage of Figaro, The 31, 50–6; construction and difficulties of 51, 53, 56; production at Covent Garden 56
Martin, Sergeant 211
Marullo (in *Rigoletto*) 81, 88
Mary Tudor 125, 126
Mascagni, Pietro 246–7
Masetto (in *Don Giovanni*) 32
Mathilde (in *William Tell*) 59–61, 63–4
Maugeri, Carmelo 122
Maurel, Victor 120, 169, 171
Mefistofeles, played by Neri 84
Mekler, Mani 252
Melchtal (in *William Tell*) 59–60, 64
Melitone (in *Forza del Destino*) 16
Meneghini, Battista 97
Merry Wives of Windsor, The 157–8
Metifio (in *L'Arlesiana*) 248
Metropolitan Opera House, New York 138, 144
Michele (in *Il Tabarro*) 215–16, 218–19, 221; played by Boyagian 220
Michonnet (in *Adriana Lecouvreur*) 248–9
Milanov, Zinka 25
Mimi (in *La Bohème*) 186–93; Gobbi sings the role 177–8; her longing for the sun 188, 191; in Act 4 191–3
Moffo, Anna 95
Molière 30
Molina, Tirso de 30
Molinari, Bernardino 237–8
Molinari, Mary 238
Mongelli, Andrea 115–16
'*Montanara, La*' (song) 254
Montano (in *Otello*) 147
Monte Ivnor 242
Montemezzi, Italo 242
Monterone (in *Rigoletto*) 79, 82, 86, 89
Monti, Nicola 40
Morelli, Domenico 146
moustaches 26
movement on stage 17–18
Mozart, Wolfgang Amadeus: his *Don Giovanni* 29, 30, 31, 36; his *Marriage of Figaro* 50–6
Musetta (in *La Bohème*) 178, 180–1, 183, 184–6, 191, 192

Museum of Ligurian Sculpture 121
Musset, Louis-Charles-Alfred de 243
Muzio, Claudia 95; as Tosca 209; as Cecilia 239
My Life 140

Nannetta (in *Falstaff*) 161, 163, 165
Napoleon, Emperor 195, 196
Napoli, Jacopo 251
Nardi (*comprimario*) 20
Nave, La 242
'*Nebbie*' (song) 250
neck, mobility of 28
Nedda (in *Pagliacci*) 169, 172, 173–6
Negri, Ada 250
Nella (in *Gianni Schicchi*) 226–7
Nelson, Horatio 197
Neri, Giulio 26, 40, 84–5, 136, 148, 182; as Grand Inquisitor 137–8; as Colline 183
Nessi (*comprimario*) 20
Nicolai, Otto 157
Nozze di Figaro, Le see *Marriage of Figaro*

Olivero, Magda 95
Olivier, Lord 154
Opéra, Paris 57
opera, vitality of 142–4
opera buffa, requirements of 40, 158
Opera Studio 56
Opera Workshop 177
organ grinder (in *Il Tabarro*) 216
Orseolo 244–5
Orta, Gennaro 67
Otello 21, 144–56; del Monaco in 22; fireworks in 150; the handkerchief in 151
Otello (the character) 22, 122, 146–7, 153–5, 179, 181
Ottavio (in *Don Giovanni*) 33

Pacini, sings in *La Bohème* 182
Page, Mistress (in *Falstaff*) 159, 160, 162
Page to the Duchess (in *Rigoletto*) 79
Pagliacci, I 21, 27, 168–76; 'mould' on the score 169, 171; Prologue 169–70; *verismo* in 171; chorus in 172; the play within a play 175–6
Paglialunga, wigmaker 26
Pagliughi, Lina 40, 84, 87

Paisiello, Giovanni 50, 203
Panerai, Rolando 220
Paolo (in *Boccanegra*) 109–10, 111, 112–13; Verdi and Boito on 112; in curse scene 113
Parpignol (in *La Bohème*) 179–80
Pasero, Tancredi 245
'Pastori, I' (song) 246
Pederzini, Gianna 248
period, the manner of each 41, 196, 205
Perosi, Don Lorenzo 237–8
Perris, sings in *La Bohème* 182
Persico, Mario 251
Petrarca, Francesco 121
Philip II (in *Don Carlo*) 20, 127, 132–3, 139, 140; the man in history 125–6; played by Christoff 129–32; in study scene 133–5; character of 139
physical presence, importance of 120, 121–2
Piave, Francesco Maria 68, 70, 109
Piccola Scala 249–50
Pietro (in *Boccanegra*) 110, 111, 112
Pinellino (in *Gianni Schicchi*) 225, 230
Pinza, Ezio 42
Piolti, Pietro *see* Perosi, Lorenzo
Pirandello, Luigi 253
Pistol (in *Falstaff*) 159, 160–1, 164
Pius VI 196, 208
Pius VII, 196
Pius XII 143
Pizzetti, Ildebrando 243–6
Pizzetti, Ippolito 246
Pizzi, Italo 157
Pizzi, Pier Luigi 220
Podic, Baldo 252
Poletti, Charles 42
Popp, Lucia 220
Posa, Marquis of *see* Rodrigo
preparation, importance of 16, 17, 99–100
Previtali, Fernando 39
Prinz Regenten Theater, Munich 220
Prologue (in *Pagliacci*) 169–72, 176
pronunciation, importance of 38, 93, 119, 135, 156
Puccini, Giacomo 57, 247; his *La Bohème* 177–93; his art of the everyday 179; his *Tosca* 195–213; his *Il Tabarro* 214–19, 221; his *Gianni Schicchi* 224–35; his *Turandot* 239

Quattro Rusteghi, I 241–2
Quickly, Mistress (in *Falstaff*) 161, 163; Verdi on 164

Rabbi (in *L'Amico Fritz*) 246
Radice, Attila 63
Radius, Emilio, 120
recitatives, importance of 30–1, 41, 44, 56, 86; Verdian 145
Refice, Don Licinio 238–9
repetition, variety in 18
Respighi, Elsa 250
Respighi, Ottorino 250
Resurrection of Christ 237–8
Resurrezione 239
Riccardo (in *Ernani*) 70
Ricci, Luigi 39, 77, 84
Ricordi, Giulio 116, 120, 144, 154, 164
Rigoletto 41, 76–94, 152; films of 77, 78, 84; timing in 80, 85, 86, 94; dangers of overproduction 80–1; stage effects for 84, 87
Rigoletto (the character) 82, 85–6, 87, 88–94; a difficult role 76, 77–8; appearance of 78–9, 85, 89–90; entrance 89; his folly 90; his duet with Sparafucile 90–1; his fall 92; need for control in playing 92–3; 'Vendetta' 93; in final scene 94; compared with Simone Boccanegra 120
Rinuccio (in *Gianni Schicchi*) 225–8, 230, 233–4; played by Kelen 220
'Riposo, Il', Gobbi's house 102–3
Risorgimento 68, 73, 121
Rocca, Ludovico 242–3
Roderigo (in *Otello*) 149
Rodolfo (in *La Bohème*) 16, 178 186–93
Rodolfo (in *William Tell*) 59–60
Rodrigo (in *Don Carlo*) 126, 127, 129–30; 131–5, 139–40; character of 128, 138
Romani, Pietro 49
Romeo and Juliet, Perosi's opera 237
Ronchetti, wigmaker 26
Rome Opera 224; *see also* Teatro Reale
Rosina (in *The Barber*) 40, 41, 42–9; her character 43; *see also* Almaviva, Countess
Rosina, Serafin's housekeeper 167

Rossini, Gioacchino 157, 158; his *Barber of Seville* 38, 40, 44, 49–50; his *William Tell* 57–66; his *Otello* 144

Rota, Nino 255–6

Royal Herald (in *Don Carlo*) 136

Ruffo, Cardinal Fabrizio 197

Sacristan (in *Tosca*) 16, 21, 195, 202

Salieri, Antonio 157

Sampaoli, Maestro 170

San Carlo, Naples *see* Teatro San Carlo

San Carlos, Lisbon 115, 139, 241–2

San Francesco 254

San Gimignano 11–12, 256

Sanine, Alexander 43

Santa Severa, Gobbi's summer home 239

Santafé (*comprimario*) 20

Sardou, Victorien 197, 202, 203, 208

Saul (in *David*) 252

Sawallisch, Maestro 220

Sayao, Bidu 95

Scala, La, Milan 77, 100, 120, 126, 159, 238, 246; Gobbi's debut at 244–5; *see also* Piccola Scala

Scandella, Misha 68, 75

Scarpia (in *Tosca*) 24–5, 195, 196, 198–9, 202–6; make-up for 24–5, 27; played by Stabile 26; his supposed birthplace 203; appearance and dress 204; entrance 204; performance of role 205–6, 207

Schaunard (in *La Bohème*) 178, 182, 192

Schicchi, Gianni (the character) 228–9, 230, 231–5; sung by Gobbi 220; played by Panieri 220; make-up for 223–4; played by Franci 224; his entrance 228; his 'Addio Firenze' 230, 232–3; voice for 229, 231; a countryman 231

Schiller, Johann Christoph Friedrich von 126, 141

Schipa, Tito 248

Sciarrone (in *Tosca*) 197, 198–9

Second World War 40, 41

Segreto di Susanna, Il 241

Sentinati, Pietro 111

Serafin, Tullio 66, 80, 84, 140, 167, 182; on role of Don Giovanni 30; on Gobbi as Rigoletto 78–9, 92; on Callas' weight 98; on *Simone Boccanegra* 112–13; and singers'

suggestions 118; his 'clean' performances of *Pagliacci* 171; conducts *Or Oss* 239; presents *Dibuk* and *Monte Ivnor* 242–3; presents works by Carabella 243

Sergeant (in *Tosca*) 198

Sette Canzoni 254

Shadwell (playwright) 30

Shakespeare, William 144, 146, 157–8

Shepherd (in *Tosca*) 198

Siepi, Cesare 91

silence, value of 17

Sills, Beverly 95

Silva (in *Ernani*) 69–73; his hospitality 70, 71; his age and character 73–4

Silvio (in *Pagliacci*) 174–5, 176; played by Gobbi 169

Simionato, Giulietta 46, 128

Simon, Michel 77

Simone (in *Gianni Schicchi*) 226, 227, 228, 232, 234

Simone Boccanegra 84, 109–25; historical background to 109; Prologue 109–10, 122; plot summary 110; produced by Gobbi 111–12, 122–30; curse scene 113; garden scene 114, 118, 122; importance of the sea in 114, 117, 118, 120; Council Chamber scene 114, 118–19, 123; study scene 119, 123; a great work 121; final scene 119, 123; *see also* Boccanegra, Simone

Simonson (in *Resurrezione*) 239

singing, some tips on 17–18

Sir John in Love 157

Solti, Sir George 56

Sparafucile (in *Rigoletto*) 82, 83, 84–5; played by Neri 84; played by Siepi 91; his duet with Rigoletto 90–1

Spinelloccio, Doctor (in *Gianni Schicchi*) 226, 229

Spoletta (in *Tosca*) 197, 201

Stabile, Mariano 26, 166, 250, 251

stance (for singing) 17, 18

Steber, Eleanor 25

Sterbini, Cesare 44

'Stone Guest, The' 36

Straniero, Lo 243

Strauss, Richard 158

supernumeraries 22, 85, 132, 190, 199, 220

Susanna (in *Figaro*) 51–6
'Swan of Pesaro' *see* Rossini

Tabarro, Il 214–19; and life at two
levels 215, 216, 219; produced by
Gobbi 219–21; lighting for 220–1
Taddei, Giuseppe 182, 250
Tagliavini, Ferrucio 40, 239–40, 241,
251
Tajo, Italo 21, 26, 40, 51, 182, 242; as
Colline 183
Talpa (in *Il Tabarro*) 215, 217
Tamagno, original singer of Otello 154
Taranto, Vito de 40
Tassinari, Pia 239
Teatro Adriano 78
Teatro Agentina 197
Teatro in musica 86
Teatro Reale, Rome 20, 26, 39, 42, 78,
182, 241, 242, 249, 252
Teatro San Carlo, Naples 169, 179,
239; Gobbi's production of *Ernani*
there 67, 74–5; its chorus 67–8
Tebaldi, Renata 25, 95, 161
Tebaldo (in *Don Carlo*) 136
Tell, William (the character) 58–65;
'Resta immobile' 63
Tell, William, in history 58–9
Tesoro, Il 251
Tiburzio (in *Cecilia*) 238–9
timing, importance of 76–7, 80, 96
Tinca (in *Il Tabarro*) 215
Tolentino, Treaty of 196
Tolstoi, Leo 239
Tonio (in *Pagliacci*) 172, 173–6;
make-up for 27
Tosca 195–213; Sacristan in 16, 21,
202; Gobbi as Scarpia in 24–5 *et
passim*; Stabile as Scarpia in 26;
played during the War 41; recorded
with Callas 99; historical
background to 195–7; opening to
Act 3 198; firing squad mass suicide
199; Callas in 210–13
Tosca (the character) 195, 196, 208–10;
a Venetian 195; elegant 208; played
by Muzio 209; demeanour of
209–10; played by Callas 210–13
Toscanini, Arturo 164, 169
Traviata, La 21, 95–108; staging of
100–1; film of 101
Turandot 239

Umberto, King of Italy 123

Vaghi, Giacomo 26, 243
Varnay, Astrid 220
Vaughan, Elizabeth 229
Vaughan Williams, Ralph 157
Velis (*comprimario*) 20
Verdi, Giuseppe 19–20; his *Forza del
Destino* 16; his *Macbeth* 19, 144–5;
his *Ernani* 67–75; his *Rigoletto* 76–94;
his *La Traviata* 98, 99–108; his
Simone Boccanegra 109–25; on Paolo
Albiani 112; on Jacopo Fiesco 116;
compares Simone with Rigoletto
120; his *Don Carlo* 126–41; his *Otello*
144–56; and Verdian evolution
144–5; his view of Iago 145–6; on
Otello's voice 154; his *Luisa Miller*
145; his *Falstaff* 144, 157–67; his
view of that opera 158–9; and on the
character of Falstaff 157; on La Scala
159; and on other characters in
Falstaff 164
Verona Arena 139, 205
Vickers, Jon 130
Vinay, Ramon 181–2
Violetta (in *La Traviata*) 95, 101–8;
sung by Callas
Visconti, Luchino 130–1
Vittorio Emanuel, King of Italy 73
Voce del Cielo (in *Don Carlo*) 135–6
voice, its understanding and use 15–18
Volti la Lanterna 243
Votto, Maestro 167

Wallman, Margherita 249–50
Webster, Sir David 58, 130, 212
wigs and wigmakers 25, 26–7
William Tell 57–66, 84; a seminal work
57–8; historical background to
58–9; difficulties of 58, 65; 'Amici
della patria' 61–2; special effects in
65; *see also* Tell, William
Wolf-Ferrari, Ermanno 240–2

Zagonara (*comprimario*) 20
Zanchetta, Agostino 251–2
Zandonai, Riccardo 122, 250
Zeffirelli, Franco 101, 212
Zerlina (in *Don Giovanni*) 31–2, 35
Zita (in *Gianni Schicchi*) 226, 227–8,
233, 234; played by Varnay 220